Luther

Luther

by
RICHARD MARIUS

J. B. LIPPINCOTT COMPANY
Philadelphia and New York

This is a volume in a series of PORTRAITS devoted to figures who have changed the world we live in. The series is edited by Walter Kaufmann, Professor of Philosophy at Princeton University.

Other volumes in the series are:
SARTRE *by Hazel E. Barnes*
WITTGENSTEIN *by William Warren Bartley III*
LENIN *by Rolf H. W. Theen*

Printed in the United States of America

U.S. Library of Congress Cataloging in Publication Data

Marius, Richard.
　Luther.

　Bibliography: p.
　1. Luther, Martin, 1483–1546.
BR325.M29　　　　230′.4′10924 [B]　　　74–12134
ISBN–0–397–01048–6

Hommage à mon père
HENRI TOUSSAINT MARIUS
Ancien combattant de l'armée belge
grièvement blessé
1914
Ingénieur en Birmanie
Enfin, au Tennessee, cultivateur des terres
et des songes pour ses enfants

EDITOR'S PREFACE

Was Luther a Saint George who fought the dragon of the Church of Rome, or a villain who destroyed the unity of Western Christendom? (Eastern Christendom, of course, had never enjoyed any unity.) Protestants usually present Luther as a kindly man, a good husband and father, and a religious thinker who was on the whole as right as the papacy was wrong. But his admirers, like his detractors, generally have extraordinarily little feeling for Luther. In fact, he was a man almost anyone who reads enough of his writings is bound to admire and detest in turn. He was neither dull nor moderate, but radical in speech and action. It will not do, however, to make a hero of the young Luther while admitting that the old Luther wrote some deplorable tracts against the German peasants and the Jews. The man was of one piece, and the writings that shock modern readers involve no betrayal of the principles on which he based his Reformation.

When the peasants revolted, Luther wrote in 1525, a mere four years after what is widely considered the high point of his career, his refusal to recant at the Diet of Worms: "There are to be no bondslaves since Christ has freed us all? What is all this? This makes Christian freedom carnal! . . . Read St. Paul. . . . This article goes straight against the Gospel and advocates robbery so that each robs his master, who owns it, of his body. For a bondslave can be a Christian and have Christian freedom just as a prisoner and a sick man can be Christians even without being free. This article wants to make all men equal and turn the spiritual kingdom of Christ into a worldly, external kingdom, which is impossible."

In the same vein, Luther admonished Christian prisoners of war who had been reduced to slavery by Turkish Muslims that they had no right to seek their freedom: "You are robbing and stealing your body from your master who has bought it or acquired it in some other way so that it is no longer yours but his property, like cattle or other possessions."

Liberal Protestants could scarcely believe that a great Christian could have written things like these. But the assumption that such sentiments are incompatible with Christianity and that Christianity entails twentieth-century liberalism is a twentieth-century superstition, of a piece with the notion of Christians in other climes and times that Christianity entailed *their* views. Luther's firm conviction that Christianity entailed *his* views was actually less naive and thoughtless, for he knew the Bible as few liberals have ever known it, the New Testament as well as the Old, book for book, having translated the whole of it and weighed every word.

It is a measure of the naiveté of legions of his admirers that few of his stands have been applauded more than his refusal to recant unless he should be refuted from Scripture—as if Scripture said with one voice: man is made just by faith alone—faith in Christ's expiation of our sins—and not at all by any works whatever. Luther took his cue from his reading of Paul's Epistles to the Romans and Galatians, where Paul interprets Habakkuk as having said that. But the Epistle of James, also in the New Testament, says: "Man is justified by works and not by faith alone." Says Luther: The Epistle of James is utter straw!

Luther chose what fitted his aims and denounced what did not. But he did not do this piecemeal, picking a verse from here and a half verse from there. In his theology he had little use on the whole for the Old Testament and none at all for the Mosaic and prophetic concern with what is often called social justice. Nor did he have very much use for the first three Gospels. The moral demands of the Sermon on the Mount, he said, were intended only to show us our incapacity for good works. The saving words are to be found in Paul's epistles, notably including Romans 13 and I Corinthians 7: "Let every one be subject to the authority that has power over him, for there is no authority that is not from God. Whatever authority there is, is from God. And whoever opposes authority, opposes the order of God, and those who resist will be judged accordingly." "Let every one remain in the state in which he was called. If you are called as a slave, have no care."

Why, then, did Luther rebel against ecclesiastical authority? Because his primary concern was not with *this* world but with salvation, and one could suffer and be oppressed in this world and be saved; but the Church, he thought, had falsified the Word of God and kept from men the tidings that they needed to be saved. He stated his position clearly in 1520 in his treatise *On Good Works,* one of the major works of the Reformation. In his discussion of the Mosaic commandment to honor father and mother, he said:

"The third work of this commandment is to be obedient to temporal authority, as Paul teaches us in Romans 13 and Titus 3, and Saint Peter in I Peter 2. Be subject to the king as the supreme authority, and to princes as his ambassadors, and to all orders of temporal authority. . . . For suffering wrong does not corrupt anyone's soul; nay, it improves the soul though it diminishes the body and one's possessions. But doing wrong does corrupt the soul even if it should succeed in this world. . . . This is also the reason why there is not so much danger in temporal power as there is in spiritual power when it does wrong. For temporal power may do no harm because it has nothing to do with preaching and faith and the first three commandments. But spiritual power does harm not only when it does wrong but also when it neglects its office and does other things, even if these should be better than the very best works of the temporal power. Hence one must resist it when it does not do right, and not resist the temporal power even when it does wrong."

A few pages earlier, Luther begins his commentary on the commandment to honor father and mother by saying of "obedience to and service of all who have authority over us [that] Therefore disobedience is a greater sin than murder, unchastity, theft, deception, and whatever may be included in that." It should be noted how remote this New Testament ethic is from the ethos of Elijah and the prophets who risked their lives defying kings.

As for Luther's frequent lack of kindliness and his impassioned wrath and hatred, he believed—like the Christ of the Gospels—in hell and damnation, and his God was no more liberal or moderate than Luther himself. Among earlier treatments of Luther I am most impressed by Ernst Troeltsch's great book on *The Social Teachings of the Christian Churches.* (The English version of this work obscures one of its greatest virtues by turning "Teachings" into "Teaching," as if all the Churches had offered the same message.) But Troeltsch's tome comprises a thousand pages, of which roughly one hundred deal with some aspects of Lutheranism.

There has long been a need for a new full-length portrait of Luther. To bring that off, his biographer must have highly unusual qualifications—including three that are rarely found together. First, one must know Luther's world: the age and the intellectual climate in which he lived, his contemporaries and the whole setting. Then one must know religion not only from books but also firsthand—and not only the milk of human kindness that sometimes passes for religion in the modern world. Finally, one must love language and be sensitive to its power, or one cannot begin to appreciate Luther's achievement; for his translation of the Bible went far toward creating the modern German language.

Richard Marius possesses all three of these qualifications in the highest degree. As a professor of history, he has prepared scholarly editions of one of Luther's most renowned contemporaries: Sir Thomas More. But while he is at home in Luther's world, his only book so far has been *The Coming of Rain,* a novel that is remarkable for its prose, its emotional depth, and its understanding of human passion. Clearly he had the gifts and the background to write an outstanding intellectual biography of Luther. Here it is: a compelling portrait of a man who did whatever he did with his whole heart and soul and power. Richard Marius has succeeded in bringing to life the man who made the Reformation.

WALTER KAUFMANN

AUTHOR'S PREFACE

HISTORY IS PARTLY autobiography, and any historian owes it to his readers to explain, as best he can, the set of mind that made him write the book he presents for their judgment.

This little book on Martin Luther grew out of my experience with my world and his during the last decade. The United States was involved in a dirty war in Vietnam. I taught students who labored under the shadow of death. Some of them were drafted to fight in a senseless and immoral cause; some of them were killed. Lyndon Johnson and Richard Nixon assaulted us with a Christian and patriotic rhetoric in which God was equated with their own perverted ideal of the American nation, young men were urged to perish in blind faith and obedience to a Presidential will to power, and grieving families were consoled hypocritically for the loss of sons who died utterly in vain.

During these bitter years, I was teaching the Reformation, presenting Martin Luther to young men and women preoccupied with the gloom and frustration of current events. My background in an intensely Christian home had taught me to seek comforting words from the religious past to inspire the present. And so I looked at Luther day after day and night after night with an almost devout intensity. I realized slowly and painfully that he had no word to speak to our time. And in my peregrinations around my state, speaking everywhere I could against the Vietnam War, I found my most hostile audiences in the Christian churches that claimed to be the heirs of the Reformation. Most pious Christians I met wanted to treat the Vietnamese as Luther treated the rebellious peasants: to destroy them without mercy as long as they were in a state of resistance to our sovereign will as a nation. Just after the invasion of Cambodia in 1970 and the massacre of four students by the National Guard on the campus of Kent State University, the Reverend Billy Graham brought Richard Nixon to Knoxville to participate in an evangelistic crusade. In a long prayer, Graham spoke in great detail to God of Nixon's Christian greatness. Some students brought signs saying "Thou shalt not kill" to the stadium, intending to hold them silently on their laps. The signs were confiscated by the police. No one had the right to quote the Bible, even silently, against the preacher.

Such was the end of at least one strand woven from the traditions of the Reformation. Increasingly the Reformation era itself struck me not as an age of gallant heroes but rather as a generation of vipers, not one of the great stepping-stones of our civilization but rather a trauma like famine or plague that our ancestors barely survived.

But at scholarly meetings in those years I kept running into clerical historians. For them the great reformers were paladins of sacred truth, and if they had faults they were only petty peccadilloes, shadows cast by greatness, to be forgiven and forgotten. This mood has been deepened by the rise of the ecumenical movement among Christians. Catholics and Protestants nowadays regularly flash hot grins at each other across crowded rooms of earnestly friendly scholars and seek to make a prostrate and demythologized Luther a historical bridge over which they can rush into the arms of one another to keep warm. This process is known as "ecumenical dialogue."

All of this is harmless enough. It is better for Christians to toast scholarship than to burn bodies. But there is a perversion in such an enterprise. To use history to buttress some present idealism is often to sanitize the past, to convert it to romance, and to grant to it also a stifling power over the present. As one of the finest commentators on Luther's thought, Regin Prenter, has noted, to make Luther speak to our times is often to fail to hear him speaking in his own. We cannot truly isolate the warm and benevolent aspects of Luther's theology from the vicious and intolerant side of the man. We cannot honestly fix on the gentle Luther of the *Children's Catechism* without also calling up the Luther who wanted to burn synagogues and destroy the homes of Jews, deprive them of the Bible, and drive them out of Europe because they would not accept the benevolent Christ of the *Children's Catechism*. And there is more besides.

This book was precipitated by a visit to our campus by Walter Kaufmann in January 1972. I had read his book, *The Faith of a Heretic,* and had admired its keen wit and independence. We met at a party and liked each other instantly, talked away the evening and the next morning, and considered the uses of the past. We pondered one of the great questions: How can any scholar use his knowledge of the past to inform people how they might become more humane in the present? Naturally I spoke of my problems with Martin Luther.

He asked me to contribute a short statement on Luther's thought to a series of intellectual biographies he was editing. I agreed on the spot, and this book is the consequence of that long and happy meeting of minds and hearts.

My debts are many, and this book gives me a chance to express some of them. I am deeply grateful to the men who taught me at Yale and remained my friends afterward: Sydney Ahlstrom, Roland Bainton, the late Hajo Holborn, and Richard S. Sylvester, the executive editor of the Yale Edition of the Complete Works of St. Thomas More. Dick and I have worked so long and so hard editing More that the saint's works have become our private martyrdom; but, like most martyrdoms, it has been a labor of love among those who suffer. *Gratias ago tibi, domine collega et fidelissime amice!*

Other friends have been constantly stimulating because of their intense interest in history and its problems and their continually provocative conversation. I must mention D. L. Dungan, Charles Garside, Jr., J. H. Hexter, C. O. Jackson, M. M. Klein, D. E. Linge, F. S. Lusby, M. J. McDonald, John Muldowny, R. V. Norman, Jr., P. J. Pinckney, and my brother John.

I am grateful indeed to Walter Kaufmann for a meticulous reading of my manuscript and for his many helpful suggestions, to Ed Burlingame of Lippincott for his enthusiasm for a book conceived almost as an afterthought during a breakfast conversation on a very cold day, and to Hilda M. Rogers, a magnificent copy editor, in whose hands a blue pencil becomes a wand.

I must also thank my dear wife, Lanier, who read my manuscript carefully and often toned down my habitual temptation to verbal exuberance. Olive H. Branch has, in her role as chief acquisitions librarian at the University of Tennessee, purchased many thousands of dollars' worth of arcane books needed for my work.

My three young sons were extremely patient at various campsites in the Rocky Mountains when their father sprawled with a yellow pad in his lap, writing about Martin Luther while they waited eagerly to go exploring on horseback. It is probably a good sign that the two of them old enough to talk came home from that summer and told their friends that their father had written a book "about somebody named after Martin Luther King." The heroes of the distant past must always be discarded after a while, and new heroes must take their place.

Most of all I appreciate the several hundred students who during the past decade have passed through History 3412, Reformation, at my beloved alma mater, the University of Tennessee, asking questions out of their experience of men long dead but yet speaking.

RICHARD MARIUS

Luther

1

ARTIN LUTHER was born on November 10, 1483, in the little town of Eisleben in east-central Germany. We should speak of the German lands rather than of Germany, for in the Middle Ages "Germany" was only a geographical expression. The political power that was said to bind the German people together was called the Holy Roman Empire. It claimed an illustrious descent from the Roman Empire of classical antiquity, and its Emperor was called the first ruler of Christian Europe. But in fact his power was as threadbare as his purse, and his authority over the Germans was only a glittering reflection, a mirage cast by sunny theory. When Luther was born, the Emperor was a diplomatic laughingstock among those shrewd Italian ambassadors who sometimes visited his wandering court, leaving a record of their scorn at his impotence.

The German lands were divided and subdivided, ruled and mis-ruled, by dozens of princes great and small who competed with each other for local power. There were a few imperial cities, such as Nurem-berg and Strasbourg, that were governed by town councils, sup-posedly not ruled by any prince but responsible directly to the Em-peror himself; in fact they were virtually independent. There were a few German territories, such as Austria or the two Saxonies, where strong princes kept up a semblance of law and order. But most of Germany was violent and tumultuous. Petty princeling fought others of his own kind in an insane battle for empty honor and worthless spoils. Martin Luther was always to view any disorder as the very manifestation of the devil, and rebellion was always in his view the energy of Satan. But the Germans of his time had raised disorder to a rule of life.

The Germans were backward both politically and intellectually in the Middle Ages, and they remained so until the eighteenth century. The civilizing influence of the old Roman Empire had only tentatively spread into the German lands. When Rome decayed, France and Italy assimilated her rich heritage and civilized the barbarians who had invaded their territories. But one can argue that Germany never did catch up with the lands where the dominion of Roman culture had been most pervasive. Luther was born in a region where most people were ignorant and superstitious. The dark, primeval forest still covered thousands of square miles around him, and it was easy to imagine that trolls haunted the gloomy depths of the woods and that demons shrieked in the darkness of the night. The witchcraft delusion was rampant throughout Luther's life. Three years after his birth the great *Malleus Maleficarum* was published by two German Dominican monks; for three centuries after that this weighty tome was the official handbook throughout Europe for the discovery and extermination of witches. Luther, like most men in his age, believed in witches and the power of crafty devils as long as he lived. For him the world was always a battleground of eerie forces, as far removed as we can imagine from the world that began to come into existence before he died—a world of cosmic order and regularity where there was room neither for miracle nor witch nor demon, and perhaps no room for God Himself.

Luther's father, Hans, was one of those hard-working, ambitious men who, in every age, climb above their origins but not so high as they want. Hans Luther had been born a peasant; but because the inheritance customs of his region favored the youngest son, and because Hans was older, he had been cast adrift from the furrow and the village. He became a miner and prospered. In fact, he did so well that he could send Martin to the university. For most peasants the university was as remote as heaven, and its rewards must have seemed just as glittering with enchantment.

Then, as now, the university offered young men a chance to move up in the world. In the chaotic division of the German lands, the people who tried to govern needed all the help they could get. A clever young lawyer could look forward to lucrative employment. He might even become the counselor of princes or emperors, and he could count on earning enough wealth to live in comfort or even luxury. He would have reputation and influence, and he would make his parents proud of him as the glow of his name spread over the region of his simple beginnings. Martin Luther was one of the most gifted men our culture has ever produced. We may be sure that his brilliance began to shine early in life. Hans Luther decided that his boy should be educated, that he would study law, and that he would take care of Hans later on when Hans was too old to take care of himself. A good son in that age was a mirror of a father's thoughts about himself, and he was a pension plan for a father and a mother alike in their old age.

Much speculation has blown about concerning Luther's relationship to his father. Did Luther take his notions of a wrathful and yet loving God from the example of his father? Did the intimidating strength of Hans Luther crush young Martin to silence, a silence shattered finally when at age thirty-four young man Luther found his own identity and his voice and proceeded to shout an old order down? Was Luther's constipation a symptom of those psychological pressures inflicted upon him by Hans, a father who could be terrible at one moment and full of love and grace in the next? Some psychologists, including Erik Erikson, have thought so. But it is difficult to know how valid such conclusions are. As a class psychologists seem unusually pleased with their hindsight, but their disagreements with one another about problems and remedies in the present are so vehement as to remind a detached observer of the angry doctrinal quarrels perpetually raging among sects of Baptists. Most historians who spend their lives pondering the irreducible, grubby details of evidence are as yet unsure whether the aid proffered them by psychologists is really a rod or a serpent.

Luther's relationships with both father and mother seem to have been unusually close for as long as they lived. They were on rare occasions harsh with him, as most parents were harsh in an age when children were considered beasts to be tamed; but they do not seem to have been brutal, and it seems too much to believe that Luther took his idea of God from his father. The sculptures of the Last Judgment on any Gothic church, the rich tissue of legend that enveloped the saints, and the Bible itself all conveyed the paradox of the loving yet furious God that came to occupy the center of Luther's theology. As for his constipation, that was probably caused by the sedentary life and the bad diet that caused plugged bowels in most scholars of that era. Luther did suffer from moody spells of depression and melancholy, which became more pronounced in his later years; but it is difficult to know if these attacks were the legacy of youthful conflicts never resolved. There was enough in the theology he espoused and in the turmoil of his days to make the strongest person fall into depression at times.

Luther did conflict with his father over his vocation. He wrote much later on that his father had decided on a rich marriage for him. We do not know the woman in question; but the prospect of marriage might have been terrifying to such a sensitive young man as Luther, especially if he was already involved in a deep inner conflict about his vocation. Obviously Hans wanted his boy to stay in the world of affairs and become a wealthy lawyer. But in 1505 Martin suddenly quit the study of law and entered the Augustinian monastery in Erfurt without telling his father until the deed was done.

He told several stories later on to explain his act. According to the most famous, he was struck down by a lightning bolt when he was caught out in a storm. In his terror he cried out to Saint Anne —the patron of miners and the mother of the Virgin Mary—for help, promising her to become a monk if she spared his life. According to another yarn, he cut his leg badly and nearly bled to death, and the sudden perception of the frailty of life drove him to the monastery. All these stories are probably true in the way tales of older men about their youth may be true—a factual incident converted by the haze of years into boundless romance and made into a turning point when it was in fact only a milestone.

If Luther's decision was sudden, it was not strange. The world of the sixteenth century swarmed with invisible powers who showed themselves in signs and wonders. A man under strain could be expected to look for a sign about his destiny. People on the lookout for signs usually find them. So it had been for centuries. Paul had his vision on the road to Damascus and stopped persecuting Christians and became one himself. Augustine heard a child's tender voice crying the refrain of a song. Bernard of Clairvaux suffered the death of his beloved mother. And much later on John Wesley (so similar to Luther in so many ways) paused to hear someone read aloud Luther's preface to the Epistle of Paul to the Romans and felt his heart strangely warmed and his life changed. Martin Luther was one of those born in every generation to feel the transient nature of life, to lament its frailty, to fear death, and to seek eternity at the expense of time. And he was always to find signs in the events of his life and in the simple things. His was a mind made for metaphor.

His age was more frantic than most. Today the popular imagination often conceives the Middle Ages in the light of the romantic writers of the nineteenth century. These people were usually fugitives from their own time, hating the dirt and the smoke and the noise of the industrial revolution, the rise of a culture built on the masses, and the irrevocable shattering of religious faith on unyielding shoals. They saw the Middle Ages through the roseate glow of cathedral windows and in the aura of serene calm that made the old Gothic and Romanesque churches cavernous refuges from the storm and stress of life in the streets outside. They treasured what they took to be a stately age of faith, and their melancholy at its departure inspired all their reverence for that vanished past.

Martin Luther would not have recognized their vision. His times were filled with plagues and wars, violence and sudden death. Men died young by our standards. Even those who lived longer than most found their vitality extinguished by years that do not seem to us to be so burdensome. Henry VIII of England was considered very old when he died, but he was only fifty-six. A sketch we have of John Calvin shows him looking aged and frail, but he went to the grave when he was only fifty-five. In our own world of germ killers and hospitals, it only takes mention of the word "cancer" to give us that stab of terror in the bowels that pervaded nearly every day in the life of medieval man, who expected death to come swiftly, without warning, and soon.

The political violence of Luther's age is too notorious to detail. Baffling economic unrest seethed within political turmoil. Capitalism of a sort had long since begun to break down the ancient social vision of a Christian Europe organized into priests who prayed and knights who fought and serfs who worked the land for the rest. The capitalist was a worm in the stately medieval woodwork, where all the carvings were assumed to be fixed by God. Thomas Aquinas had taught that God made men unequal and in their proper station, and nearly everybody believed that heaven and earth alike existed in hierarchies where some were set higher and some lower for time and for eternity. If God put anyone on a certain level, that person should be reverent enough to stay there. But the capitalist hankered to get rich, and riches could carry him from the barn to a bought title of nobility. Aristocrats who founded their pretensions on land and blood discovered to their consternation that they were being thrust aside by merchants and bankers who clawed their way up in the world on talent and profit. Bankers lent money at interest in contradiction to the familiar prohibition against usury in the Christian Church. Interest was seen by Christians as a vicious way of taking advantage of a brother's need, and many Christians—including Martin Luther—could never understand that if one followed the precept "Neither a borrower nor lender be," the new economy would not run. The capitalist was well hated, and probably not until the nineteenth century did he begin to feel truly secure in Western society.

Before the Reformation, Europe was beset by almost two centuries of hard times. Businesses failed. Wealthy men became destitute overnight. Money, so necessary to the economy, flowed erratically. There was a shortage of precious metals unrelieved until the age of discoveries brought the bullion of the New World to inflate the economy of the Old. Peasants were ruthlessly exploited by a frustrated nobility that was finding it harder and harder to locate wealth enough to provide its traditional pomp and circumstance.

By Luther's time the desperate days were passing away for some peasants and for townspeople in the German lands, and the economy was beginning to improve. The success of Hans Luther in the mining business is a small illustration. He found it possible to rise from the peasantry into the class of prosperous small businessmen, men who in his day and ours have become councillors of towns (as he did), warming the pride of one another by their labored assemblies over small matters. Even the peasants who remained on the land were finding a better life. Many of them had served in the Italian Wars as paid soldiers. When they came home, they brought with them confidence and a self-esteem and ambitions that their ancestors in darker times had never known. The harvests seem to have been fairly good in those years; the peasants had surpluses to sell, and the expanding towns gave them markets for their grain and coins to ring in their leather purses.

We seem to know a couple of things from our contemporary experience that might help us to understand better the society of Luther's day. One is that any kind of change may make people anxious. The greater the change, the more anxious they become, even if the change is for the better. Promotions are likely to cause ulcers. A new job and a new town, a new house and sometimes a new wife, are likely to drive the most sturdy American executive to drink or to psychiatry.

We cannot measure the anxiety of Europe on the eve of the Reformation, though the literary remains show that mood of brooding melancholy to have been both strong and widely prevalent. But we must not assume that it was all caused by violence, disease, and sudden death, though all of these contributed their share to the stew of anguish. Many changes were improvements, and Germany especially shows evidence of stretching and yawning and waking up after several centuries of stuporous hardship and darkness. A swell of change was running beneath the old certainties. Brisk winds were picking up, and no one could tell what storms those winds might bring. So people worried and consulted oracles and looked to the future with foreboding.

We also know today that social groups experiencing a slowly rising standard of living are likely to have an even sharper rise in their expectations. The more they have, the more they want, and they want it faster than they have been getting it. Often an indefinable point is reached when society or their own energies, their work or their times, cannot possibly provide the substance of their dreams immediately. Then we are likely to have revolution.

Martin Luther was to grow up amid the grumblings of peasants for freedom from their old feudal obligations to rapacious lords. But the peasants were in fact better off than they had ever been before. Luther was to grow up amid the furious complaints of the German business classes against the extravagance of the Pope at Rome. We may glory today in the beauty of Renaissance art in Rome, especially in the Vatican; but the Germans at the time believed they were being handed the bill for high living, cavorting, and extravagance by the Pope and his cardinal henchmen, and they deeply resented every glittering coin that fell out of German hands into the Roman coffers. The more gold and silver left the German lands, the less German bankers and German merchants were going to have to stack in German countinghouses. So they complained; but in fact these monied classes were more prosperous than they had ever been before.

The German princes and dukes and counts and the city governments had wrested almost sovereign political power from the Emperor, but they lived in dread lest the Emperor find substance for the enthralling shadows of his power and steal their authority away. And so every political force jealously guarded what power it already possessed and hungered for more as insurance against nameless fear.

So everywhere in the German lands there was a pent-up desire for something more, and there was a terrific anxiety lest those who already had something might lose what they had. It was a tense and disorderly situation swept by fear and desperate hopes, and in such confusion and change a passionate man might raise a standard and passionate souls would rally around it from far and near, seeking a ground on which to stand, a foundation that would not be moved in the wind or tumbled by earthquake. It would have to be a religious standard, for it was a religious age, and only religion offered the vocabulary, the rhetoric, and the moral authority that would sanctify greed and anoint violence, comfort hearts afraid of change and yet changing, and set the engines of revolution in motion.

This was the world that Martin Luther forsook when in 1505 he entered the orderly tranquillity of the monastery to dedicate his life to seeking salvation. He was like those who seek the solitude of their own way in our present wild century, a quiet refugee from the tumult of desperate and confusing times.

2

IT HAS ALWAYS seemed natural to Martin Luther's biographers that he should have entered the monastery. The monastery was the place for a man to withdraw from the world and to give his life to saving his soul. It had an old and for the most part honorable history.

As soon as the Roman Emperor Constantine stopped persecuting Christians and began persecuting their enemies, some hardy and heroic souls fled to the desert to live in solitude away from a world that had suddenly become too easy. Many lived as hermits and tormented their bodies for the sake of their souls. Gradually some came together in communities, and still more gradually various rules were set up to help monks live together in an orderly and pious way. By the time Benedict established his famous monastery on the great, bare escarpment of Monte Cassino in southern Italy in 529, the orderly Roman world had died. The monastery became the only place where men could find literate companionship and the regulated life that had elsewhere disappeared. The tranquillity of the monastery was a natural haven in a world where conditions were so chaotic that no single man could do anything about them.

The monk became a hero in the violent centuries that followed. The common man had a desperate time struggling to exist; he could not give long and serious attention to the devout and holy life. He was taken by lusts so easily assuaged that they could hardly be resisted; virginity in the Middle Ages was exalted as an ideal, but few people after the age of puberty possessed it. It was a violent time, and men had to be violent themselves to keep from becoming the victims of violence. People in the world had no books and no time to read them had they been available, and little knowledge of letters had both time and books been plenteous.

The monk lived apart from this tumultuous world. He could cultivate his mind and his soul, enjoying both leisure and rude comfort. Most monasteries tried to follow some form of the rule Benedict had given to his monks. This was a schedule that provided hours for prayer, hours for study, hours for physical work, hours for eating and sleeping, hours for singing and hearing the Mass before the altar. The good monastery was one where the routine was faithfully carried out without sloth or grumbling. Unlike the peasant, the monk could always look forward with some certainty to what he would be doing tomorrow, and that assurance gave him in his day the same security that now underlies the orderly functioning of our bureaucratic civilization. The aim of the routine was to tame evil in the monk by asceticism, a life of careful discipline and restraint. It is one of the great good fortunes of Western civilization that study came to be considered as a way of disciplining the body for the good of the soul. Monks learned Latin and copied old manuscripts, both pagan and Christian, thus transferring the wisdom of classical antiquity to later generations, including our own. And so monasticism flourished for better than a thousand years.

But monastic culture was already dying when Luther became a monk. Only in Germany and in Spain was it still lively enough to attract a man of his genius. Both of these regions were behind the times.

Elsewhere in Europe the grand old abbeys, monuments to the best in medieval piety, were becoming shabby and dilapidated. When old monks died, to be buried in the graveyard of the monastery or else under the floors of the church to rot in anonymity, there were few young men to replace them. The usual monastery in England or in France or even in Italy housed a few monks whose prayers resounded through great hollow spaces in chants of thin and echoing sadness.

Another ideal had seduced the European consciousness, the ideal of the active life in the world. The world had its rewards for those who worked in it and had a little luck. People were beginning to be proud of the associations that bound them to other men in the pursuit of wealth and social order. Nationalism of a sort was beginning to claim the loyalties of men. It was certainly not the ecstatic and religious nationalism that swept Europe like a feverish plague in the nineteenth century, complete with sacred hymns and imperishable vows to the nation and flags that transubstantiated cloth and color into the very reality of the state itself. But in the sixteenth century there was an ever widening sense of common birth among some peoples, and that sentiment is where nationalism begins. Gifted men were finding pleasure and reward in devoting themselves to corporations that embodied secular aims—the city of Florence or the English monarchy or the cantons of mountainous Switzerland. Whatever it was, men felt themselves called to serve in the world of here and now, and their ideal of the active life eroded away the old ideal of withdrawal and contemplation. So monasteries—those stony bastions of reverent quiet—fell into cracking decay.

In England, Thomas More, like Martin Luther, entered upon the study of law and thought of going into the monastery. But he remained in secular life. In 1516 he published a work of enduring interest, his *Utopia*. This little book purported to be an account of an ideal republic discovered on an island off the coast of the New World by one of the seamen who had gone sailing with Amerigo Vespucci. Here everything was done in the light of reason and natural religion. There were monastic orders in Utopia, but the monks spent their lives looking after the sick, repairing roads, mending bridges, hauling dirt, and doing other hard work for the society at large. They were not the withdrawn and isolated men of the Benedictine ideal, singing away at their prayers in the wilderness. And though Thomas More tremendously admired the Carthusians, whose boast was that they never needed reforming because they had never been corrupted, he did not join them, though he did as a student live in their monastery and subject himself to their discipline. In an earlier century he would probably have taken their vows and remained with them; but, like his Utopians, he saw a higher ideal of serving God by serving in the world, and his respect for the Carthusians seems more like nostalgia than desire. More's later references to monks were often tinged with contempt; for instance, he called Luther "a mean and base little friar," as though there were something about friars themselves that made them unworthy to contest with kings. An earlier age would not have found it so.

Respect for monks elsewhere was largely gone. They were the butt of endless jokes. The friars—wandering preachers who took vows of poverty, chastity, and obedience—were almost stock characters in the comedy of the period. Giovanni Boccaccio, in his *Decameron,* made them experts in seducing silly women. Writers of less genius made monkery and vulgarity synonyms. Monks were like the Negro butlers and maids in those dreadful and sickening old plays that used to be put on in American high schools. When a black face appeared, the audience got ready to laugh. So with monks in the Renaissance. Peo-

26

ple had not laughed at Francis of Assisi or at Dominic, and, in a way, laughter was ringing in a new and more secular age.

In Germany the old ways held on longer than elsewhere. Martin Luther entered the monastery to seek the salvation of his soul, just as similar men had done in previous centuries. And the Augustinian house, the so-called black cloister at Erfurt, appears to have been thriving.

He proved to be a good monk, advancing rapidly in the esteem of his brother monks and his superiors. In April 1507, when he was twenty-three years old, he was ordained to the priesthood.

The priesthood held a monopoly over the sacramental system of the Church. A sacrament was a ceremony devised by the Church to give Christians strength against the special moments of uncertainty in their lives. There were seven sacraments by this time: baptism, confirmation, the Mass, penance, ordination, marriage, and extreme unction. They were considered to be vehicles of divine grace to help the Christian pilgrim make his journey from earth to heaven. In a way they were like transformers, in that they received God's infinite and terrible force and reduced it to a form that would help men without killing them. Each of the sacraments shared in the nature of Christ, for each was an incarnation of sorts—an invisible spirit or power, clothed and communicated in a physical form that could be perceived by the senses, just as Christ had been divinity clothed in flesh.

The greatest sacrament of all was the Mass. When Christians were uncertain about the meaning of the harsh world around them, they could share in the Mass and believe that they were sharing the flesh and blood of Christ himself and that the world itself possessed a mystical and spiritual quality beyond the brute impressions of the senses.

Like other religions of antiquity, Christianity had developed a cultic Communion meal of bread and wine. The first three Gospels and Paul's first letter to the church at Corinth hold that the meal was instituted by Christ himself. Very shortly it became not a meal but a ceremony performed by a priest. And from an early time Christians believed that on this occasion, Christ was somehow especially present in a powerful way. Early, too, came the custom that only the priest should drink the wine, token of the blood. The common herd got only the bread, and even this they could not touch with their foul hands. The priest put it on their tongues.

By 1215 the belief in the special presence of Christ in the Mass had become the doctrine of transubstantiation. This formidable word means that the substance of the bread and the wine changes by miracle. No longer is it bread and wine; it is the actual body and

27

blood of Jesus. It has the taste, smell, feel, and look of bread and wine, but that constancy of appearance is part of the miracle. God, knowing we would be sickened by the taste of raw flesh and blood, stoops to our weakness by keeping the elements in their familiar form. The form, however, is only a saving illusion. Christ himself is there in real flesh and blood, and there are no bread and no wine at all in the Sacrament. So decreed the Fourth Lateran Council, called by the greatest medieval Pope, Innocent III. And since then Catholic orthodoxy has held that this has been the true faith since Christ and the apostles.

Our age can hardly grasp the awe before the Mass in medieval people who took the rite seriously. Martin Luther took it seriously indeed. The first thing a new priest did after his ordination was to perform the Mass. Luther was so terrified that he nearly fainted. Psychologist Erikson leaps on Luther's fright with both feet. The occasion was one of semipublic celebration. Hans Luther had ridden in with a company of friends to witness the great moment, and he brought with him a handsome donation for the monastery. He and his dearly beloved son saw each other for the first time in two years. Erikson lays Luther's terror on the presence of his father; psychologists take fathers seriously.

But this is modernity speaking against a history Erikson and all the rest of us cannot truly get into our souls. If someone handed Erikson a ticking bomb, told him that it was powerful enough to blow up him and his study and all the other people in his building, and kindly asked him to hold it for a few moments, he would most likely tremble. Luther held God Himself in his hands during the Mass. And in an age when God was more than an abstraction or an oath, it was enough to make any sensitive man quake. Luther's father undoubtedly added to the discomfort of the young priest; but God as Luther conceived Him contributed the tremendous mystery that nearly overpowered him.

Hans did his part to make the occasion grim. The father still smarted because his dear son had gone against his wishes. After the Mass, the two of them sat with the rest at dinner in the great monastery refectory. It was supposed to be a joyful time, but Hans could not contain himself. And when his son began to explain the terror of soul that had brought him to be a monk, Hans burst out, "Better hope that it was not a trick of the devil." These words, so Martin wrote much later on to his father, "went deep in my soul and stayed there as though God had spoken." And God did such things: He spoke with unexpected voices, and men besides Martin Luther paused to hear Him in maids and children and in dreams and perhaps also in the grumbling of fathers.

The question of Luther's God at this early time in his career deserves some comment here. His God was filled with contradictions that sometimes seemed to war against one another. He was fierce and terrible, but He was also loving and good. He hid Himself in the darkness, and yet He was the God of light.

Monotheism requires that we take the terrors and delights of life and fit them together in the same design. Polytheism allows us to assign different forces to different gods; these gods may quarrel with one another, compete, and fight, giving us a convenient explanation for the rise and fall of kingdoms, the lightning that smites the earth, the waves that beat angrily against the shore, or the sun that pursues a lordly way across the crystal heavens, extinguishing the shining stars in his path.

Monotheism requires a greater leap of the imagination, a reconciliation of the darkness and light, health and plague, under some general principle. And if the God is a person with a name and a mind, the problem of explaining the warfare we perceive in nature becomes immense, dreadful, and finally baffling. Whether the people of an age perceive God more as blessing or scourge depends on an indefinable and intangible spirit whose parts we may perceive by detached observation but whose whole we can only feel. In the end Luther's thought was remarkable because he managed to affirm both the love and terror of God, the revelation and the mystery, the light and the dark, making the mystery the very sign of God's presence among men. The Christian suffered as Christ had suffered, and God was seen to be blessing men in just those tribulations where the human reason in its feeble powers could see no blessing at all. The Christian suffered as Christ had suffered, and so the Christian should rejoice in his adversities, for they were a sign that God was with him.

But this great paradox was not clear to Luther when he became a priest, and he saw God with fear and trembling and in a state of dread that threatened to exclude love altogether. We have already mentioned some things in this time that provoked many people to fear the terrors of divinity. Theology added to the mystery and symbolized the spirit of the age, not creating the atmosphere of dread and mystery but expressing it in the religious terminology that was the vehicle of most thought. Luther had imbibed enough theology to make him faint before the Mass.

He was trained in the school of nominalism. In an earlier time a form of realist theology had predominated. "Nominalist" and

29

"realist" deserve some explanation, because they convey attitudes about God and His relationship to man and help us understand Luther a little better.

Each doctrine had many forms. But "realism" is generally the notion that all the universal concepts by which we define our world exist as real ideals in the mind of God. If I apply the concept "man" to one of my fellow creatures, it is because God possesses in His mind such a concept. Nothing is a man that does not conform to the idea that God has in Himself as to what a man must be. Individual men change and pass away as do all things on earth; consequently, they are not truly real, for reality is the same now and forever. God's idea of man endures eternally the same, and so the idea is much more real than its copy who may live on earth hardly more than threescore years and ten.

And when I recognize another man to be a fellow creature, it is because my mind is in some way in tune with God's mind either by direct divine illumination or by some indirect means. Thinking becomes possible for me because there is something similar in God's mind and in my own, just as the mirror held to the sun will reflect the same light, however imperfectly. Learning usually becomes recognition in this scheme of things; my mind responds to images implanted in it by God, and when I see John Jones I know him as a man because he corresponds to an idea of "man" already set in my head.

Realists have a habit of thinking that man's reason may gain a fairly large knowledge of God without the aid of revelation. From a practical standpoint, the realist is likely to be quite sympathetic to the notion that God has spoken to virtuous men in all religions; for if any mind is correctly disciplined to reflect on the nature of experience and the world, that mind will arrive at many correspondences with the mind of God. The very act of good thinking becomes in some sense an act of communion with the divine, for valid general concepts have their origin in the divine intellect.

The nominalists asked a very simple question: How do we know that these general concepts really exist in the mind of God? And they gave that question a very simple answer: We do not know anything about God's mind except what He chooses to tell us, and He has not chosen to tell us how He thinks. God is so different from us, so much more potent than we are, so pure compared to our impurity, so wise compared to our ignorance that we cannot apply our feeble reason to anything about Him. What are general concepts like "man" or "chair" or "tree"? They are but names (hence the name "nominalist" from the Latin *nomen,* meaning name). We can use the names effectively enough to communicate with one another, but we can have no idea whether these names have some sort of eternal and defining existence in the mind of God. No real comparison can be made between our being and the being of God. No analogies can be made between our minds and God's mind. When we engage in thinking, we can have no idea whether we are sharing in the mind of God or not.

The nominalists felt that God was a tremendous mystery, holy and exalted beyond all human reasoning. The violent and chaotic experience of the time probably led them to such a belief before they made philosophy about it, for any God who sponsored such a world must appear to be veiled in shrouds of darkness. The only way men could know anything about God was to listen to what He told them. God did speak in a revelation that men could trust—in Scripture and in the tradition and authority of the Catholic Church.

In some cases the nominalists developed a fine talent for hair-splitting. They were always seeking to prove that the powers of our reason were strictly limited in divine matters, and sometimes they asked questions that annoyed the pious. Could God have become incarnate in a stone or an ass? Could God command someone to hate Him and then condemn that person for his hatred? The questions have the air of the frivolous about them, and they help to explain why Luther had such a lifelong aversion to philosophy. But they were serious questions in their way, intended to show man the limits of human reason. God could do anything He wanted to do, and if He wanted to be incarnate as an ass, He could do so without the approval of man's understanding as to what things were appropriate and polite for divinity. Whatever God *does* binds man to certain obligations, and whatever God commands, man must obey. In fact, the notion of God suffering on a cross, bleeding and dying the death of a criminal, is hardly more reasonable than the suggestion that God could become incarnate as a stone. In this sense the nominalists prepared the way for Luther's feeling about the incapacity of human reason, though in other respects that we shall see, he differed from them profoundly.

Now with this veiled and terrible God of almighty power and mystery hulking above the world, it became extremely important to men to be sure that they were getting the right revelation. Satan was out to trick the world into hell. A God utterly beyond the power of reason to comprehend Him was a terror, for there was no way to measure Him or to predict Him, to see if what He did fitted human standards of fair play and decency. Hence Luther's stabbing fear at his father's suggestion that he might have been deluded by Satan to become a monk. It was simply no good to say, "Oh, God would not permit such a thing to happen!" That was to use reason, human standards and measurements, and the infinite and terrible God Luther worshiped was beyond all such petty efforts of the mind of man.

And so at least from that time on, Luther's quest in life was one of terrible simplicity. He must find a revelation that was sure, a Word of God that was authentic, that he could cling to knowing that here God had spoken and that he had heard Him aright. It was a search for certainty beyond reason, and it led him to rebellion against a Church that in his mind exalted reason and the traditions of men over God's Word.

3

THE TEN YEARS between Luther's ordination in 1507 and the outbreak of the Reformation in 1517 have been called his years of silence. They were the years of quiet ferment and seeking when many things were happening that would shape his world-historical importance.

In the winter of 1510–11 he was sent to Rome with a fellow monk on business for his order. He was in the Holy City for only a month, and this was the only time in his entire life that he was to leave the German lands. Even so he was most happy in Rome when he was attending a German church and associating with other Germans.

Luther was always a provincial. The fact that he was a brilliant man was not enough in itself to broaden his mind or to mitigate the terrible propensity of all provincials to think that the sun shines only on them and that their convictions are the rule of the world. Luther had little sense of history and even less sense of the great inhabited earth. He could hold that Almighty God for His own mysterious purpose damned nearly everybody to hell merely because he himself had little personal knowledge of the multitudes condemned to perdition. They were always abstractions to him, and we can bomb or damn abstractions with few qualms. It becomes more difficult to condemn people we can look in the eye, whose humanity we have experienced ourselves, whose numbers we have seen. Tolerance is usually the possession of the urbane. Luther had no sympathy at all with the world of courtesy where gentlemen observe the proper forms and let each other live. He equated tolerance with cowardice, urbanity with hypocrisy, and respect for one's adversaries with a lack of conviction. We see him running like a baffled sheep with his flock of fellow Germans in Rome, and we may wish that he had mingled a little more with cultivated Italians and learned something from them about manners.

As it was, he hated the Italians. He thought the Italian clergy profligate and superficial and downright blasphemous. He complained that Italian priests rushed through the Mass like the wind. When he had scarcely begun his own celebration of the rite in one of the great churches, impatient priests behind him were hissing at him to get a move on, probably because they were in haste to rattle off the Masses they were paid to sing for the dead. Their piety was as cold as a machine.

Yet Luther himself was enthralled with the mechanical observances of touristic piety. He rushed all over the city, visiting holy places, adoring relics from the saints, even climbing on his knees the holy stairway claimed by tradition to have been in the palace of Pontius Pilate in Jerusalem. Christ himself had ascended it, so the legend said, and it had been conveniently transported from the Holy Land to Rome for the benefit of Roman Christians and their visitors.

Relics were already beginning to be mocked by the time Luther went to Rome. Chaucer had made fun of the credulous who worshiped sheep's bones when they thought they were worshiping the bones of saints. Erasmus of Rotterdam, Luther's older contemporary, mocked the guardians of the shrine of Canterbury for preserving the handkerchiefs Thomas à Becket had supposedly used to blow his nose. Some shrines held milk from the Virgin Mary's breast. Many had a thorn or two from the crown of thorns spiked down on the head of Jesus before the Crucifixion, and there were enough pieces of the true cross around to build a rail fence across Europe. In some places the pious pilgrim could look on some of the very mud God had scooped up to fashion Adam. Thomas More was enraptured by a handkerchief made by the Virgin Mary herself, sewn by her own hand in fine stitches More admired. Just outside of Rome one could see a plaster cast of Jesus' footprints where he had stood to confront Peter when Peter was fleeing from persecution. (I have seen this relic myself; Jesus appears to have worn about a 14-D.)

In Luther's time relics were tied up with indulgences. As we shall see, indulgences were linked to the Catholic doctrine of purgatory. But the real meaning of the cult of relics was probably more subtle. Religious people believe in an invisible world, a realm removed from the ordinary senses of humankind. But there is a limit to how much most of us can be devoted to this invisible world without demanding some evidence of its presence, evidence that we can see and maybe touch. Saints and their relics were associated with miraculous stories of wonderful things that had happened when at divine moments the icy screen between the seen and unseen worlds was broken down. Christians who saw the relics, who stroked them with devout fingers and kissed them with pious lips, were seeking some palpable assurance that the miracles they had heard about so often really had happened in the same world where we all live, a world that is so painfully ordinary and hard, so unrelieved by any sign that we are important in the cosmos. If I am shown some of the milk from the Virgin Mary's breast, for a moment I may feel closer to her and her serene mercy; and if I am shown a chunk from the true cross, the events of the sorrowful treading of Christ from Jerusalem to Calvary swim before my eyes, and for a little while I can believe more profoundly that they really happened.

The problem is that though the religious mind often craves these visible manifestations of the invisible world, they may prove to be terribly unsatisfying when they do appear. It is perhaps much like other human expectations. The person who has never been to the Swiss Alps may conjure up in his mind visions of a snowy paradise where his soul will float in clean, clear air; but when he arrives he finds a pall of automobile exhaust in the highest passes, litter along the roadsides, and the Swiss everywhere—all likely to reduce his delight in the heavenly spectacle of the mountains. So it is that the enjoyment of things in prospect is often greater than the pleasures of possession; and if we translate that common experience to a religious dimension, we may understand why relics generated so much motion and so little real piety. Some looked at the milk from the Virgin's breast and found that it resembled ordinary powdered chalk. And they saw that the pieces of the true cross looked like very common wood; and in some way that they could not truly express, they were vaguely disappointed. So pilgrims made their long journeys to shrines in Rome and elsewhere and discovered, as Chaucer apparently did, that the trip was more pleasurable than the visit.

No one in our history has ever wanted to be more in communion with the invisible God than Martin Luther did. He threw himself into the cult of relics with the same energy with which he did everything. There were more relics in Rome than anywhere else outside of Palestine, and he tried to see them all. But he was not satisfied. His comment on climbing the holy stairway is instructive: "Who can tell if it is so?" His vague disappointment was the honest reaction of a sensitive man who came seeking something and went away empty-handed and yearning for something more.

Luther was to move in the other direction, exalting God and the unseen spirit to the point that man's communion with the divine was built on invisible faith. In the process, the cult of relics and all the other paraphernalia of shrines and holy places designed to ease the intercourse between visible and invisible were swept away. His inner evolution was not unlike the development of religious consciousness in the Hebrew people in the Old Testament, who, it seems, found the adoration of the bull-calf god unfulfilling and turned instead to the worship of an awful and invisible Jehovah, whose dwelling was behind a veil in their Temple in an empty room called the Holy of Holies. One can never possess the invisible, and so one is less likely to be disappointed in an invisible god.

Before his Roman visit, Luther had been transferred from the monastery at Erfurt to the University of Wittenberg, where he was to be a professor. Here, in 1512, he took his doctorate. It was an important degree in the Middle Ages because it gave the theologian the sanction to publish his views. In the age of the printing press, newly dawned on Europe, publication was more important than anyone in 1512 could imagine. Luther always had an eye for the significance of his own experience, and for the rest of his life he was proud of his doctorate. The degree made him a teacher to the Church, and he regarded it as a seal for the ministry of reformation he later found thrust upon him.

Wittenberg was a squalid little town located on infertile land at the fringes of nowhere. Its university was the brainchild of the elector Frederick of Saxony, a shy, withdrawn, and finally mysterious man whose personality comes down to us as a confusion of shadows. He seems to have wanted a university to compete with the great University of Leipzig in the neighboring territory of ducal Saxony. Ducal Saxony was more important in every way than electoral Saxony except that the prince of electoral Saxony cast one of the seven votes that made a new emperor on the death of the old. Frederick collected relics and professors and cultivated silence. He sent word to the Augustinian order at Erfurt that he could use a teacher or two from their cloister, and they sent him Luther.

By spending the rest of his life in Wittenberg, Luther, with his sparkling and powerful personality, was assured of being able to dominate the lesser minds around him, and so the streak of provincial intolerance that was so powerful in him could run unabated until his death. But his isolation also gave him the freedom to follow the instincts of his own mind and heart without having them blunted by crowds of the urbane and the articulate, those men wise in the ways of the world who are always able to tell the young with great authority to walk in the footsteps of their fathers. Luther was a sort of William Faulkner in his time, a genius with words, always treading to the different drummer pounding a tattoo in his own heart, able in his isolation to grow wild and true to himself.

In time he was happy enough with Wittenberg, perhaps because his physical surroundings never seemed to mean much to him. But his introduction to university teaching was bitterly unpleasant. Before he took his doctorate, he had to teach Aristotle's logic and physics. That experience filled him with frustration and then with fury against the Greek philosopher, and his later life was deeply colored by it.

The explanation of his anger is simple enough. Aristotle is the master of those who think that the world is an orderly place no matter how chaotic it may seem. He taught that man's reason was his glory and that human reason was adequate in itself to perceive the nature of things. The world we see, hear, taste, feel, and smell is the real world, and the impressions we gain from common sense are true. Everything in the world exists for a purpose, and a sensible man can find that purpose merely by looking for it. Trees exist to give shade, lumber, and fruit to man. Man exists to live with his fellows in society. Truth, virtue, and all the other moral values are open to reason; and when we know what is right, reason can help us do the right thing.

Aristotle believed in God, but his God was impersonal and abstract. He would never think of speaking to God or calling Him by name or asking Him to change something. His naturalist philosophy was a rebellion against the irrational impulses of Greek antiquity that found personality in every spring of gushing water and in every breath of wind. Personal polytheism may seem quaint and romantic to us, but the strain of satisfying so many conflicting gods was a burden to humankind, and polytheism is always unsatisfying to a few who want to arrange the world in a single order of being. Aristotle spoke of God as the first mover and the reason behind all things, but he spoke always with the same detachment that one might use today to discuss the age of the moon or the composition of a gas. He loved God only as one might love geometry or the orderly shining of the stars in the clear night sky. It might be said that he did not really believe in an invisible realm at all, for to him true reality was always wrapped up in sensual experience. He believed in the eternity of matter, and he did not truly believe in the immortality of the soul because he did not think the soul could exist without a body to express it. Even qualities like beauty, always so hard for ordinary men to define, were in Aristotle's mind associated with forms the intellect could understand. He was one of the first to set down rules for drama, and the fact that he did so shows his belief that the most moving experience of the

37

Greek world was, on reflection, open to understanding by the analytical mind.

Luther considered man utterly wretched and miserable, and though he could respect human reason for devising ways for society to exist on earth, he felt utter contempt for the claims of philosophy to unravel the enigma of the universe and the nature and destiny of man. He was always tremendously awed before the mystery of things. Aristotle, with his explanations of everything under the sun, was to Luther a charlatan, a kind of huckster of the intellect, offering a worthless tonic to cure a deadly sickness. Luther always knew God as a person with a name and a will, acting, speaking, giving grace, withholding grace, sustaining the world by His power and directing it till doomsday. Aristotle's God never spoke, never listened, never comforted, never judged, never interfered with the orderly course of nature. Christians had begun to rediscover Aristotle's thought by about the year 1000, and many were entranced with his rules for logic that made orderly and systematic thinking possible. Everyone recognized that there were dangers to the faith in his philosophy, but many believed that they could sort out the benefits from the perils and use Aristotle's help in the coherent expression of Christian doctrine. But to Luther, mixing Aristotle with Christianity was as foolish and dangerous as mixing poison with water. Aristotle taught an excessive pride in human reason; Luther thought that such pride kept men from God and damned them to hell.

And so it was with relief and devotion that Luther turned from Aristotle after his doctorate and began to lecture on the Bible. From then until the end of his life the Bible was his book, and we cannot begin to know Luther's thought unless we know something about the Scripture that informed him at every moment.

Hardly anyone reads the Bible any more, though most still profess to revere it. Consequently, it is nearly impossible to set ourselves in Luther's chair and to approach the Bible as he saw it.

The grand assumption of Christians in his time was that the Bible is the consistent revelation of a single God. That view had been held for centuries, and it was to endure in the West until modern times. But the attempt to reconcile everything in the Bible always caused difficulties. Does one practice holy war as Joshua did when he massacred the citizens of Jericho to the last child, sparing only one whore and her household? (He saved the whore because she had hidden his spies, though the Bible is discreetly silent about how the spies happened to be in her house.) Or does one practice the ethic of Jesus, who told his disciples to turn the other cheek and blessed peacemakers? Does one cheer for Elijah, who supervised the slaughter of 450 priests of Baal, and for Samuel, who cut Agag into pieces before Jehovah? Or does one listen to the counsel of Micah the prophet, who asked: "And what doth the Lord require of thee, but to do justly, and to love mercy, and to walk humbly with thy God?" Does one follow the practice of Ezra in the Old Testament, who treated the Moabites as a people who were cursed by God and who could not share the divine promise to Israel? Or does one remember Ruth, the woman of Moab, who became the great-grandmother of David, the greatest of Israel's kings? Does one follow the general Old Testament view that there is no life after death? Or does one accept the New Testament teaching of resurrection with its promise of everlasting life in a pearly white city? In the Book of Exodus God's people are supposedly commanded by the deity Himself, "Thou shalt not suffer a witch to live"; and later the witch of En-dor brought the shade of the prophet Samuel back from the grave to pronounce doom on King Saul and his minions. But in the New Testament, familiarity with demons leads to such torments that no one could possibly practice witchcraft. Which view does the Christian accept? The questions can be multiplied by the hundred.

In our modern liberation from the tyranny of the sacred, we may say easily enough that the Bible is really not a consistent book at all. It is, rather, a motley conglomeration of sublime feeling, glorious prose, exciting history, opaque and meaningless mystery, bloodcurdling superstition, and simple trash. There are a few erotic poems scattered through its pages, and there is some exalting religious verse that has inspired the ages. There are tales of epic grandeur where heroes bestride the earth, and there are delightful little vignettes such as the story of how the Ark of the Covenant came home to Israel from the Philistine lands. Some books, such as Ezekiel, are so confused that medieval professors considered it a sporting challenge to lecture on them.

The Bible was collected by pious men with different motives in different epochs. That all these writings found their way into one book is largely a matter of accident. Most of them remain at odds with the temper of our times. Nowadays translations of the Bible pour off the presses, and they are avidly bought by people who seem to think that informal English will make the great sacred book of the West more meaningful. But the Bible remains the same underneath, no matter what language is used to paint its realities, and not even slang or paraphrase can remove its inner contradictions and difficulties.

Medieval expositors wrestled hard with the Bible. Their problem was to make it consistent. To do this, they arrived at the so-called "fourfold interpretation" of the text. This meant simply that they would look at any passage in the Bible in four different ways and choose the one or ones most edifying to the Christian community.

For example, they might stick with the literal meaning of the text they were treating. When Joshua fought his bloody crusade against Canaan, he was fighting for the right of Israel to settle in the Land of Promise, where God's purposes would be revealed to all the peoples of earth. The story was worth studying in itself because it was exciting, and it assured Christians that they worshiped a God who wove the threads of history—even those colored bloodred—into a tapestry of splendid beauty and meticulous design. The literal meaning was never completely given up by medieval expositors, and it helped mightily to preserve a powerful sense of history in the Judeo-Christian tradition nearly unique in all the civilizations of the world after the fall of Rome.

But the medieval interpreter also had the authority of Paul the Apostle to put the literal sense aside in appropriate cases. Paul had said, "The letter killeth, but the spirit giveth life." So the medieval mind turned enthusiastically to spiritual interpretations of the Bible. The essential Platonism of Christian thought in the West after about the year 250 aided in this process. The Platonist was always likely to see the visible and ordinary things of life as signs and symbols of an invisible and extraordinary realm of reality. Scripture became, for the Christian who had become saturated with Platonism, a conglomerate of sign language, prodigious with many kinds of divine revelation.

Most favored of all the spiritual senses was allegory, for it gave the luxuriant medieval imagination the freedom to flourish like a jungle plant. If we take Joshua at Jericho as an allegory, we can see Christ assaulting the fortress of Satan, and Jericho becomes a symbol of the gates of hell that cannot prevail against the Church of God. The blast from the horns that brought the walls tumbling down is a symbol of the irresistible Word of God that destroys the powers of darkness. The capacity to find such an allegory of Christ in the Old Testament gave Christians in the Middle Ages a pleasure not unlike that experienced by the mathematicians of the eighteenth-century Enlightenment. The chaotic phenomena of a mysterious world were seen, on reflection, to be parts of a grand unity comprised of ever-recurring themes or ever-constant laws.

Allegory allowed some embarrassingly erotic parts of the Bible to be understood in a sense safe enough for the meekest nun. The Song of Solomon is an explicit and beautiful love poem; but by the time Christian expositors got through with it, the little poem had become a chaste rhapsody between Christ and his bride, the Church.

This particular allegory may yet be seen in the headnotes of some editions of the King James Version of the Bible. "Thy two breasts are like two young roes that are twins," exults the lover. And the King James Version solemnly assures us that here "Christ setteth forth the graces of the church."

Allegory could take the bite out of the uncertain moral examples of many Old Testament heroes. When King David lay dying, his counselors sought to warm him up in a way that had not failed to heat the king before: they put a young girl named Abishag in bed with him. When David made no response, they knew that he was indeed close to death, and they made plans for the succession.

As far back as Jerome, the great Bible commentator and translator, this story was shocking to Christians preoccupied with chastity. Jerome said that Abishag was really an allegory of wisdom. An old man could hug wisdom to his breast without having passion aroused in his body. And in Luther's own time, Thomas More thought that allegory was the only possible way to make sense out of this passage.

Scripture could also be taken in a moral sense. In the case of Joshua at Jericho, one learns obedience and humility. The Christian should do exactly what he is commanded to do by God, and God will do the rest. And Scripture could be taken as a reservoir of hope, which, heaven knows, men in the medieval world badly needed. The idea that the River Jordan is the symbol of death that the Christian must cross to get to heaven is retained in many venerable American songs. It would have been perfectly at home in the medieval pulpit or lecture room, where expositors sought passages in the Scriptures that would tell their listeners about the bliss of the life to come.

In spite of the flexibility granted by spiritual interpretations, Scripture still caused problems. Heretics were always popping up. (The word "heretic" simply means a person who makes a choice, and the heretic was anyone who thought that there was some choice besides the Catholic Church.) Heretics were always quoting Scripture against the established order. It is not quite true to assert that the Reformation delivered the Bible to Christians after they had been deprived of it for centuries; but it is true that Catholic authorities did not hanker to distribute the Bible to the masses. The masses were dangerous and hard to control, and they were likely to read things in Scripture that made them more dangerous still.

From the very earliest times in the Church, even before the New Testament was assembled, there was developed the idea of tradition that helped impose some restraints on careless or dangerous Scriptural interpretation. Tradition may be defined as the cumulative power of custom in the Church. It was the experience of Christians from generation to generation, examined, reflected upon, sorted out, and passed on. Custom received its authority by the devout fiction that it had originated with the apostles, who had taken it from Christ. The Fourth Gospel concluded with the remark that Jesus had done so many things that the world probably could not hold the books that would have to be written if his acts were all written down. And so it was easy enough to believe that Jesus had passed on many teachings to the apostles that did not happen to be included in Scripture and that the apostles in turn had passed these matters on to the Church at large. Easy and comforting. Thomas More could share in the Mass and believe in his heart that the very gestures of the priest at the altar had been handed down through the centuries from Christ himself!

So custom could speak where Scripture was silent, and custom helped to interpret Scripture in such a way that Scripture did not conflict with what the Church was doing and thinking. Custom taught Christians to come to church on Sunday rather than on Saturday, the Jewish Sabbath commanded by God in the Old Testament to be observed by His people. Custom taught Christians to abandon circumcision, although God had told Abraham that circumcision was to be an everlasting covenant. Custom held that the doctrine of the Trinity is clearly stated in the Bible, although in fact it is not. Custom taught Christians when to observe Easter, although there is some confusion in the Gospels as to when Christ was crucified, and there was a great deal of perplexity among early Christians about when the Resurrection should be celebrated. And so it went. Whenever there was a problem, Christians tried to solve it by turning to customary usages.

In the Middle Ages, when God seemed so close to earth, custom in all the realms of life—in common law, in government, and in theology—possessed a divine authority even in small things. If the custom displeased God, people thought that He would not allow it to continue. Consequently, if a custom had continued for a long time, it was thought to be God's will for it to be preserved. The sense of history was so foggy and confused in the Middle Ages that no one could really tell when a custom had originated, so the tendency was to say that all customs went far back into antiquity; and in the case of those customs controlling Christian faith and practice, it was easy enough to argue that they had come from Christ himself. Supposedly a great unwritten tradition was handed down from age to age, and by Luther's time many people thought that tradition contained much more than Scripture itself.

With tradition so powerful, Scripture came to be quite subordinate to it in spite of the pious affirmations of loyalty to Biblical authority all through the Middle Ages. In fact, Scripture was reduced to a mere repository of proof texts called up as the occasion required to support an argument, whether the text really had anything to do with the issue or not. Allegory allowed almost any verse to be made a proof text for almost any doctrine. Did the papacy need to support its claim that it owned complete spiritual authority over all Christians and that kings should not meddle in the religious life of their subjects? Well, there is the rather mysterious text of Luke 22:38 in which the disciples, on the evening before the Crucifixion, say to Christ, "Lord, behold, here are two swords." The popes took this to mean that there are only two authorities in the world: an authority over things subject to time, which is government; and an authority over things eternal, which is the papacy. Since the two swords are distinct, the powers that govern the earth should leave the popes alone. (The popes could not return the favor by leaving kings alone, since kings were mortals, subject to sin, and required the help of the papacy just as ordinary Christians did.) The point is that Scripture was used by nearly everybody to prove nearly anything that needed proving without regard either to the history of the text or to the context in which something was found.

To gain some idea of how Scripture was used in the Middle Ages, we might imagine a pompous gentleman, popular on the after-dinner circuit because he is able to recite Shakespeare from memory for every occasion. "Much ado about nothing!" he might roar at some squabble in a civic club. "To be or not to be! That is the question!" he might gravely tell a group thinking about organizing a Little League baseball team. "Out, out, damned Spot!" he might cry if his dog wandered into the living room and jumped up on his guests. We might all hear a lot of Shakespeare from such a man. But we would learn more about Shakespeare's work if we sat down and read the plays from beginning to end, studied their language, examined their characters, and ruminated about their themes and their internal organization.

So it was with the Bible in the Middle Ages. Men knew its words and could recite them on every occasion. But they did not know it as a book. They found in it only a collection of divine quotations, and they were sure that in its pages they could find one for every need.

By Luther's time, the humanist scholars of the Renaissance were teaching a different approach to all literature, both classical and Christian. These men knew a great deal about the Roman world where the New Testament had originated. More and more of them were learning Greek, and some were even studying Hebrew. With their new linguistic and historical tools, they began looking critically at Jerome's Vulgate, his Latin translation of the Bible that had been used for centuries. In 1516, Erasmus, the greatest scholar of them all, published a printed text of the Greek New Testament. He provided a set of notes to his text, some of them critical of the Vulgate. Luther and others studied the text and pondered the notes, and they saw that the Church of the New Testament looked quite different from the Catholic Church of their day. Whether these differences were essential or not remained to be seen.

By the time the Erasmian text appeared, Luther's own conception about how to read the Bible had already been formed. In October 1512, he began lecturing on the Psalms in a style that would remain consistent with him for the rest of his life in referring to the Bible. He treated the Psalms as entities that must be studied as a whole to be understood and tried to elucidate the literal meaning of the text. From our point of view his lectures are not literal at all because he found Christ speaking in nearly all the Psalms. For him, the Psalms were an elaborate commentary on the life, the Passion, the death, and the Resurrection of Jesus.

Yet if he did use allegory in this sense, it was an allegory strictly limited when compared with the efflorescence of the medieval theologians. And even at the first, Luther is quite free from any pretensions about deriving philosophy from the Bible. He wanted to know what God had said and done. The best way to gain this knowledge, he thought, was to study the Bible, which he regarded as a history of the acts of God, and he used one part of that history to illuminate another. In the historical sense, his method was literal. He was searching for the difficult inner consistency I mentioned earlier as a necessity for those Christians who take the Bible to be the revelation of a single God. In the next few years he lectured on Romans, on Hebrews, and on Galatians. And by 1518, when the Reformation was heating to the boil, he believed he had found the theme that held all the Bible together.

*L*UTHER NOT ONLY taught the Bible in the classroom to university students; he preached regularly from the Bible in the pulpit to congregations drawn from the public at large. Many of these lectures and sermons have come down to us. They reveal several common themes.

Most prominent is a sense of profound abnegation. His burden was the helplessness of man before sin, the terrible distance of man from a holy and awful God, the total dependence of man on Christ the redeemer. Always he put stress on the interior life, the secret motives of the heart that can be concealed by outward acts. In one of his earliest sermons he expressed an insight that was to become celebrated when he repeated it again and again in the Reformation: Even good works may be sin. He meant that a work that is only outwardly good, done in pride and without the fear of God, is no good work at all. The thought is not original. The Pharisees, with their pride at keeping the law in the time of Christ, provided a model for everyone who ever wanted to avoid hypocrisy or belabor hypocrites. (At least that is the picture of the Pharisees we gain from the prejudiced witness of the Gospels.)

Still, there is something so earnest and so constant in Luther's humiliation of man that we must pause before it. He was appalled by the sin of Adam. He groaned that sin had cast all Adam's progeny away from the face of God. In these works Luther is the great psychologist, the man who studies the soul with no illusions and no pretense. Everywhere he looked he found greed and pride, so that the most glorious achievements of mankind were seen to rest on the ashes of selfish desire.

Later on in his life he claimed to have passed these years in a miserable and incessant struggle to cleanse himself from sin. He resorted to confession time and again, so he said, seeking by the sacrament of penance some way to the liberation of his soul. Penance was supposed to relieve Christians of the guilt of sin incurred after baptism. And an old Luther recalled himself as a tormented young man confessing all the sins he could remember, receiving absolution, departing, and running back to the confessional almost at once, wearing his confessors out with his guilt. He would recall some other evil thought, some hidden wickedness, some sinful deed that he had left unconfessed, and back he would go to pour out his heart and to beg forgiveness.

We do not really know how to judge this account of himself as seen from the perspective of age. When Luther told these stories, he had lost his hold on the world at large. He was the patriarch of Wittenberg, surrounded by a swarm of eager young students who crowded in with him at table and took down every word he said between bites. They were youths eager to find drama in their hero—and fans who require drama from their idols usually get it.

But it is difficult to find evidence of a titanic struggle in the written works of the young Luther that have come down to us. He looks very much like a young man of great intelligence developing his thought in a rather normal and undramatic way. Yet there was enough in the theology of the period to inspire the fear of hell in the staunchest human heart, and Luther's memories may have been more accurate than the surviving documents might lead us to believe. For if one takes hell seriously—its black flames and eternal torments, its horrible thirst and unendingly disagreeable company—one must beseech God for escape from such a destiny. Can the sinner do anything by himself to save his soul? Luther looked very deeply into the Christian gospel and examined the nature of the human heart, and he concluded that man could do nothing, nothing, nothing at all.

Christ became the center of Luther's theology, and his view of man revolved around the pole the cross made in history. Here, as in our view of the Bible, we find a great gulf fixed between ourselves and Martin Luther. Jesus has become a name we apply to any current ideal of man. In our own century Jesus has been depicted as a soldier sighting down the barrel of a rifle in a World War I poster. He has been a great scoutmaster for the Boy Scouts, and he has been a kindly Rotarian in the minds of the business classes. He has been a rather vacuous-looking shepherd in thousands of picture books for city children who have never seen a sheep, and he has been a rock singer in several stage productions that have attempted to translate the New Testament into the language of beats and hippies. Some people claim that he was married, though there is no evidence that he was; others make him one of the ascetics who produced the literature of the Dead Sea Scrolls. Some have made him a political conspirator, and some have thought that he was a revolutionary who failed. Someone has said that Jesus is what we call the face we see reflected back at us when we look down the deep well of history to that distant water we can never truly reach. But all of this is to say that we take him no more seriously than we take a billboard along the highway, and we can hardly grasp the significance of the very name of Jesus to Martin Luther.

To Luther, Jesus was the incarnation of the God who had made the world, given order to chaos, flooded evil humanity, and set the rainbow in the sky as a token both of His mercy and His wrath. Jesus was the human form of a God Old Testament man could not look on and live. And Luther, intoxicated with his vision of God, was astonished by the way that terrible deity, who could melt the world with a breath, had shown Himself among men in the Jesus who had died on the cross, a death that was necessary if any human being was to be saved. It was not a heroic death that one might expect if a god must die. It was, rather, the most shameful and humiliating death the ancient world could devise, full of lingering suffering, flies and clotting blood, torturous thirst, and running public excrement. And God Himself had suffered this death because no one on earth could be redeemed without it.

To Martin Luther, the cross said something final about the nature of man. For surely if there had been any capacity whatsoever within man to help win his own salvation, the cross, with its shame and its agony for the Son of God, would not have been necessary. So the cross, standing in its deep hole in human history, was a crude and eternal sign that fallen man was wicked in every thought and every deed and required the grace of God for salvation. It was a grace so necessary that no one could be redeemed without it, so complete that no one could do anything to earn it. No one could help grace help him once God had granted it, and no one could relinquish it. In the overpowering way Luther interpreted it, the cross meant a theology of predestination. The working of the cross was finally beyond all the power of reason to comprehend, and not even the greatest philosophers, unaided by revelation, had ever imagined that the cross would be the way God chose to work with the world. The cross perpetually humiliated the power of human reason to decide

47

what is decent and orderly for God. With its mystery, terror, and glory, the cross was the sign that God was working out His own purpose in creation, a purpose filled with darkness and triumph and incredible, unimaginable victory; and in that cosmic drama, individual men became only tools in an unseen hand.

Possessed by such a stern theology, an earnest seeker must ask this question: How can I know if I am predestined by God to be saved? The early English Puritans kept diaries to record their every inner feeling, seeking for evidences of their election to salvation. When they detected within themselves the right sentiments, they could assume that they were among the predestined. They were not far removed from Luther's mentality.

For Luther first taught that the proper attitude toward God was one of harrowing and abject humility. Go into your soul; examine every thought. Question the motive behind every deed. Find the wickedness that is there. Find in yourself nothing at all worthy to be called good. And in that prostrate humility, you will find grace. All men are tempted to pride. Some are even proud of their outward humility. But the true Christian is one who is always becoming more aware of himself as a hateful sinner, more conscious of God, who alone is holy and good. God has pronounced man to be a sinner, and the cross shows just how great that sin must be. The true Christian is one who agrees with every particle of his being in the judgment that God has pronounced against him.

Several notions from the Bible play a part in this rather grim evaluation of mankind. What is the law of the Old Testament for Luther? It is what the Apostle Paul declares it to be in the book of Galatians and in the book of Romans. The law is the schoolmaster to bring us to Christ. By trying to keep the law, we recognize our impotence. Though by endless struggle we may achieve outward conformity to the law's demands, we can never in our lives arrive by our own efforts at the inner purity, the simplicity, and the unselfishness the spirit of the law requires. So we are humiliated by our very effort to be good; and in the midst of that humiliation we despair of our own powers, and so make it possible for Christ to save us. Only when we admit our sinfulness can Christ save us. Thus the Christian, in Luther's words, is both sinning and justified at the same time; for in this life he cannot free himself from the limitations of human flesh, and yet he is justified in that he acknowledges his helpless state and calls on God for salvation. God saves only sinners, and in Luther's view sin becomes the basis for our fellowship with God, since God will not have anything to do with those who come to Him claiming righteousness.

If we try to put Luther's thought into some contemporary mode that we can understand, we find it to be like the fear of presumption that seems to be attached to both superstition and religion. We may say, "I've never been sick a day in my life!" Then quickly we knock on wood or else repeat the verbal equivalent of the knocking: "Thanks be to God." Our unspoken fear is that the gods will strike us down for presuming that our health has come from some special power of our own when it is really in their hands. We must not threaten the place of the gods by assuming that frail things like ourselves are equal to them. On the contrary, we must recognize our inferior station and hope that they will receive our humility as an offering and not strike us down for our presumption.

Luther's notion seemed to be that he would not dare claim a shred of goodness that would make God count arrogance against him and cast him into hell. This fear would account for his frequent confessions. He did not want to leave anything in his heart unscanned lest God judge him for his oversight. If he could search himself thoroughly enough and hate his flesh completely enough, surely that full abjection would be a certain sign that God had granted him grace. In the tedious process of this humiliation, he discovered a wisdom that was greatly to affect his later theology of faith. He learned that even humility can be a great deal of work.

In the meantime, his views of man's low estate drove him into rebellion against an important current of late medieval theology. This particular line of thought, associated with the name of Gabriel Biel and others, tried to make room for man's free will under a sort of umbrella of God's sovereignty and grace. The impetus for this reasoning came from a common desire we can all understand today in the threatening world of B. F. Skinner. These thinkers wanted to provide a place for human freedom and dignity. At the same time they wanted to make God just, for it was a cardinal article of faith that the God who revealed Himself in the Bible and in the tradition of the Church was a God of justice. Yet how can God be considered just when He predestines some to damnation and some to bliss before they are born? Even Luther said that his first impulse was to hate such an intolerably autocratic deity.

All Christians agreed that God had the absolute power to do anything He wanted. The seemingly futile and silly arguments that God could incarnate Himself as a stone or an ass were attempts to express in striking ways God's unlimited power. Gabriel Biel and his disciples, and the nominalist school in general, did not have much faith in the power of the unaided human reason to discover divine truth. But they did believe that reason could sort out the data of revelation and arrive at some probable conclusions about the way God had chosen to work with the world.

God had chosen to be a loving father, they believed, and a loving father did not do outrageous things. Though He could do anything He wanted, God had in fact bound Himself to a certain order within which He would work with men. He had revealed that order to the Catholic Church. Within it He chose to redeem humanity by the Incarnation of Jesus Christ, by his terrible death on the cross, and by his glorious Resurrection. He chose to establish an infallible Church to announce the truth until the end of time. And by a supreme act of grace, He chose to allow man to possess some free will. God was so powerful that He could grant the dignity of liberty to humankind. Some even said that a man could love God with all his heart and soul without the help of grace, but this was an extreme position. For most people, the freedom God granted to man was more limited than that, but for all of them it was the possession of freedom that made men responsible. God, then, was just when He judged men according to how they used their freedom of choice. And so His justice could be affirmed in the way Christian tradition said it must be.

We must be careful not to equate these Christian theologians with the Platonists of ancient Greece, who made man an immortal soul, preexisting, almost a god in himself, and who planted in him an autonomous free will that spontaneously followed the intellect. The Platonists saw man as covered with glory and tended to regard sin as ignorance rather than malice. Most late medieval Catholics never pretended that man's freedom came from himself. It was a gift of God, and it was usually a very limited freedom, hardly more than the liberty to accept what God graciously gave. Once that freedom did move to accept God, God helped the Christian to do good works and to gain the merit that would lead to salvation. The late medieval theologians were preoccupied with what was called the "first grace." How did man get himself into a state where he and God could be brought together by God's grace?

Nearly everybody in Luther's time held that man was so fallen and miserable that he could do no good deed of itself worthy of credit by God. So in the midst of his stress on good works, the Christian theologian of this time knew a dependence that would have been quite foreign to Plato or, for that matter, to Aristotle. For even if the outward act was good, the Christian could perceive failures in his motives. I may give alms to help the poor out of real compassion, or I may give to the poor only because I enjoy the feeling of superiority giving allows me. I may minister to the sick because I have sympathy for them, or my visitation may be made only to build my reputation.

Often in good works, good motives and bad motives are so mixed that no one can tell which predominate.

God, in this view, did not judge works finally on their intrinsic worth. Rather, he judged them in a relative sense, measured against man's capacity, and nearly everybody agreed that that capacity was weak. No man could do a perfectly good work, but every man could do his best; and if a man really did do his best, God counted the result as sufficient. He was a decent God who did the fitting thing according to what He had revealed about Himself. Works became good, then, because God accepted them as good, in much the same way a loving father will accept a painted squiggle as a work of art because it is done by his six-year-old son. God is a Father who wants to bless His children; and when they do their best, He rewards them as if their works were perfect.

It all sounds very simple and easy, and this scheme of things had the advantage of making grace necessary while at the same time requiring effort on man's part. Certainly most people were satisfied with this arrangement and lived in the comfortable and conforming piety that has been the mark of most men since the beginnings of human religion.

But there was one dreadful question that, when asked, could turn the pious heart to stone: How do I know when I am doing my best? That question cannot be answered in any realm of human activity. Indeed, the very use of the sentiment, "Well, I did my best," is often merely an excuse for failure. In the later Middle Ages, no one could be sure when he was doing his best in the sight of God. That meant that no one could be certain that he was going to be saved. For Luther, doing one's best was tied up with being humble. And he could never rest assured that he was humble enough.

There was a moral value to this uncertainty, and such people as Gabriel Biel and Thomas More tried to affirm man's place in society as a moral and responsible person. The very uncertainty about one's salvation could keep people somewhere between presumption and despair, in a continual tension to try to do good works. Presumption, as I have said, has been regarded as blasphemy against the gods in nearly all religions; but it was also a menace to the social order in an age when religion was viewed as a necessary restraint, helping to keep society from falling apart. If I presume that I am going to be saved no matter what, I am likely to be lax in observing the moral law. I may drift about here and there, eating, drinking, and being merry, and my responsibility to my neighbor—a responsibility that makes me a good citizen—may float away in a haze of overconfidence about eternity.

But despair is also a threat to society. For if I believe myself doomed to hell, I may as well enjoy life while I have it here in this world. Hell endures forever, and so in this fleeting world I may as well drift about here and there, eating, drinking, and being merry. We are able to understand something of the late medieval hostility to resignation and despair when we consider the hippie communes of recent days and the outrage they have provoked among conservatives. The hippies lost hope in any of the goals proclaimed by tradition to be worthy. They pulled out of society to seek happiness now, believing that they might as well enjoy the present just because tomorrow looked so bleak. One consequence of their defection has been a rash of commencement speakers urging new graduates to believe in the system and to contribute to it. For if everyone gives up, the system will fall. And so it was in the sixteenth century when despair about one's salvation could lead one to abandon the larger requirements of civilized life in a mad drive to enjoy the present before it was too late.

From a pastoral point of view, this uncertainty allowed moralizing preachers to belabor their congregations with endless sermons on striving. The theology behind the moralizing was directed to the intentions of the heart. Do your best, and God will give you grace. But do not stop to congratulate yourself that you have already done your best. Doing good works becomes a habit. That habitual striving, cooperating with grace, strengthens the soul. Thus not the outward act alone but the inner condition of the soul remained important to all theologians of the period.

But common people rarely stop to listen to subtlety, and most preachers are likely to pander to what their people will understand. In this rush of moralizing, people were likely to think that they could do enough to earn their way into heaven. If I go on pilgrimage to some far place, if I give generously to the poor, if I attend Mass and confession regularly, wear a hair shirt next to my skin, leave money to the church in my will, send my sons into the monastery and my widow into the nunnery and have myself buried in a simple monk's cowl, I will look like a true Christian. And so the crude equation was often made, "If men think I am doing my best, God must surely agree with them."

Luther was always deeply offended with these popular notions about the nature of merit and piety. He was also increasingly uncomfortable with a theology which held that anyone had a natural capacity to make God a debtor. If God must save me when I do my best, then I have some capacity—however slight—to make God obligated to me. And that notion did not fit Luther's experience.

For Luther found that he could not come to God with anything other than what God gave him. God Himself was dark and terrible with mystery except in that shaft of light that had fallen on the world in Christ. The natural man, cursed by sin, was so blind that he could not even see that light unless God opened his eyes. To ask the totally blind from birth to do their best to see was not only a cruel mockery; it was also an affront to the God who alone possessed the power of light and vision. Man could only dare to hope in the predestinating power of God, who alone chose, redeemed, and preserved the sinner without any deserving at all on the part of the sinner himself.

And so even before the outbreak of the controversy over indulgences in 1517, Luther had arrived at a conviction of man's absolute dependence upon God that made man much more abject than the prevailing Catholic theology would approve. His view was also radically opposed to that glittering idol of humanity set up in the sun of the Italian Renaissance. He held to the grim belief that God was gracious to some and not gracious to others and that God's purpose in predestination was known only to Himself and hidden from man.

Predestination was never a stranger to all Catholic theology. Paul the Apostle preached predestination in his epistle to the Romans, and four hundred years later Augustine of Hippo, the greatest theologian of the Church, made predestination a pillar of his faith. Thomas Aquinas also believed in predestination, a fact that Luther seems never truly to have understood, for he attacked Thomas for preaching the goodness of reason and the necessity for good works.

But everyone before Luther seemed to combine predestination with works in a way that provided a place for merit. Augustine and Thomas alike taught that God predestined some and gave them the power to do good works and to earn merit and so brought them to heaven by grace alone, but a grace impelling the elected Christian to serve God. A current of electricity sent through transmission lines will drive a train along the rails to its destination, and without electricity the train will not move one inch. Yet when the power is flowing into the engine, the train must move, and it does so by means of wheels turning around in response to motors being turned by electricity and converting that invisible force into a motion everyone can see. So grace, in the view of Thomas and Augustine, flows into the Christian heart and generates merit that drives the Christian to God. Sacraments, vigils, chastity, pilgrimages, discipline, and all the other paraphernalia of piety thus have a place, for grace uses them as engines for the earning of reward. From a social point of view, anyone who claimed to be a Christian must be able to demonstrate some outward evidence that he was moving toward his goal.

Already by 1517 Luther's view was turning to a hostility toward the very word "merit." The only evidence anyone could have for his own election was a sincere and abject humiliation in his heart, a humility that made him despair of any power whatsoever of his own and drove him to God for relief. The true Christian was one whose sentiments were fully those of the prophet Isaiah: "But we are all as an unclean thing, and all our righteousnesses are as filthy rags; and we all do fade as a leaf; and our iniquities, like the wind, have taken us away." If we continue with our analogy of the electric locomotive (admittedly almost four centuries out of place!), we might say that for Luther man's engine was wrecked and stalled and required a power completely outside itself to drag it safely to its destination.

Humble confession of abject impotence was the sign that grace had already begun to work in the Christian's heart. Only when we are able to make that confession with a completely sincere heart does God grant His righteousness to us. And indeed it is God Himself who humbles us to make that confession possible in the first place. We may say in a somewhat analogous way that only the person who admits that he has cancer can be helped by medical science; but it takes a doctor to diagnose the case in the first place, to tell us what we must tell ourselves and him, that we are stricken and near to dying and need his help. But this is a weak analogy, for to Luther the important thing was not to save this life but rather to save the soul. And the healing of sin—the disease all men have—does not come about by any power within ourselves. Both our recognition of our sin and our turning in despair of ourselves to God to receive His righteousness are processes in the mysterious purposes of God for all His creation, steps in a glorious destiny we cannot see. But if the destiny is hidden, the hope for what will come blazes in our hearts and lights the path we walk in this world.

What was truly revolutionary in Luther was that on the eve of the quarrel over indulgences, he began to see his own earnest striving for abject humility as a work, an attempt to earn salvation by the rituals of abnegation. He was apparently slowly working out another conception when he was struck by an unexpected crisis that speeded up the wrestling of his mind and made him first a reformer and then a heretic.

5

ARTIN LUTHER WAS PROPELLED onto the European scene by a dispute about indulgences. It was on the face of it an unlikely occasion for the rupture of the Catholic Church and the beginning of a long and bloody period of religious strife.

In fact the quarrel over indulgences was like the pistol shot that felled an archduke in 1914 or that earlier shot fired in the morning calm of Lexington, Massachusetts, in 1775. It came as a tiny explosion in a world that had slowly been filling with gunpowder dust. Fire jumped from grain to grain of swirling circumstance until an ancient order had been blown away forever.

An indulgence was part of the mechanism of the sacrament of penance. Penance, as we have seen, was the sacrament that restored the Christian to communion with God and the Church when he had sinned. In early Christianity there seemed to exist a glittering expectancy that baptism would blot out sin forever in the life of the Christian. This optimism was quickly flooded away by reality. For a time the theology of baptism seemed to fix on the notion that no sin committed after baptism could be forgiven. Christians tried to postpone baptism as long as possible. The Emperor Constantine, first Christian ruler of the Roman Empire, put off baptism until he lay dying. His seemed to be a common practice, but it had its dangers. We do not customarily know the hour of our death, and though the comforts of a deathbed baptism must have been great indeed to those who expired gracefully and by degrees, they were not of much value to someone thrown from a galloping horse to die of a broken neck.

Baptism was slowly moved back until it was regularly administered at birth. Little children were not to be deprived of its immense power, especially in a time when death was more likely than not to carry off the child before he could become an adult. So penance was developed to deal with those sins committed after baptism. It was, said Jerome, the second plank thrown to the shipwrecked sailor. He meant that baptism was the first.

Penance developed slowly. By about the eleventh century it had become the monopoly of the clergy. No longer could one devout Christian confess his sin to another and receive the consolation that a loving brother might always give to one in need. Ordination and the increasing isolation of priests from the common life had converted them into spiritual aristocrats, in charge of the sacraments. And under that priestly dominion, penance became a ritual with three steps.

First, the sinning Christian felt sorry for his sin. Good penance required a sorrow called contrition. Every Christian might feel sorry for his sin because sin put people into hell forever. But sorrow originating out of selfish fear was not enough. True contrition was sorrow that arose from a genuine love of God. God the loving Father was separated from His children by their sins, and the good child wanted to restore his fellowship with God and was sincerely sorry that the fellowship was broken.

In that mood of sincere contrition, the sinning Christian went to his priest and undertook the next step in penance. That was confession. In confession the sinner indulged himself in one of the stranger pleasures of Western civilization: He poured out a story of how bad he had been. The priest heard him out in stern sympathy, perhaps admonished him to do better, and granted him absolution in the name of Christ and the Holy Catholic Church. Now the sins were forgiven, and the Christian could believe that those sins would not cast him into hell. But there still remained the final step in the rite: satisfaction.

The origins of satisfaction are lost in Christian antiquity. It probably began in those days when the Church was a powerless sect in the midst of a hostile Roman world. In those tight little congregations scattered through the Empire, the bonds of fellowship and dependence must have been very close. Any sin was likely to break this precious communion. Some sins—such as betraying the congregation in times of persecution—could bring horrible death on one's fellow Christians. Even some sins that did not bring the authorities to drag one's brothers and sisters to death in the arena struck other Christians as horrible enough. These were such transgressions as burning the Scriptures, cursing Christ, or participating in sacrifices to

56

other gods, especially to the spirit of the Emperor. Persecutions never lasted very long. When they were over, many who had forsaken the faith were filled with guilt and remorse, and they clamored for forgiveness and return to the fellowship of the Church. Those who had suffered at the hands of a traitor or who had been shocked in their pious hearts by his iniquities had the right to ask for some proof of his sincerity. Satisfaction may have arisen as something the offending party did to show that he was indeed contrite.

I recently met a boy who had been exiled from a hippie commune in Tennessee for insubordination. Before he could rejoin his congregation, he had to demonstrate a change of heart. He was roving about in the Smoky Mountains near Knoxville, gathering herbs and selling them to flatlanders like me. He appeared at my door early one Sunday morning looking a little like John the Baptist, offering me his herbs and his story and asking meekly for a vegetarian meal. After six months of this cold and windswept humility, he was to be readmitted to fellowship with his spiritual kinsmen in the commune. Though he had had his troubles, he wanted very badly to get back to his people. Between his bites of tomato sandwich and his gulping of milk he confided to me his conviction that his commune offered the only chance he had for happiness. Alas, before his probation was up, the local sheriff raided the commune and hauled away its leaders for making their clan lie down in green pastures of marijuana. But in a way, all the elements of the early Christian experience were there insofar as the commune was concerned. Here was a persecuted group, and persecution gave the denizens of the commune a powerful feeling of solidarity. And of course the excommunicated boy seeking herbs in the mountains was doing a work of exemplary satisfaction.

Satisfaction probably had the additional psychological benefit of reassuring the sinner that he was indeed contrite—else why would he be going on this tedious pilgrimage? It allowed the normal, healthy human being—who is always rather lax and shallow in religious matters—to shrug off his guilt feelings and look to God with some confidence. "Of course I fornicated with the scullery maid, but God's teeth! I went on the damned pilgrimage to make up for it, didn't I?"

It was only a step from this view to the notion that satisfaction itself was a punishment for sin, a punishment not demanded merely by the Church but by God Himself. Here the prevailing sense came to be that if one did not punish oneself enough for sins committed here on earth, one would have to be punished for them in purgatory after death.

Though penance was a great psychological help to the shallow Christian, it had its psychological problems for the earnest. Who was to know if the sinner was truly contrite? In retrospect, it seems that penance put the sinning Christian in an abominable situation. Love a perfect God, and be dismayed for the breakdown of fellowship between you and Him. Know that if the fellowship is not restored, He will cast you into a black, hot hell forever. But do not let the fear of hell drive you to confess your sin, for that craven confession does not count.

It all reminds me of that old folktale of a fairy who promised a wealth of gold to a young maid on the condition that the girl not think of liver sausage while she was digging up the treasure in the basement. Otherwise the gold would vanish. The very admonition made her think of liver sausage if only because she did not want to think about it. And so she never got the gold. So it was with the fear of hell and penance. One could hardly confess one's sins to the priest and not have presentiments of hell lurking around somewhere in the back of one's mind.

The doctrine of purgatory offered a handy escape from the problems of penance. It is a doctrine not to be found in Scripture, and it hardly existed during the first several centuries of the Church. But people did pray for the dead, and this ritual was strong and enduring. The question must arise, "Why are we praying for our dead friends?" If they were in hell, prayer would do them no good, for no one ever escaped hell. If they were in heaven, they did not need prayer. So it was decided that they must be in purgatory, an intermediate state between heaven and hell, a place where the imperfect Christian was purged of all the residue of sin he had not been able to cast off on earth. From purgatory the refined soul would finally emerge spotless into paradise, there to contemplate the perfect vision of God forever.

Purgatory took a long time—sometimes thousands or millions of years—to do its purifying work for most souls. It was thought to be a pretty painful business. The imagery of purgatory got mixed up with the vocabulary of goldsmithing and smelting. That meant a lot of fire and a lot of beating. Though purgatory might well be seen as yet another boon from the merciful God Christians worshiped, it seemed also to most to be an altogether unpleasant prospect. By Luther's time the average man probably feared purgatory more than he feared hell.

The greatest difficulty about purgatory is the very nebulous character of the doctrine, founded as it is on no clear Scriptural authority and arising in ecclesiastical tradition only in response to that popular liturgical practice, prayers for the dead. It was hardly mentioned by the theologians who set up the standards of Christian doctrine for about four hundred years after Christ. So the doctrine of purgatory resembled a free-floating balloon drifting in the theological sky. Anyone with air enough to blow in its direction could make the doctrine drift, and if there was anything medieval popes did have at their command, it was air—air to inflate their own claims to spiritual authority to ridiculous size, and air to inflate any doctrine into its most profitable dimensions to suit their pretensions.

Indulgences were always profitable to the popes. And what the popes finally did was to shift them from one division of the penance business to another, from satisfaction on earth to satisfaction in purgatory.

In the late eleventh century, the Turks had seized the Holy Land—Palestine with all its shrines and relics and blessed names so revered in the pious imagination. Pope Urban II decreed a crusade against the infidel, and he called on Christians to go down to Jerusalem and slaughter Turks to the glory of God.

To encourage enlistment, he issued a plenary indulgence, or, as we might say, a complete liberty with regard to satisfactions previously imposed by priests on all penitents of the Church. The Pope meant that if, say, a priest had imposed a pilgrimage on a penitent, that penitent could go down to Jerusalem and massacre Turks in place of going on the pilgrimage. Any satisfaction imposed by any priest could be dropped by the authority of the Pope if the penitent went on the Crusade instead. The Pope thereby asserted his almighty authority over the lower clergy, since he usurped for himself their customary function of judging what satisfaction was best. He also harnessed some of the chaotic energy being expended by pious Christians who were by then running antlike over Europe, doing satisfactions for their sins.

What the Pope decreed and what many Christians thought he meant were very different things. On the surface the Pope was only using a judgment about what satisfaction was best. But the very concepts of holy war and plenary indulgence, combined with the vivid expectation that the world would soon end, made some Crusaders imagine that if they were killed in battle, they would fly directly to heaven. Their notion represents popular piety, and it was not an official teaching of the Church. But again and again in the history of the Church the papacy has added to its authority by elevating to doctrine notions held by common Christians. For the moment the papal indulgence was consoling to men going so far from home, and popular piety seized on it with the grim zeal that makes some travelers today buy accident insurance in airports so that they may ease their fear of flight with ruminations about the bargain their death would bring.

By 1300 Pope Boniface VIII, whom Dante confidently expected to arrive soon in hell, fell into financial need. The Church was searching around to answer the same brutal question secular rulers were asking: How can we get enough cash to keep going? The dire problem arose in a world where the economy was changing from barter to transactions in money. Secular rulers could sell titles of nobility, and they could tax new business enterprises, and they could charge fees for the services they gave their people. The Church did not have all these resources. But it did have spiritual benefits to give, and popes hit on the notion of requiring some offering to be made in exchange for the blessings. Pope Boniface decreed a jubilee indulgence for Rome. A visit to the innumerable relics there would cancel the requirements imposed by all other priests as satisfactions for sin.

The papal extravaganza was a huge success. Pilgrims flocked into Rome from all over Christendom. Like tourists of all times, these avid wanderers spent a lot of hard cash journeying from church to church, admiring the relics of the saints and receiving spiritual rewards rather painless to win and rather pleasant to possess. And what Christian could resist dropping a few coins into the collection boxes set next to a vial of milk from the Virgin Mary's breast or the chains that had bound Peter when he had lain in prison?

The practical effect of the jubilee indulgence was to assert the right of the Pope to decree indulgences any time he wanted rather than only for some event of world-historical importance such as a Crusade. It was also to extend the indulgence to anyone, including women, who came to Rome. Again the popular piety that prized the indulgences and the papal power that profited from them were finding common goals. By responding to that piety, the Pope was inserting himself and his office even more directly into the religious life of the average Christian. The papal treasury achieved a comfortable fullness. The Pope lessened the authority of all priests under him, replacing their judgment about satisfactions with his own and in the process strengthening the papal monarchy. Naturally enough the sacrament of penance became more impersonal and more mechanical when it was removed in this way from the priest, who was likely to know the offender and the offenses for which forgiveness was required. If the parish clergy was demeaned by the end of the Middle Ages, one of the culprits was the papacy.

In 1343 Pope Clement VI decreed that only one drop of the blood of Christ would have sufficed to redeem all mankind. But Christ shed not one drop but a torrent. Thus there was a surplus of merit in a universe where God allowed nothing to go to waste. That surplus constituted a treasury. And the Pope, who had been given the keys of the Kingdom of Heaven in the person of the Apostle Peter, suddenly discovered that those keys would also unlock the treasury of merits. The Pope could transfer its benefits to anyone he wanted to help. He made this transfer in the grant of an indulgence, substituting the merits of Christ for the sins of the penitent Christian. When the Pope began speaking of conferring *merit* in the indulgence itself, the matter was becoming serious indeed. The doctrine of indulgences was more than an administrative matter now; it was an affair of cosmic significance.

The amazing thing is that with this rapid swelling of the doctrine, indulgences were not formally applied to purgatory until 1476. At that time Sixtus IV, one of the more fabulously corrupt popes of the Renaissance, succumbed to his perpetual desire for more money and to the demands of popular piety and made the indulgence reach to purgatory itself to release pent-up and suffering souls who yearned for access to heaven. The logic was already implicit in the doctrine before Sixtus IV defined it. Surely no one could limit the power of the merits of Christ to this world. And since the Pope assumed the power over this celestial treasury of merits, surely he could extend that power to the poor souls in purgatory. The Church was a communion. It was one body, and one part of the body shared in the life of all the rest. A sweet smell offered the nose will delight the mind; a burn on the finger makes the whole body cringe. And so if anyone living in this world should win an indulgence, its benefits could be transferred to some loved one in purgatory. So it was that popular piety greeted the papal definition of 1476 with enthusiasm.

In theory indulgences were never "sold," though I speak of their "sale" as a matter of convenience. But an indulgence was *announced*. People did what they could to show their goodwill in response to the charity of the Pope, for only a person of goodwill could receive the indulgence. But then the most convenient way to demonstrate goodwill was to make a contribution of money. The indulgence changed hands. Money changed hands. There were even tables to advise the public what constituted suitable gifts for the various levels of the population. Princes paid more than paupers, merchants more than mendicants. But in theory no "sale" was involved. Still, the collection of money was sure enough for bankers to lend money to the popes against the security of cash yet to be collected from indulgences, and the energetic men who went out to distribute certificates of indulgence to the people understood that they were not supposed to return to their bishops with coffers as empty as the pockets of Christ.

During the Renaissance the popes found themselves especially hard pressed for money. Like other princes ruling in cities of the Italian peninsula, they had embarked on a colossal building program. They were patrons of the arts and collectors of very expensive books, and they decorated their chambers and their churches with the work of the best painters and sculptors they could find. The work of a Michelangelo or a Raphael was not donated to the papacy for nothing; artists expected to be paid and to be paid well.

By 1517 Europe was passing into a period of sudden inflation, and all governments were becoming more frantic in their relentless search for funds. But at some indefinable point before this, many Europeans had passed into a mood of profound dissatisfaction with the way spiritual blessings were being hawked about Europe like so much Baltic herring. Probably the dissatisfied were a minority; but when someone arose to speak sharply, it would be seen that others were around to echo those sentiments of outrage. And so it was in the autumn of 1517 when indulgence pitchmen came peddling their wares in the German lands.

6

*L*UTHER'S DISPUTE over indulgences began with the ambitions of Pope Julius II. Julius was the crusty old man who was elected in 1503, perhaps (we really do not know) because the cardinals were deadlocked and hit on him as a compromise. A man of his years—he was sixty—would surely be expected to die soon. The pope elected before him, Pius III, had lasted only a few months in the miasmal air of the Roman summer. It might be hoped that Julius would soon follow him into the other world. And in the meantime those murderous Roman families who ruled the cardinals and had taken the papacy as a prize to be handed from one to another could settle on someone to their liking. So Julius was duly elected. But if shrewd ecclesiastical politicians expected him to wrap a shawl around his knees and sit still on the papal throne until death gently carried him away, they were disappointed. Julius discovered that supreme office in the Church was the elixir of life. He set out on a decade of the most aggressive and vigorous leadership the papacy had known in centuries.

He fought wars, made alliances, and settled the ecclesiastical problems of Europe with a wary political eye on the interests of the papacy. Among other things he agreed to the marriage of the young man who would become Henry VIII of England to the Spanish widow of Henry's older brother, Arthur. Her name was Catherine of Aragon, and her marriage to Henry was strictly illegal according to the canon law, the constitution of the Roman Church. The canon law held that God forbade anyone to marry his brother's widow. But Julius needed the help of both Spain and England to chase the

63

French out of Italy, where French power was threatening papal independence. Julius was never a man to let a little thing like the canon law stand in the way of his partners in alliance. He claimed the right to set the law aside and did so with a dispensation.

Julius also embarked on an orgy of embellishment and building in the city of Rome. Perhaps it was the only orgy of which a man of his years in that time was capable. Whatever his motives, he set out to be remembered. And no one who visits Rome today can avoid the stunning success of his enterprises. It was at his patronage that Michelangelo painted the ceiling of the Sistine Chapel. And it was for him that Raphael painted his great frescoes in the Vatican palace.

The most ambitious project in his plans to beautify Rome was his decision to build a new church over the supposed tomb of the Apostle Peter in the Vatican. The church then on the site was shabby and decrepit and old. Julius wanted a church worthy of the first pope. Such a grand edifice would increase the stature of popes themselves and emphasize their connection to Peter, who, according to the Gospel of Matthew, had been given the keys of the kingdom by Christ. A large and important body of Catholic opinion was opposed to the claims of the papal monarchy; and whereas other popes had assembled theologians to argue for their almighty power in the Church, Julius would assert that authority in stone and concrete, gold and silver, wood and brass. So the church of Saint Peter in the Vatican was projected and designed; and in 1513, as work was getting well under way, Julius died.

He was succeeded by a soft, pink, youngish man by the name of Giovanni de' Medici, an indulged member of the famous Florentine family. He took the name of Leo X, and it was on his startled and uncomprehending head that the Reformation was to fall.

Leo was a peaceful soul, well educated in classical literature, a good comrade, well liked by people who knew him, much given to the pleasures of good living, more moral than most popes of the Renaissance, but limited, as urbane men often are, by the perilous conviction that all the men who count in life are reasonable and that every man has his price. He loved to hunt and play cards and converse with his friends. He is supposed to have said on his election to the holy office, "God has given us the papacy; now let us enjoy it." When he lay dying, his last words to those standing around his bed were, "I wanted to make you all happy." Yet his piety was probably sincere enough, and he very much wanted to see the Vatican church go up to the glory of God, Peter, and himself.

But how was the money to be raised? A great issue of indulgences was proclaimed throughout Europe.

The conditions of the sale had to be negotiated with the various governments involved. By this time governments were beginning to understand something about economics, and they knew that a lot of gold pouring out of a country was likely to lead to unhappy consequences. Indulgences might be looked on as an Italian export, and countries such as France, Spain, and England were strong enough to regulate them so that the balance of payments would not be upset.

Poor Germany—hopelessly divided, riven with internal discord, supposedly ruled by an emperor but in fact ruled by dozens of petty princes—could not resist papal economic maneuvering. Germany in 1517 was much like China in 1895. A potential giant, she was so badly ruled that she was a victim always in search of a robber.

The papacy won the cooperation of young Albrecht of Brandenburg, an archbishop with ambition to collect as many bishoprics as he could. The more bishoprics he held, the more money he could take from his episcopal lands. But he needed money to buy permission from the Pope to hold several bishoprics at once, for the canon law held that a bishop should rule only one bishopric at a time. Only the Pope could grant dispensations to this rule. So Albrecht and the Pope found themselves in need of each other. And Germany was lying there like a bank with the vaults open and all the guards asleep.

Indulgence pitchmen turned up nearly everywhere, and Germany rang with the jingle of coins and the rustle of indulgence paper. Presumably purgatory experienced a considerable draft as souls went whooshing out of it and into heaven.

One of the indulgence peddlers was John Tetzel. Tetzel was a Dominican monk, evidently not very intelligent, a rotund, middle-aged man who had grown up in a system much as a fish grows up in water. He did not seem ever to understand that other men could grow up in something else. He was like salesmen from time immemorial: He thought that he had a product worth buying. Selling it made him a good living and a respected name around his lowly and envious peers. If he exaggerated the benefits of his goods—indeed, going far beyond the warranty issued by the manufacturer—he was only saying things his customers delighted to hear.

"Even if you have deflowered the Virgin Mary, an indulgence will free you from punishment in purgatory!" So he is supposed to have said. The claim was not so farfetched when we consider that the Virgin was often painted with voluptuous naked breasts and that Christ had said that whoever looks on a woman to lust after her in his heart has already committed adultery.

"When the coin in the coffer rings, a soul from purgatory springs!" Another supposed line from Tetzel. Well, why not? The

Church had opposed teachings of instantaneous release from purgatory by the indulgences. But what is time to God? It was an age of exalted spirituality combined with the grossest sensual excesses. Why should the solid and comforting ring of the coin not be a sign of the flight of an imprisoned soul just as the ringing of a little bell at the Mass was a sign of the transubstantiation of the bread and wine into the very body and blood of Jesus?

Tetzel may have claimed that the indulgences were good for sins not yet committed—a position abhorred by good Catholics and nowhere claimed by any pope. But again, what was time to a faith that considered past, present, and future to be but a single moment to God, for whom all being was eternally present?

There are in all supernatural religions elements contradictory to one another. In Christianity one reason for the religion's astounding vitality has been the utter confusion of wildly variant tenets of theology that intelligent men have patiently tried to reconcile, achieving ever new combinations in the process. Everything that Tetzel is supposed to have claimed for indulgences may be justified on theological grounds that some Christians professed to believe, and so Tetzel's promises had a plausibility at the time that they now lack. He combined these serious issues with a blatant and superficial spirit and a mercenary lust that contradicted Luther's experience of God.

It was ironic that Tetzel was not permitted within the territories of Frederick the Wise. Frederick had a stupendous collection of relics that he had zealously put together over the years. He had parts from the bodies of nearly all the apostles and a vial of milk from the Virgin's breast and other assorted fragments of holy things. He had won earlier papal indulgences for his relics, and he did not want any competition from this new issue being touted over the German lands. He was strong enough to forbid Tetzel to come into Wittenberg and to make his prohibition stick.

But Tetzel set up his standard and his collection box at Jüterbog, only a few miles away across the nebulous Saxon frontier. Some of Luther's townsmen naturally enough went over to drop their coins in the coffer and to return with certificates of indulgence and a great deal of smug confidence.

Luther was never able to tolerate any important experience different from his own. He was enraged at the peddling of indulgences and by what he heard Tetzel was claiming for them. In his thought one spent years yearning for God, studying the Scriptures, examining every deed and every motive of the heart, and asserting one's terrific badness and God's boundless mercy and love. But here was Tetzel selling release from punishment for a few coins! Here were Luther's own fellow townsmen flocking to buy this supposed release, whereas Luther believed that the true Christian should be willing to accept any punishment God might give. Again his thought expressed itself in paradox. The Christian who loved his punishment because he believed he merited it was the very Christian who had experienced the mercy of God. There was nothing in this painful concept about release by barter.

Luther did what the ecclesiastical etiquette of the time required when one was offended with something going on in the Church. He wrote a humble letter to his archbishop, who happened to be Albrecht of Mainz, a man whose interest in reform was approximately the same as a wolf's concern for sheep. Luther enclosed ninety-five theses or propositions for debate for the pious consideration of the archbishop.

Each of these theses might be termed a headline. The supporting evidence would be brought forward in the debate itself. It is extremely doubtful that Luther ever intended that a formal academic debate take place on all his propositions. They constituted a short, pungent, witty, and provocative position paper that might be the general introduction to a serious discussion of the matter. It is difficult to avoid the feeling that Luther had no clear aim in mind at all when he wrote the theses other than to call attention to an annoying abuse in the Church. They look very much like something dashed off to vent his spleen, but they were powerful nevertheless. They struck at the very roots of papal sovereignty.

Luther said that the Pope cannot remit any penalties except those he imposes himself. This meant that the Pope could, say, tell a Christian to go on a pilgrimage and then change his mind and tell him to stay home. Or the Pope could impose a penalty for eating meat on Friday and revoke the penalty if there was a reason for doing so. But nobody ever claimed that the Pope could send anyone to purgatory. Consequently, Luther's thesis meant that the Pope could not free people from purgatory, since their release was completely in the hands of God. Luther's statement was mild enough; but the meaning of it was revolutionary, given the pretensions of the popes from 1476 on.

The sentiments limiting papal power are repeated several times in slightly different ways in the ninety-five theses. In my opinion this repetition lends credence to the notion that the theses were not designed for true debate but were a succession of running heads that even a bishop could understand. It was comic-strip theology, though a comic strip of a very high order.

The Pope could pray for the soul imprisoned in purgatory, just as any priest could pray for the souls in his parish, Luther said. But no pope could say to a soul, "Get thee gone from this place of purgation." What Luther was implying was the same thing that conciliar thinkers had said earlier: The Pope is not sovereign over the Church; rather, the Pope is the supreme pastor of the flock, and his most important duties are prayer and spiritual consolation of the people of God.

Throughout the theses one theme is constant. Religion defined by outward observances alone is worthless. True religion is an affair of the heart. Inner religion is always productive of outer acts. But these outward acts did not drive true Christians to mechanical piety—such as the purchase of indulgences. True inner piety made men contrite and devout. It made them give to the poor or lend to the needy; it was generous and not selfish.

The tone of the ninety-five theses gets more and more snappish as Luther advances through the issues. One can imagine him writing furiously, becoming more and more annoyed as he goes along.

In theory the Pope's power to give indulgences rested on the so-called "treasury of merits" that we have noted. In this treasury were stored not only the surplus merits of the blood of Christ but, by this time, the surplus merits earned by the saints now in heaven. Luther denied that the treasury of merits existed. The true treasure of the Church is the gospel of Christ. That gospel is the word that man, helpless and wretched in sin, may nevertheless be saved by the unmerited grace of God.

At the very last Luther turns vehement scorn on the Pope himself. With such claims for indulgences shouted everywhere, it is hard to give the Pope due reverence. If the Pope could free souls from purgatory, why does he not do so out of Christian love? Why does he demand money for doing this merciful deed?

One of Luther's wittiest suggestions concerned endowments bequeathed to the Church by Christians in their wills. For centuries people had been leaving money to pay priests to say Masses in perpetuity for their souls—Masses intended like prayers for the dead to release the souls of the testators from the pains of purgatory. But when a plenary indulgence was granted to such a soul, the Masses and prayers were no longer necessary. If the Pope's claims were true, that soul had now risen to heaven. Everybody agreed that prayers for souls already in heaven were not necessary at all. Then, inquired Luther, why not give the money for these unnecessary Masses back to the heirs!

Why, asked Luther, does the Pope not build the church of Saint Peter with his own money, since the Pope is richer than Croesus? Why is the Pope so stingy with the blessings he claims he is able to give? Why not give them to all Christians a hundred times a day? This was the reduction to absurdity of the papal claims about the supposed authority to grant indulgences at all. And in effect it struck back at the arbitrary decision of that indisputably greedy and corrupt old man who had been Boniface VIII, who called for the jubilee indulgence of 1300 and who by that act asserted that the Pope could issue indulgences whenever he wanted. Floating around in Luther's ridicule was the supposition that the Pope could not make decisions on his own about something so important as the sacraments of the Church. And if the Pope's monarchical authority was limited in such a manner, he then could not assume any power that the consensus of the Church did not grant to him. Thus the ninety-five theses condemned the theory of papal monarchy that popes had struggled ardently to assert at least as far back as the investiture controversy of the eleventh century and, depending on how we may interpret certain texts, perhaps much longer than that. These issues about the place and power of the papacy in the Church were probably vague in Luther's mind when he distilled the ninety-five theses from his boiling pen. But it was not long before they were clear to him and clear to Europe at large.

Today when we examine closely the meaning of the ninety-five theses and discover how radical they were, we still find it difficult to be moved by them. Our world has changed. Probably their most important power when Luther wrote them was that they made people laugh. Even their laughter is cold today. To laugh at events requires that we be charged with a sense of those events so that the incongruity that makes for wit about them snaps at our brains. Today the issues of indulgences and papal power are dead to most of us, and we cannot laugh at what we care so little about.

But when the ninety-five theses appeared, Germans greeted them with absorbed attention and with the kind of belly laugh that makes one man chortle to another, "Listen to this!"

Within only two months people all over the German lands were listening.

7

ONE OF THE MOST furious scholarly debates
of recent years still rages over the way
Luther's ninety-five theses came before the public.

The traditional view holds that on the eve of All Saints, October
31, 1517, Luther nailed a printed broadside containing the theses
onto the church door at Wittenberg. It was a normal procedure when
one wished to announce an academic debate. And the magnificent
picture frequently painted and drawn of stern, heroic, dauntless
Martin Luther pounding the theses to the door with his great hammer
is irresistible. The symbolism is overpowering! One man with his
trusty hammer knocks the old order down, and in the motion pictures made of Luther's career the pounding hammer never fails to
resound like a cannon in the ghostly church on the other side of the
door. It is an image as powerful in its own way as the picture of little
George Washington holding his hatchet and facing up to his father
while a felled cherry tree lies in the background, newly chopped
off its slender stump.

Supposedly someone copied the theses off the door, translated
them from Latin into German, and had them reprinted in bundles
and strewn over Germany. They made Luther a hero overnight.

In the last decade a German Catholic scholar, Erwin Iserloh,
has questioned this picture severely. Iserloh is very sympathetic to
Luther in the current mood of Catholic ecumenicity. But he points
out a few interesting facts, and he has succeeded in raising a bellow
of outrage from those current disciples of Luther who cannot bear
to lose a single glitter of their idol's glamour. To my mind (and

here everyone must study the evidence for himself) Iserloh's arguments are compelling.

In his later life Luther talked endlessly about his career as a reformer, and overzealous students sat at his table and tried to write down his every word. In not one case did he ever speak of posting the ninety-five theses on the church door. In several of his own works Luther reviewed the beginning of the controversy, and again he is silent about any public posting of the theses. He recalls that he did preach to his people about what grace and remission of sins really were, and he seems to have discussed the matter in private with his associates and to have sent copies of his theses to learned friends. But none of this equals the public act of hammering the theses onto a church door and calling for a disputation.

Iserloh holds that the story of the nailing of the theses to the church door comes from the pen of Philipp Melanchthon, who wrote a short summary of Luther's life a few months after Luther died. Melanchthon was a professor of Greek, a fine theologian, and one of Luther's closest colleagues for many years. He was to become celebrated as the "teacher of Germany" when he tried (mostly without success) to restore public education to German children after the Reformation had virtually destroyed the old system of ecclesiastical schooling. But Melanchthon had not yet come to Wittenberg when the theses were written, and he could not have been a witness to the event. The argument made by some that he surely would have been corrected by eyewitnesses had he been mistaken about the posting is an unwarranted inference from silence. Nearly thirty years had passed by the time he wrote. It is not at all certain that any eyewitnesses were still around. Melanchthon made other errors in his account of Luther's life, but no one seems to have corrected him. And even if corrections are offered, they are no guarantee that any author will think enough of them to embody them in a revision.

Luther himself always claimed to have gone through channels, and Iserloh takes him seriously. Iserloh concludes that the theses were not posted, and the gushing of counterargument from zealous Lutheran scholars such as Kurt Aland has only convinced me that Iserloh is right.

We are somewhat handicapped because Luther himself never regarded the indulgence issue as nearly as important as his "discovery" of the gospel and all that came afterward. He frequently regretted that he had still been a convinced papist when the Reformation began, and he admonished readers to be careful when they consulted his early works. The indulgence issue was just a beginning, and only a little later on the source of the conflict tended to be submerged in the flood that poured from it. Were Luther alive today he would probably laugh at all the ink spilled over something he would have regarded as terribly unimportant—how the theses came to public attention.

History always aims at a plausible reconstruction of the evidence from the past. We can never be completely certain about our knowledge, for the effort of writing history is a little like trying to work a very complicated jigsaw puzzle when most of the pieces are lost and those pieces we have are warped and discolored by age. Kurt Aland points out that in October 1516 Luther complained of needing two secretaries because he was writing letters nearly all day long; yet from that year we have today only twenty-one letters from Luther's hand. And so we must take the fragments of evidence that we do possess and try to put them together both honestly and with a certain humility, knowing that many will remain unconvinced by our work when we are done.

Having read Luther and Iserloh, I believe that events might have gone something like this: Luther was enraged at what he heard about Tetzel's indulgence hawking at Jüterbog. Luther himself was in the midst of a great wrestling over the nature of man and the wrath of a holy God. Tetzel's ridiculous preaching about the ease of escape from purgatory angered him in the way historians are likely to be angered today if someone tells them that any child can do history. In that angry mood, he did what one might expect from one of so vehement a temperament: he fired off a letter on the subject to his Archbishop.

But Albrecht of Mainz was a noble of the Church while Luther was only a little monk, a nobody in a wretched little school in a wretched little place. Certain conventions of the time had to be observed for any communication between two men of such disparate ranks. So Luther's letter became obsequious and so sticky with flattery that our stomachs are nearly turned by it. (The letters of Erasmus affect us often in nearly the same way!) Such was the demand of that formal courtesy in whose dreadful efflorescence the Middle Ages finally choked to death.

Luther never liked these conventional formalities. One might say that he was as honest and crude as a peasant's wooden table. But his temper was akin to the spirit of the Renaissance that was yearning to find spontaneous and natural expression amid the rigid and cold jungle of images left over from a petrifying medieval tradition.

Perhaps almost as an afterthought, he conceived the idea of presenting his views on the subject in terms far more pungent and detailed than would have been possible in a direct letter to so esteemed a person as the Archbishop. By presenting his arguments in the form of serial theses for debate in academic surroundings, he could avoid disrespect to his spiritual lord, and he could also make the claim that nothing he said was a firm tenet of his beliefs. It was a safety device often employed by writers of dialogues during that century and afterward, and both Erasmus and Galileo resorted to it. One could say something potentially dangerous but, if pressed, one could retort that the remark was not truly meant. The theses were not a dialogue, of course. But we do know that Luther was reading the *Julius Exclusus* of Erasmus at about the same time he was composing the ninety-five theses. Here Erasmus had written a thunderously satirical dialogue against old Pope Julius, who arrived at the gates of heaven only to be turned away by Peter, who did not recognize him. Erasmus had not signed his name to this dialogue, though he never flatly denied writing it, and Thomas More wrote him discreetly inquiring what was to be done with a manuscript of the work in the handwriting of Erasmus himself that had come into More's possession. From this little dialogue, Luther might well have taken the notion of phrasing his thoughts on indulgences in a form reasonably safe in a world where heresy was punished by horrible death. Hence he could utter such sentiments as these:

When our Lord and Master, Jesus Christ, says "Repent," he means that all the life of the faithful man should be repentance.

The pope cannot forgive any sin; he can only make known and testify to God's forgiveness.

The priests who, when someone is dying, issue penances for him to do in purgatory act stupidly and wickedly.

These weeds—namely, penances changed into the pains of purgatory—were sown evidently while the bishops were fast asleep.

Christians should be taught that if the pope knew the greedy crookedness of the indulgence preachers, he would prefer to let Saint Peter's Cathedral be burned to cinders than have it erected with the skin, body, and bones of his flock.

Christians should be taught that in conferring indulgences, the pope needs and yearns for fervent prayer for himself instead of their money.

So Luther wrote his theses in haste and sent them off to his Archbishop.

Luther was probably taken with his own composition and had a few copies made for the edification and amusement of his friends.

As the weeks wore on in an ominous silence from the Archbishop, he seems to have sent copies to a few other scholars in the German lands, even as scholars nowadays will send copies of their papers to others in the field. An important difference is that it is not at all certain that Luther had the copies he sent printed. They were probably drawn up by hand.

But his friends must have passed them around. Indeed, it is just possible that the theses may have made a great hit with some of the underlings who served the Archbishop himself. Albrecht was not amused. He had much to lose by any dispute that made ordinary people mistrust indulgences. But it could well be that some of his own agents, who might not have admired Albrecht as much as he admired himself, did their part in surreptitiously passing the theses around in Germany. They were translated from Latin to German several times. And if we assume that copies were passed from hand to hand by the almost ubiquitous agents of the Archbishop himself, their swift circulation may be a little more understandable. But perhaps the ironies of history cannot be pushed so far.

The fact is that within a couple of months the theses were spread widely over the German lands, and they provoked tremendous sympathy. The pious sixteenth-century disciples of a Christ who had driven the money changers out of the Temple were now presented with a keen and witty statement of what their own convictions ought to be. And almost instantly the silly teachings about indulgences exploded, leaving only limp and irredeemable pieces on the ground.

Almost in a twinkling, Martin Luther became a famous man.

8

*L*UTHER FOUND HIMSELF in the position of many who have become public figures overnight. He had to explain himself again and again. Being a man with a seething mind, he thought out the things he said several times. And so he found himself thinking new things—forbidden thoughts—and much to his own genuine amazement, he was set adrift from the ancient communion of the Catholic Church.

Luther always denounced the scholastic theologians of the Middle Ages because they mingled reason with faith. But the essence of scholasticism was to use reason to sort out the articles of faith. The schoolmen wanted to present a coherent view of Christian doctrine with no contradictions in the sum of things believed. The truly fundamental scholastic question was always something like this: If I believe A, can I also believe B? And it was precisely this step-by-step way of approaching a problem that led Luther out of the Church.

His questions about indulgences might be paraphrased in this way: If I believe that salvation comes by the grace of God to men who cannot deserve it in the slightest way, can I also believe that the Pope can free souls from purgatory when a coin rings in a box? A scholastic theologian could easily have believed in some form of predestination, and in fact most did; but he might as easily have held that the indulgence was the means by which God accomplished His eternal purpose, the indulgence itself being predestined. Luther's intuition told him that the dreadful and holy God he worshiped could not act in such a frivolous way. Indulgences were to him a contradiction to the grace of God.

Now, when he was asked to explain himself, he had to keep asking other questions of his assumptions, translating his convictions about the nature of true religion into a coherent commentary on Church teachings and practice. The process continued to the end of his life.

His first chance came at Heidelberg in the spring of 1518. Luther was an Augustinian monk. Pope Leo X had a distaste for monks, but he also had a mind for the niceties of bureaucratic discipline. If an Augustinian was upsetting things, his superiors in the order should bring him to heel—or else. For Leo, cultivated man that he was, isolated in his education and in the luxuries of Italy, telling the Augustinians to take care of Luther was perhaps a little like ordering garbagemen to take care of some problem at the dump that was smelling up the neighborhood. Leo did not have to be involved himself; he could keep on playing cards and hunting and doing other important things. A great convention of the Augustinian order of the German lands was set for April in Heidelberg. Luther was summoned to give an account of himself.

He made a great impression at Heidelberg. John von Staupitz, Luther's spiritual mentor and a leader of the Augustinian order, was still convinced that Luther's opinions were orthodox. He had known the young man since Luther's entry into the order in 1505 and had often given him counsel. And now he wanted to present his Luther in such a way that the dangerous question of the nature of the Pope's authority over purgatory would not come up. Like many another teacher, Staupitz could not truly understand the destiny of a unique and beloved pupil, and he thought that if he could simply turn the discussion aside from the indulgence mess, everyone would see the Luther he knew and realize that he was a gifted and orthodox Christian.

Consequently, Luther presented some theses on free will and grace and argued them before a crowd of his fellow monks. He must have done so with pleasure because these were the real issues of theology to his mind, and they were much more important than the status of indulgences.

Here familiar themes came out. God's law does not save anyone. The law shows men how much they sin because the law defines what sin is. The righteous man is one who confesses his sin and understands that he should be damned. No one is free to do good. We are all free only to do evil. Only when the sinner despairs of his own capacity for righteousness can the grace of Christ work in his heart. The cross of Christ is everything. To the Christian that cross means suffering and mystery. But the cross is also the grace that brings salvation.

Here Luther again attacked Aristotle for his confidence in human reason. We can understand Luther's reasoning already from what we know of him before this moment. How could reason conceive the cross? And what good was the cross if man's will could do anything on its own? One must feel that Luther enjoyed his assault on those who thought themselves educated because they understood Aristotle.

At Heidelberg Luther seemed tolerant, patient, and good-humored. Somebody called out, "If the peasants heard this, they would stone you to death!" I am not sure that anyone knows just what Luther said to provoke this outburst. Most likely it was an opinion that he was to repeat again and again: People should stay in the status in which God has placed them. The life of the true Christian is suffering. No one should expect anything else. When a man does suffer, though he is innocent, his affliction is a sign of the blessing of God. Not sentiments that would sit well with peasants in turmoil, yearning for better treatment in this world. The issue was serious enough, and it would become lethal. But now when that anonymous voice cried out from the audience of rapt monks, everyone laughed. Luther laughed, too. The old men were bewildered; the young men were captivated. One of the young men was Martin Bucer, the later reformer of Strasbourg. In 1529 he was to side with Ulrich Zwingli of Zurich in one of the great confrontations of the Reformation, and Luther was to rebuke him face to face and reject him as a Christian brother. But now the world seemed at springtime, and under Luther's sun green things seemed to be growing everywhere.

It is not difficult to see why. We have already mentioned that the later Middle Ages were choking to death on forms. Chivalry, piety, dress, death, poetry, even meals, were marked by elaborate and ossified conventions that seem quaint and picturesque to us today. But the formalities were a dreadful burden to people who had to suffer them or else admit to no status in the world. And if one does put so much stress on observing all the forms, human nature experiences an oppression that may be too much for it to bear. Our own generation has witnessed the revolt of blue jeans and rock music against the stultified conventions of the gray flannel suit and the contrived dignities of slow dancing to the soft music of very large bands. We are now observing that revolt itself has become an institution, and Luther's movement was to be brought to living death by the same fatal process. But like the revolts of our time, Luther's began as a quest for honest and free expression against the conventions of stultifying dignity and restraint. What a grand power it was to argue primarily from Scripture when most previous disputants had come into intellectual battle dragging a whole baggage train of ancient authorities, Fathers, philosophers, and theologians! And what force it must have had to announce that the will of God ran the world when men were frantically scurrying about trying to run things on their own!

There are recurring times in our history when men are consumed with the responsibility of striving and the ethics of a success built on the mastery of traditional forms. During these periods people are likely to believe that the very order of the universe depends on their willingness to follow the old and intricate ways with meticulous care. But there are other times when people learn with relief that civilization does not depend on themselves and that if they live spontaneously, doing what they feel is right, the skies will not fall. Luther's first, fresh, beautiful proclamation was that God was free and sovereign over all the complex forms by which men tried to keep the spiritual peace of the world. And many devout young men heard him gladly.

To see Luther at Heidelberg is to see what he might have been— a witty, warmhearted young theologian debating calmly and easily certain propositions that had always found shelter, however scant, within Catholic orthodoxy. Had he been left alone after Heidelberg, he might by now have retreated to the footnotes of history, to become the property only of those few specialists who would have devoted their lives to the study of his obscure works, a dimly recalled Martin Luther become the horn on the nose of this or that professional academician charging headlong at some adversary on the decent and quiet turf of scholarly meetings where reputations are made and broken in a tiny world.

But the Church's authorities in high places found themselves in much the same situation as some American university presidents in the hectic decade of the 1960s. They lived in an orderly institution, faithful to old ways they thought were sacred, and any breach of discipline had to be punished and the guilty made to admit their errors in public. They might have hung back on the indulgence matter, correcting the worst abuses as they ultimately were forced to do, letting the caldron cool down in Germany until the affair that Luther had stirred up became only stagnant water. But they were men whose own position depended on the firm support of their underlings. They wanted to get Luther perhaps because as long as he survived, their own self-confidence was bound to suffer. And certainly they were enraged at him because he had punctured a very profitable industry with a stab from his pen.

So Luther was summoned to the south German city of Augsburg in October 1518. Now he would confront not sympathetic fellow monks but Tommaso de vio di Gaeta, called Cajetan, and Cajetan was a cardinal of the Church. Their meeting was a disaster.

Cajetan's attitude was a reflection of the spirit prevailing in Rome. How dare this little monk protest against what had been decreed by many people who were more important than he was and who knew so much more than he did about what was good for the Church! It was very nearly a standard reaction by the bureaucratic mind that seems to be the same in all ages. High churchmen wanted to hustle Luther down to Rome, intimidate him into a recantation, and, failing that, burn him.

But Germans were by now intensely interested in the fate of Martin Luther. They could look back on centuries of financial exploitation by the popes. Luther said that the German lands had become the Pope's milk cow. Papal law courts were an abomination. Any question involving clergymen or matters of religion (including marriage, one of the sacraments) was heard before judges who were clergymen. The case could always be called down to Rome on appeal, and if some poor layman had a petition against a priest or a monastery or a cathedral chapter, he then had to pay his own expenses to travel to Rome, to present his case afresh before haughty ecclesiastical judges, and to support himself during the long delays in procedure. In Luther's case it was hard for Germans to believe that anyone opposing the view of the Pope on indulgences could receive a fair trial in the Roman courts.

Government in our day is strong enough to defend us from most of the tyranny of clerical pride. Government regulates marriage and divorce, government courts will hear any case involving clergymen accused of criminal acts, and no government in the world today will burn a man to death because some ecclesiastical establishment proclaims that person unfit for the society of decent human beings. But in Luther's time the confusion of German politics made a flabby defense against the intrusions of the Pope's judicial authority.

John Huss, a religious dissenter from Prague, had been summoned to a church court at the Council of Constance in 1415. He had opposed the authority of the Pope. The Emperor Sigismund gave him a safe-conduct (we would call it a passport) and promised

79

him a fair hearing at Constance. Huss went in the hope of debating his views before the Council. But once there, he found that churchmen had persuaded the Emperor that no promise need be kept to a heretic. Huss could not debate; he was ordered to recant. And when he stood by his faith, he was burned at the stake. His followers at home were outraged. They went to war, and Bohemia and southern Germany were burned and bled by the Hussite Wars for a generation.

The smoke from those wars still burned in the nostrils of some Germans. If the Pope hauled Luther off to Rome and burned him, the Germans might have to pay the price in blood and fire while the Pope went back to his hunting and his games. Even strictly orthodox Germans were frightened at that prospect. The elector Frederick of Saxony had an eye for political reality. And he seemed to regard his professor Luther with a proprietary air as he viewed the relics he had gathered in his great church. He had no wish to see Luther go down into Italy, where no German could protect him. And he certainly had no relish for the civil war that might result. So the meeting at Augsburg was arranged with Cajetan, who was in Germany on other business.

Even so it was a dangerous moment for Luther, perhaps the most dangerous of his life. Cajetan arrived in town with a swarm of retainers. Luther could have been kidnapped. Augsburg was not far from the borders of Italy, and he could have been out of the reach of German authority in a night. He heard rumors on every wind and took brazen insults, and his friends at Wittenberg feared for his life.

Cajetan was nearly fifty years old, elderly for his time, a short man with a short man's aggressive and uncompromising confidence in himself. He had been an expert debater in his younger days. Once his students hoisted him on their shoulders and carried him through a cheering crowd after he had soundly thrashed his opponents in an academic disputation. He was an ardent defender of the papal monarchy. That monarchy had, after all, recognized his worth and made him a cardinal. He had served as a papal diplomat, successful in courts where men kept their tongues and their daggers oiled. He had written learned commentaries on Thomas Aquinas. He was a prodigy grown old and more careful for his reputation than for the future, and he possessed that specious importance of very good, second-rate men who vaunt themselves because they are so close to the center of power.

His attitude toward Luther was that here was a young man needing correction and that correction required only a stern word from the almighty tongue of the great Cajetan. In the retrospect of history he seems arrogant, inflexible, condescending, and opaque; but he was probably a standard product of any bureaucracy, seeing life set down as a series of orderly channels through which one passed with bowing respect to get what the bosses might condescend to give. He could not truly take Luther seriously because in Cajetan's world the people one took seriously had rank, reputation, and power and moved serenely through life on a cloud of ceremony.

Luther was a nobody, a type to offend bureaucrats in all ages because his case had become a public matter. Every bureaucrat worth his desk knows that the public cannot understand anything, that it needs to trust the organization and its leaders, and that anybody within the organization who takes his case to the people can have only bad motives.

Cajetan demanded that Luther recant. Luther asked that Cajetan prove him wrong. Cajetan, very much annoyed and impatient, quoted papal pronouncements on indulgences. He included the declaration of Pope Clement VI that there was a treasury of merits that popes could dispense by means of indulgences. Luther disagreed, holding that Cajetan had misinterpreted popes, Scripture, and tradition. Cajetan waved the arguments away. Luther had only one choice —to recant. Cajetan had not come to Augsburg to argue with an upstart. He had come to judge and decree and get on with his proper business, which did not concern Luther at all. When Luther was ready to recant, Cajetan would hear him.

Luther was left to cool in his rooms, there to talk with a few theological small fry from Cajetan's entourage. They came to tilt with him and to drop snide threats. His friends worried. Rumors abounded that plots were afoot. Finally Luther was persuaded to leave town for his own safety.

The interview with Cajetan was fateful. Here was the majesty of the Roman See delivered to Luther in the form of an arrogant cardinal who treated Luther like dirt under his feet. Luther was not made to take such insulting condescension. That attitude on the part of his adversaries was always to sting him to fury. He went away from Augsburg smarting from the cavalier handling he had received, bitter and frustrated and spoiling for a continuation of the fight, a man who believed that he had been unjustly put off, evidently burning with all the things he might have said had he only had the chance.

Cajetan's citations of papal authority worked in an opposite way from that which he had intended. Luther seems not to have given much thought to papal decrees or even to the papacy in his earlier lectures and notes. He condemned wickedness in high places and attacked the pride and luxurious living of prelates in the Church, but these blasts were a part of the sermonic lore of the time. There is nothing in the documentary evidence to suggest that moral corruption in the Church had occupied Luther's mind in any extraordinary way. He took the Pope to be the head of the Church without defining that headship very clearly. He did not use papal decrees to clarify the Scriptural text, for he preferred both early and late in his life to explain one Scriptural passage by reference to another. He did not even seem to ask the questions about the nature of the papacy that had buzzed about Europe in the previous century when many Catholics argued that a council was sovereign over the Pope and that the Pope was only a kind of ceremonial head of Christendom.

Now, by putting so much stress on what popes had said, Cajetan drove Luther to study the papal utterances and the papacy itself. He came to believe that Cajetan was right! Popes had disagreed with Luther's convictions about indulgences and the treasury of merits. But whereas for Cajetan papal pronouncements were enough to end the debate, for Luther they only proved that popes had erred and erred catastrophically.

This conviction was not yet heresy in 1518. Since 1870 and the first Vatican Council, all Catholics have been obliged to believe that when the Pope speaks as bishop of all Christians, he cannot be wrong in matters of faith and morals. But in Luther's time there was still debate on this matter.

I have mentioned the idea of the general council several times. In 1415 the Church had been divided for a generation among rival popes. There had been two and then three popes, all able to claim some form of valid election, each damning the others, each claiming a unique sovereignty over all Christians. The mess was horrendous, and it had finally been cleared up by the Council of Constance (1414–18), which managed to get rid of the three rivals and appoint a new Pope altogether. It also issued a decree that the authority of the Council was superior to all other authorities in the Church. In another decree it called for a Council to be summoned every three years to hold the Pope responsible for his acts in the meantime.

The Council of those days was made up of bishops and abbots, and it was a sort of parliament in the Church. It was founded on an old Roman notion necessary for any parliamentary order: that collective wisdom, assembled in representative assemblies, is better than the opinions of one man. Few propositions would be harder to defend from historical examples, but it is always an attractive idea to those who do not happen to be emperors, popes, or presidents. The typical conciliar thinker believed that the true Church was the whole body of Christian believers. Since all Christians could not meet in one place, their representatives had to come together and exercise authority for the whole. In a proper Council, God's guiding spirit would see to it that truth prevailed against error. Christ had promised to send his people the Spirit of God, the Comforter, who would lead them into all truth. A majority vote was usually seen as deciding how that spirit was leading. In theory for most Catholics, the Council did not proclaim new doctrine. It only defined and thereby made clearer those propositions that the Church already believed.

The difficulty in this elaborate theory was that a valid Council was supposed to be called by a pope or an emperor. The popes held that only the papacy could call a Council, and the emperors after the Council of Constance lacked the prestige or the power to oppose this view very seriously. In the fifteenth century the popes wrestled against the conciliar movement and gradually prevailed against it. The Pope was in office all the time and had a great judicial and psychological advantage over a Council that met only when the Pope called it. From the very first the papacy refused to call a Council every three years as Constance had decreed. No Pope wanted to risk calling a Council that might try to enforce the decrees of Constance, limit the Pope's authority, and perhaps throw the incumbent out of office altogether. By 1462 the popes had asserted themselves into such power that Pope Pius II could decree that anybody who appealed to a general council over the Pope was a heretic. Like Hitler's march into the Rhineland in 1936, this pronouncement fell on a world that was much too preoccupied with other matters to resist, illegal as the declaration was according to the spirit of Constance.

Yet this proclamation, blunt as it was, could have no real effect on a true conciliarist. He would simply hold that no Pope had the power to make such a pronouncement. And so in Luther's time many devout Catholics still believed that the final authority in the Church was the Council, that popes could err though Councils could not, and that a Council could depose a pope for any reason it saw fit. (It had been held for centuries that a Council could depose a pope if a pope fell into heresy.) Thomas More in England went to his death believing in the power of the Council over the Pope, and he was even willing to entertain the notion that perhaps the Catholic Church could get along without the Pope altogether. Yet he was England's greatest martyr for the old Church when Henry VIII led England out of the Roman communion.

So Luther could have been a conciliarist, and many Catholics would have cheered him on and rallied to his cause. The trouble was that in the winter of 1518–19, his restless quest for vindication led him to doubt the authority of Councils! And if he professed doubt in both Pope and Councils, there was hardly a place left for him in the Catholic Church.

9

THE ECCLESIASTICAL MACHINERY in Rome spun in futility for a while after Cajetan's failure with Luther. Everybody agreed that something ought to be done, but nobody knew exactly what, and there was always pressing business nearby to make churchmen less interested in affairs in distant Germany.

The chief character in the Roman drama, Pope Leo X, was not truly interested in the play. He thought it was just another monkish quarrel, and he did not like monks. Monks were always attacking each other with the peculiar bitterness that is the property of those saintly people whose profession is to be better than anyone else. Leo had been trained as a humanist to enjoy good literature and good talk spiced with epigrams and classical allusions. Medieval theology is most emphatically not good literature, and though its subjects—God the Father, Son, and Holy Spirit, together with various angels, archangels, and demons—do possess a certain epic grandeur, they are not as much fun as the comedies of Terence or the satires of Juvenal. Yet a dose of theology was necessary if one were to see what Luther was all about. To Leo theology was castor oil. He longed to enjoy life, to be with his friends, to preside lightheartedly over the Church. He was really a very lazy man, and he seems never to have had the slightest notion of the true issues of the Reformation. To him it was always a matter of a loud, rude, arrogant German monk disturbing the peace.

Leo did understand politics. In January 1519, the German Emperor, old Maximilian I, caught cold on a hunt in the mountains and abruptly died. The papacy was always nervous about emperors. The official title of the Empire was "The Holy Roman Empire of the German Nation." Emperors had a bad habit of being dazzled by the Roman part of their name, and many of them had tramped down into Italy with plundering armies to make their title good. Any time a foreign army marched into Italy, the Pope found his own independence menaced. So Leo wanted a new emperor who would be too weak to meddle in Italian affairs, a sober man, a man without a dangerous imagination. It is probably not flattering to anybody to record that his choice for the imperial succession was the elector Frederick the Wise of Saxony. Frederick was so shy, so withdrawn, so quiet that he is still shut up in a cloud of mystery. What kind of man was he? No one can tell. But Leo X decided he was safe.

The Pope sent a messenger with the golden rose, a papal decoration of honor. Would Frederick be a candidate in the coming imperial election? Would he be emperor? Frederick was himself an elector. Perhaps he knew the headaches and the heartbreak in store for anyone who took the position seriously. Perhaps he knew his own limitations. He was not a leader of men. Perhaps he shuddered at the thought of making a speech. So far as we know he never made one in his life. Whatever his reasons, he did not choose to run.

The papal emissary persisted. If Frederick would become a candidate, the Pope would appoint a cardinal of Frederick's own choosing. Was this a bid to make Luther a cardinal? Possibly. One of the best ways to silence a critic is to promote him. Hot young blood often cools in the lofty altitudes of high position. The air seems to be clearer up there, and in sight of the entire mountain range of problems, judgments become more cautious, and men in looking down into the depths tend to cling to their perches. Luther had not yet said or published anything to make it impossible to wear the cardinal's hat. A man as strong as he was could have dominated the college of cardinals, pushed through a reform or two, written some respectable theology, and so become venerable and influential. He might well have become pope in time, and we might know him today as a bright portrait by Titian or even Michelangelo and as the subject of a German monograph introducing his thought in three volumes.

But all these speculations burst before the prick of fact. Frederick would not be emperor. He nominated no cardinal. And so it was that the most terrifying candidate the Pope could imagine was elected to the great title. He was Charles of Spain, grandson of Maximilian and scion of the grand old house of Hapsburg. When he was elected in July, he was already King of Spain, Duke of Burgundy, and chief of the scattered Hapsburg lands in the region of modern Austria. And even as the electors were meeting, Hernando Cortez was in Mexico assembling allies and preparing to march overland to destroy the Aztec empire and to bring its gold and its vast lands under Charles's sway. Charles needed the gold; he was nearly broke. He had to borrow the money from south German bankers to bribe the electors—including Frederick the Wise—to vote for him.

Charles was chivalrous, devout, and possessed of a political ambition that was to wound Europe almost to death. He was the very incarnation of that lethal pride condemned by classical man, an insolence that made him try to do more than human power has any right to expect. He was Ikaros flying against the sun, and in the end he fell. He was the only emperor of the German lands who abdicated his throne and retreated to the monastery, there to contemplate his defeats in this world and to prepare his soul for the triumphs of the next. But in 1519 he was determined to make his new imperial title good. He was only nineteen years old at the time, and at that age the dew is still on men's hopes. Charles sought to unite all Christians behind his own aspirations.

But within days after the election, Martin Luther stood in Leipzig to enter a fateful debate that would divide Christians even more than they had been and make the dreams of Charles only figments of that stern and dreadful madness that seems for a while to be reason only because its shape is so grand.

The debate was the spectator sport of the medieval intellectual. People flocked in to see debates even when they had no idea what was going on, and they cheered for their champions with enthusiasm. We have already noted that after one such disputation in his youth, Cajetan was carried off on the shoulders of his admirers. Duke George of Albertine Saxony had his eye on the prestige of his University of Leipzig, and when the prospect of a debate against Luther's positions came up, Duke George courted it for his town.

The originator of the debate was John Eck. He was a professor at the University of Ingolstadt, a man who showed all the virtues and the vices created by the ardor for disputation that made medieval university life so distinctive. Eck was learned and industrious, and he had a mind like a cracking whip. He could snap off quotations from the Fathers by memory to buttress his arguments, and he had a gift for irony that made him fun to hear. But he was also superficial and arrogant, uncompromising and glib, and his intent in debate was to win at any price. He attacked Luther all his life and wrote voluminously against him. One looks in vain for any spark of genuine human sympathy or warmth in the works of his that have come down to us, tomes that lie largely unread and forgotten in such places as the quiet stacks of the British Museum.

Eck challenged one of Luther's associates, Andreas Bodenstein, who took the name of Karlstadt. The University of Leipzig seems to have had some qualms about allowing the notorious Luther to debate in its orthodox precincts. Karlstadt was acceptable only because his reputation was dimmer. Luther was invited to come along, but he was not at first given permission to speak.

Karlstadt is one of those people in history who at once inspire pity, admiration, and contempt. There was something of Everyman about him. He was the Willy Loman of the Reformation, and the account of his life might be called *Death of a Theologian*. Nothing ever turned out right for him, and the list of his failures is a rosary of disaster. Yet he had some interesting ideas, and there is much more in his thought than one might think at first glance.

He was somewhat older than Luther. He seems to have had a high opinion of his own powers, and in the early years of the Reformation he stood loyally by Luther and thought himself essential to the cause. Such loyalty would have meant death if things had not gone as well as they did. And so one must grant to him the courage, or at least the vigor, of his convictions.

Karlstadt may have thought that he should be the real leader of the movement. But his talents were too limited for the task. He somewhat resembles the would-be leaders of causes during the 1960s. He saw in ever more radical positions a way of taking command over events that seemed to be slipping away from him, into the directing hands of others he thought inferior to himself. There is something fiercely aggressive about Luther's personality; there is something almost frantic about Karlstadt.

In the end he and Luther split, and they came to hate each other with that special fury reserved for former allies in a hard cause. Karlstadt wandered hither and yon in Europe. He died at last in misery, almost forgotten, and Luther gloated over his end, declaring that Karlstadt had maliciously talked himself to death. (Actually he died of the plague.)

But at Leipzig Karlstadt was to carry the standard against Eck. And so he did for a week. His debating was a catastrophe. He could not make a point without checking it in a whole library of thick books he had brought with him. Eck would stalk back and forth before the lectern, cracking off his arguments, depending on his truly amazing memory, stabbing and slashing with his rapier tongue. Karlstadt would stumble, falter, look up references, and read them back to Eck. Luther, devoted to Karlstadt at that time, claimed that he carried his end of the argument very well. But the gallery was listless and bored. By the end of the week Eck came around to beg Luther to enter the debate. Winning against Karlstadt had no glory to it.

Duke George granted his permission. Poor Karlstadt had to step down. He believed that he had been right and that he had done well. Luther took over, and Karlstadt would have been a superman indeed had he not felt humiliated. But now the crowds had the show they had come to see.

Eck won the Leipzig debate. Maybe that is a meaningless statement even in a formal sense. The transcripts were submitted to the faculties of various universities to be judged, and the judgments were ambiguous. Theological arguments are built on assumptions that finally can be neither proved nor disproved. We cannot prove that there are fairies in the woods or angels in the dark, but we cannot disprove these notions either. Today when we are confronted by someone who makes assertions that we can neither prove nor disprove, our temper is to listen politely and to move on to other things.

But one can argue whether some of one's religious assumptions are in harmony with the rest. Luther claimed to be a good Catholic. Eck argued that Luther's new positions were not in keeping with Catholic doctrine, formulated as it had been by the great and saintly teachers of the Church through the long centuries since Christ. By now Luther was arguing in public that no Christian had to be subject to the Pope. In private he was saying that the Pope was the Antichrist.

Eck laid down a barrage of quotations to prove that the Fathers of the Church who interpreted Christianity in the early centuries of its history had supported the divine ordination of the Roman See. When Christ said, in Matthew 16:18, "Thou art Peter, and upon this rock I will build my church," he meant that Peter should be head of all the apostles. Tradition held that Peter had founded the Church in Rome. Tradition also held that Peter's supremacy was handed on to his successors, the popes, who ruled over the bishops, successors to the apostles. Eck presented Augustine, Cyprian, Jerome, and a cloud of other ancient witnesses who, he argued, had supported the supremacy of Rome.

Eck made some other judgments about history. Luther claimed that the Greeks had been Christians although they had not acknowledged the supremacy of Rome. He was speaking of the communion we today call the Eastern Orthodox Church, the Church that had been located in the Byzantine Empire of the eastern Mediterranean, with its chief city at Constantinople. Eck said that the Greeks had often recognized papal supremacy during the first centuries of the Church, and he asserted that those who denied it were damned. By the time of the Eck-Luther debate, the Muslim Turks had conquered the lands where the Greek Church held sway. Eck maintained that the Turkish conquest was the punishment of God against the Greeks for not recognizing the papacy. The argument had some force at a time when the Turks were advancing slowly up the Balkan Peninsula and everyone in the audience expected Europeans to have to fight them soon on German soil.

But the main weapon in Eck's arsenal was tradition. Luther was going against the teaching of the Church since the time of Christ. He could not be right when he had so many witnesses against him. Tradition was a part of divine inspiration. God would not let so many generations of saintly men err until only Luther rose up to correct them.

In reply Luther took up two general lines of attack.

One was simply to doubt that the authorities rolling so glibly off Eck's facile tongue had really written what Eck claimed. The problem was in fact very difficult. There were copying errors in the handwritten books that even in this early age of printing remained the staple of libraries. But more important than the slips of dozing monks was the fact that the literature from the ancient Christian past was curdled with forgeries and with cases of simple mistaken identity. A standard work on the sacrament of penance was supposedly written by Augustine, but it was really from about the eleventh century. A sermon on the washing of feet was attributed to Cyprian, who died in A.D. 258, but it was really from the twelfth century. Eck repeatedly quoted the works of a "Saint Dionysius," supposedly a disciple of Paul the Apostle who was converted by Paul at Mars' Hill in Athens. "Dionysius" had written on the celestial hierarchies, a work of mystical speculation that fascinated many in the Middle Ages. He said that there were ranks of angels and archangels in heaven reaching to God and taught that the same hierarchical order ought to be duplicated in the Church on earth, some being higher and some lower. Papalists interpreted "Dionysius" to mean that the Pope should rule as head over the Church on earth just as God ruled over the realm of heaven. But the works of "Dionysius" had been exposed as an elaborate forgery for a couple of decades before Luther and Eck met at Leipzig, and even such a devout Catholic as Thomas More would not use them in debate as Eck did. And so it went with many another supposedly ancient work of theology.

The science of editing depends on a profound knowledge of history and of the historical evolution of language. Men in the sixteenth century were only beginning to develop skills that could tell them if a book was old or new, and they had few tools—such as historical dictionaries—to help them. We have no trouble today recognizing Hemingway's style as different in time from that of Dickens, Dickens's style as different from that of Richardson, or Richardson's style as different from a medieval *chanson de geste*. But only a very few sixteenth-century scholars could make similar distinctions at sight. Often Reformation debates were to be clouded as a result.

Much more important in 1519 was Luther's other position. The Fathers of the Church were but men. They had often disagreed among themselves. Even if Augustine had taught that the Pope was the head of the Church, Luther would confute the saint with the apostolic authority of Paul, who wrote to the church at Corinth: "For other foundation can no man lay than that is laid, which is Jesus Christ."

Luther turned to Scripture for an authority older than tradition, and he set Scripture against tradition. He would take the word of a theologian only when it fitted the word of Scripture. At Leipzig Luther called Scripture the "divine law," and naturally enough everyone recognized the divine superiority of Scripture over any other literature.

Luther's way of depending on Scripture alone was a tactic that was, to some extent, taught by the humanists of the Renaissance. These men, often pious and devout, were fatigued with the complications of theology in the later Middle Ages. Most of them craved simplicity. "Back to the sources!" they cried, recognizing that the earliest manuscripts were the best sources of knowledge about the ancient past. Erasmus had extolled Scripture, and he had taught that the good Christian could get all the theology he needed out of the Bible. Luther held that since Scripture was closer to Christ than the Fathers who had interpreted Christianity to the Roman world, he would trust the Bible more than he would trust their books. Later on, in a sulfurous tractate he flung against Henry VIII of England, Luther was to thunder that he cared not for a hundred Cyprians, Jeromes, or Augustines if they did not support their doctrine with Scripture.

The problem was how Scripture was to be understood. Luther never could see all the conflicting currents that run through the New Testament, though he did repudiate the stress on good works of the Epistle of James. He believed that the Fathers had many unresolved disagreements with each other. He stressed their conflicts to show that the Fathers were only men and could be rejected when they were wrong. But he thought that all the disagreements of the apostles with one another had been resolved by the time the New

Testament came to be written—an assumption the New Testament itself simply will not support. From his assumption of harmony throughout Scripture, Luther concluded that the meaning of the sacred text was abundantly clear.

John Eck and other Catholics could retort quite correctly that Scripture was not clear at all. (At least it is not clear if one insists on taking the Bible as a consistent revelation from first to last as all Catholics did.) Catholics would overcome this cloudiness in the sacred text by the means I have already mentioned. They resorted to the consensus that had gradually developed out of tradition. Some things had not been clear to the Fathers. But slowly, slowly the right opinions prevailed, and the Church recognized them as truth. Even those Fathers who had previously disagreed with this or that point of doctrine would piously submit if they were transported through time and shown the agreement that had developed after them.

The Catholic argument was always that God would not let His people stray from the truth without correcting them. This process of correction went on in history as false notions were weeded out and good theology was preserved and more clearly defined. This way of reasoning secured the notion of a God ceaselessly active among His people, but it had its dangers.

It worked to sanctify the historical process, and it led to a dismal rigidity in Catholic thought. If something had endured in the Church for a long time, it could not be changed or doubted, since the very honor of God would be at stake. Thomas More held that even the adoration of a relic over a long period of years was proof that the relic was genuine; otherwise, God would have revealed the fraud to His people. Tradition naturally tended to become more and more elaborate with the centuries. Catholic apologists were placed in the hard and sometimes silly predicament of having to prove that everything in the present tradition had really existed in the heart of the Church from the time of Christ. A few did say that God had given the Church new revelations from time to time, but that idea was a dangerous threat to the doctrine of a unique Christ and a unique historical Incarnation. Most held that everything did come down directly from the time of Christ, either in the Scripture or in the tradition that was passed along with Scripture in the Church. Tradition, in this view, could never be contradicted by Scripture itself. If Scripture *seemed* to contradict tradition, the interpreter was simply wrong. If he prayed and studied, he would find that the apparent contradiction was resolved. And of course he had the tools of spiritual interpretation that I have already described, tools that permitted him to read into Scripture anything necessary to keep it in harmony with Catholic faith.

But Luther stood firm on his belief that Scripture did flatly contradict the tradition of the Church with regard to the papacy. He held that Matthew 16:18 did not put all Christians under subjection to the Pope. The rock on which Christ promised to build his Church was the faith Peter professed, not Peter himself—and certainly not the papacy. If Peter had not received any special authority over the other apostles, he certainly could not pass on a nonexistent supremacy to his supposed successors, the popes. The papacy is not in the text, and Luther held that tradition cannot put it there. Tradition is only the word of men, he said, and it must give way before the Word of God embodied in the divine Scripture.

Eck pointed out that the Hussites had also abandoned the papacy. Frequently during the debate he tried to associate Luther with those Bohemian heretics of a century before. The Hussite Wars had burned over the soil of ducal Saxony, and their name was a curse in the mouth of southern Germans. It was very much like the tactics of Senator Joseph McCarthy or Congressman Richard Nixon, who once tried to equate liberals and Communists in this country by saying that they believed some of the same things. The implication was that if they shared some beliefs, they must share all points of doctrine, and if John Eck could make that charge stick, he would prove Luther to be a heretic.

Eck got more than he could have hoped for in return. Luther was enraged by the unfair nature of Eck's charge. In his typical headlong, fighting way, Luther roared back with the declaration that there were many good things professed by John Huss. Huss believed in the Holy Spirit, the Holy Catholic Church, and the communion of saints. No one could condemn these articles of faith merely because Huss had held them. Neither could Eck condemn Luther as a Hussite merely because Luther happened to share with Huss the conviction that it was not necessary to salvation to be subject to the Pope at Rome.

The outburst was innocent enough. But in Leipzig, Luther's pronouncement about Huss brought an outcry in the hall. Duke George jumped up from his seat and swore. There was a murmur of anger among the spectators. And when Luther went on to claim that the Council of Constance had erred in making a blanket condemnation of Huss, he offended beyond recall those Catholics who had seen in the infallible general council the antidote to the absolutism of the papal monarchy. Eck could now chortle and preen himself, for he had made Luther admit that a Christian could talk back to the authority of centuries and reject the assemblies of multitudes.

Luther's admirers have always relished the Leipzig debate because their hero stood on his own judgment against the authority of the ages. To some he has seemed like a Copernicus or a Galileo, bringing in a new age. But there is an important difference. Copernicus and Galileo both made assumptions that could be dispassionately verified by anyone who accepted mathematics as a basis for argument. But Scripture was a different order of reality. Luther believed that Scripture was clear to all true Christians—just as Galileo believed that the language of nature was mathematics, which could be evident to anyone who took the trouble to learn it. But Luther's claim has never been supported by any empirical evidence. Christians have never since Luther agreed with each other on how the Bible should be read. For all their arrogance, Eck and other Catholics were defending an important proposition. By defending tradition, they were seeking to argue that God is not only alive and well but that history reflects both His will and His mercy in such a way that Christians of rather common sense can perceive the divine working in the order of things.

At Leipzig Luther held that tradition was often wrong. And so he raised the thought that God had allowed devout and seeking men, saints of the Church, known and unknown, to err and to err disastrously for centuries. The necessary consequence was that God was a dark mystery revealed only partly in Scripture and only partly in the Christian heart. For what kind of God was it who allowed the darkness to endure for so long and corrupt doctrine to be devoutly held by saintly men? Everyone agreed that God was mysterious and that some of His ways were beyond the power of humankind to understand. But Luther's position was to lead inevitably to a notion of God's mystery so opaque that it finally became not merely opaque but a matter of indifference to most men.

10

By the time Luther arrived at Leipzig, his thought had evolved to his mature position on the way of salvation. He had earlier believed that the Christian was to humble himself as completely as possible before God. The true Christian was one who sincerely hated himself. That self-loathing was the very sign that Christ was in his heart. The true Christian took note of the dreadful evil in his corrupt nature, confessed it contritely, and yearned for divine mercy in much the same way a criminal pleading guilty of a charge today in court will throw himself on the mercy of the judge.

But by sometime in 1518, Luther perceived one Scriptural text that spoke to him in a powerful way. The text was Romans 1:16–17: "For I am not ashamed of the gospel of Christ: for it is the power of God unto salvation to every one that believeth; to the Jew first, and also to the Greek. For therein is the righteousness of God revealed from faith to faith: as it is written, The just shall live by faith."

Before this time the righteousness of God had been to Luther the righteousness by which God was exalted above man's sin in divine holiness. That righteousness made God an implacable and terrible judge, and before it weak and sinful man must be condemned to hell. By humbling himself abjectly, the sinner might be assured of God's mercy. That humiliation was itself a frightening uncertainty, since no one could ever be sure that God had made him examine every act and every thought sufficiently to vanquish all his pride.

But in his study of this text from Paul the Apostle, Luther began to see a different view of the righteousness of God. Now righteousness became a part of the gospel. The gospel was a gift. Man had not earned Christ. And it was not a steady process of self-abnegation on man's part that made God send Christ into the world. The gospel was from first to last an act of grace, of God's giving to man a sovereign gift of salvation. And humility was not the key that made the gift effectual. If righteousness was a part of the gospel, then, like the gospel, righteousness had to be a gift.

Luther looked at his own experience and knew that righteousness did not free men from sin in the daily life. As long as we live on this earth, we are subject to the curse of Adam. Our flesh is weak, always tending to rebel against God and to follow the designs of the selfish human heart. Sin permeates not just our bodily functions but our entire personality. Man is not divided into a higher nature and a lower nature, a spirit that strives for God and a body that drags him away from the divine. All our nature is corrupt. Even our most righteous thoughts are soaked with evil because they so often spring from selfish motives. And our best deeds reek with pride. So righteousness is not to live without sin but rather a divine gift by which God treats the Christian as someone pure—much as a Presidential pardon granted in the United States does not assume that the person pardoned is guiltless of the charge that has taken him to prison but simply declares that the person is to be treated as if he were innocent, and the law can take no further vengeance on him.

Christ, in Luther's thought, becomes both the agency of God's pardon and the reason for it. God took human flesh in the person of Jesus. In that flesh he suffered all the penalties of sin, including death itself, but he was without sin. And in the Resurrection he conquered all the powers of darkness. It is through Christ and for the sake of Christ that God will pardon members of the human race, whose nature Christ assumed. For Luther, the life, the suffering, the death, and the Resurrection of Christ are the triumph of God's creative purpose over the dark forces of Satan, who has always tried to frustrate the grand design of God. Christ himself is both man and God. His victory is both for humanity and for God the Father and maker of the world.

Now when God sees the sinner who is also a Christian, He imputes the righteousness of Christ to that person. The notion is somewhat like the old Roman idea of the patron and the client. The patron was a member of the aristocratic patrician class; the client was a plebeian, a common citizen. The patron passed on the benefits of his status to his clients. Consequently, the clients were not treated as helpless men on their own; rather, they were considered to be men belonging to somebody important, and they were treated according to his standing rather than their own. So it is with Christ and his clients, the true Christians, according to Luther's way of looking at things.

But how did one gain these benefits from Christ? That was the great question. Luther's answer was always that God chose some men out of His inscrutable will to possess grace, the righteousness of Christ. Now the grace became not merely humility but faith.

To speak of "faith" seems simple enough because we have heard the term "justification by faith" so often that we think we know what it means. We sometimes fail to see just how overpowering was the concept of faith in Luther's mind and how it embraced every aspect of the Christian life.

The Catholic conception of faith in his time tended to identify faith with a belief that the propositions of the Christian religion were true. Faith was something one asserted in a creed. "I believe in God the Father Almighty, Maker of heaven and earth: And in Jesus Christ his only Son our Lord. . . ." Faith is assent to the Word of Scripture. It is assent to the tradition of the Church. Faith distinguishes what is Christian from what is not. All Christians must have faith, but all who have faith are not Christians, for James said, "Thou believest that there is one God; thou doest well: the devils also believe, and tremble. But wilt thou know, O vain man, that faith without works is dead?"

To be living, saving faith, in the Catholic view, something else is required. The extra factor is love. The proof of the need for love was taken from Paul's words written to the church at Corinth: "And though I have all faith, so that I could remove mountains, and have not charity, I am nothing." Faith without love was, in theological language adapted from Aristotle, "unformed faith." Faith with love was "formed faith," and only "formed faith" was adequate for salvation, for only love performed the works that made faith good.

What Catholic theologians were trying to avoid was the dangerous notion that the Christian could be saved from hell if he merely agreed in his mind that creeds, Scripture, and tradition were true. They were trying to keep Christianity from becoming a mere science where the heart is not moved to love and devotion and the good of others by what the mind accepts. I may, for example, know a great deal about organic chemistry or the framework of Plato's philosophy; but this knowledge does not necessarily make me an honest man, a good father, an obedient subject, or a helpful neighbor. And if Christianity was assumed to be a matter only of creedal statements, the Christian would be anyone who mouthed his belief. Love attached to faith was the impulse that made the Christian form his entire life around the precepts taught by his religion. Love, then, led to righteousness and, from a social point of view, to good citizenship.

But what Luther called "faith" went far beyond an assent to general propositions of belief. Faith is the personal acceptance of a Word spoken by God to the individual Christian who asks for some special benefit. The Canaanite woman of Matthew 15:21–28 believed that Jesus could heal her daughter's illness, and he did. The blind men in Matthew 9:27–31 came to Jesus believing that he could give them their sight, and he did. The Roman centurion of Matthew 8:5–13 came believing that Jesus could heal a tormented servant, and he did.

So for Luther faith meant that the sinner should come to Christ asking for forgiveness of sin, believing that Christ could forgive him and make him righteous. If the Christian possesses the trust of those others who sought benefits from Christ, Christ will grant his request, too, and he will be forgiven. So when the Christian looks at Christ, he must hear every promise Christ spoke as though Christ had singled him out from all the world and spoken directly to him. He must believe in his heart that everything Christ possessed is now his own. Where the Christian fails, Christ has triumphed. Every Christian must say, "I must believe in my heart that Christ has gained the victory not for mankind but for me."

Luther's great motto was always "Let God be God." In his earlier thought, he held that God alone was holy and man had no merit at all. The attitude of the true Christian was complete abnegation before that dreadful deity. "Justification" meant that the Christian became convinced in his own heart that God's verdict against the evil of the human race was just.

But in the gospel of Christ, Luther heard not wrath but redemption. And redemption was a free gift. The Christian must believe in that gift with the same certainty with which the earlier Luther believed in the power of God's anger. This belief does not merely lead to righteousness. It *is* righteousness in itself, for here the Christian recognizes the way things are, letting God be God, a God of mercy, trusting the Word of God spoken directly to his heart, living in free and spontaneous gratitude to the Christ who has given salvation to those who do not deserve it at all. This faith binds the Christian to Christ. Indeed, it is not too much to say that such faith *is* Christ, for only Christ in the human heart can provide such a faith. Wherever that faith is found, there also is Christ. And when God looks on the Christian, He sees not a sinful creature but rather Christ, the champion and the patron of those who possess faith.

Most Catholics misunderstood Luther. They thought he was saying that it was enough to believe creedal statements to be saved. And when he taught that no one could do good works, his enemies claimed that he was saying Christians could live like the devil.

But for Luther, Christ and faith always went together. It was inconceivable that the Christian could willingly, wantonly, and habitually do things that were contrary to the nature of Christ. My fingers are a part of my body. I did not do anything to join them to myself, for they were given to me when my body was formed. But the effortless quality of their attachment does not mean that I will go around deliberately smashing them with hammers or burning them in fires. By the nature of human life, I may sometimes smash a thumbnail or burn a finger; but I quickly recoil from such experiences because they are contrary to the life that holds my body together.

So it is with sin and the Christian. Christ is the Christian's life. And Christ does not go about telling lies, blaspheming God, murdering, fornicating, envying, stealing, or hating his neighbors. These evils are contrary to the very nature of the Christ present in faith in the Christian's heart. And though one may stumble into such sins because of the weakness of human flesh, there is a greater power striving within that makes the Christian hate iniquity. If one can sin and take sin serenely and dwell with sin in comfort, to Luther's mind that person is not bound to Christ in faith. A thumb that does not hurt when it is hit with an ax is dead. But on the other hand, the person who hates his sin, who longs for communion with Christ, who yearns for true fellowship with God, can have the certainty of faith. Detesting his sin, the true Christian looks to the promise of the resurrection when the corrupt flesh inherited from sinful Adam will be transformed into the spiritual and unsinning body of eternal life.

One important consequence of this fresh emphasis on the Christian who is justified even though his flesh may drag him into sin was to undermine the monastic enterprise of which Luther himself was a part. The monk left the world so that he might be isolated in the monastery from the common life where temptation lay always in the way. By making sin so completely a psychological affair, a matter of the intentions and impulses of the mind and heart, Luther attacked the notion that sin was more present in the workaday world than elsewhere. Sin was not a substance of some sort that the Christian could retreat from in the way one might withdraw from a flooded valley. Sin infected man's mind, his heart, his artistic creations, and every bodily function. Yet for the Christian, Christ was present wherever sin was present. Christ in the Christian's heart always testified that sin was not a natural state but rather a corruption that would be purged. So with sin and Christ present together everywhere, to go into a monastery to escape sin became a damning illusion. The monk who cultivated humility apart from the world became, in Luther's view, as arrogant and as selfish as the Renaissance man in the world who cultivated fame. In each the location of sin was in the selfishness of the human heart that set itself up as an idol in the center of the universe; sin has almost nothing to do with the location or the status of a human body.

Faith itself is a gift, and the question must naturally arise, "How do I get it?" Always for Luther faith is not something one wills to have but rather a recognition that Christ is present in one's heart. And Luther's concept usually seems to be that if one yearns for grace and faith, the yearning in itself is a sign that grace and faith are present. Luther's theology is always for those who feel themselves in battle with sin, and it is to tell them that the battle has already been won in Christ. Luther's justification by faith is most emphatically not for those who make up the great majority of human beings, who feel rather indifferent in religious matters except in emergencies, who take any theology with a casual stretch and a yawn. His view of faith is a comfort to the afflicted, and it has little but condemnation to offer to those who already feel comfortable with themselves.

Some inconsistencies remained in his thought. Luther talked from time to time as if the Christian could lose the salvation God gave. He was likely to speak in this way in his sermons and in his tractates destined for the common people. This idea seems to contradict the conviction that God's works are unchanging and eternal. Perhaps the explanation is simply that nobody can live as if he truly believes that his life and the world are fully determined by some exterior power. Perhaps Luther took exhortation in the same way he understood the law of the Old Testament; that is, when the preacher told people what they should be doing, they understood how little they could do, and so they were humbled, and God's grace—the gospel—would then become operative in their lives. But such a calculated view of Luther's exhortations does not really seem to fit the temper of the sermons and the tractates in which he exhorts so vehemently.

There is the simple historical fact that predestinarians as different as Francesco Petrarca and Karl Marx have been exhorters. It is almost as if they were obsessed with the necessity of seeing the secret process of destiny made manifest before their eyes. Luther had once believed passionately in relics that made visible the invisible world of God. Later he longed for Christians living in faith to declare the invisible order that the relic had not been able to reveal. It is a sign of his failure—or perhaps the failure of the human species—that as his life drew on, his mood changed. Again and again he stressed that, insofar as outward acts were concerned, Catholics lived as well as his followers. What he came to profess was no moral superiority but only that he had the true theology; his followers proved quickly enough that they were no more saintly than their adversaries. This gloomy recognition was different from his earlier confidence.

In a sermon preached in 1519 on how to die well, Luther advised the dying person not to seek to know if he were numbered among the elect. Such questions refused to let God be God, for only God could know the destiny of the soul. The dying man was simply to keep Christ ever before his eyes and to trust. Gabriel Biel, Thomas More, and Erasmus all gave the same advice, and they were all orthodox Catholics. It may be that here Luther fell back onto an old idea that if one were too concerned with one's own salvation, one thereby made an idol of oneself and one's destiny. Luther did, after all, preach that the Christian should be willing to be damned if God wanted it that way. But he went on to say that anyone willing to suffer hell for the glory of God would certainly be redeemed. Such complete humility could only be a sign of the presence of Christ in the heart of the Christian. There are ways of making all the pieces of Luther fit together, and his ardent disciples have used them to prove the consistency of their master. Yet this sermon on dying does seem quite different in temper from the certainty of faith that Luther was otherwise claiming at the same time, and the effort to make him fully consistent seems strained. Luther spoke as the moment might dictate. Though always in his reflective moments he considered certainty in faith to be the sign of the true Christian, his own understanding of that certainty wavered with circumstances.

In 1518 and in 1519 he seems to have come into an especially vivid sense of Jesus the incarnate Lord, who as God met him face to face on the gloomy and difficult landscape of earth. The sense that Christ shared human life, endured its temptations, and suffered the cross gave Luther the glorious sense of acceptance in creation that in different ways has inspired men as diverse as John Wesley and John Muir. And in the way this immense relief has come upon so many, for Luther the awareness was of a power outside himself, something that came sweetly to him when he was almost in despair, a peace with God that overwhelmed the powers of darkness attacking his soul.

Christ was always the center and the circumference of his experience, the Christ of the Gospels, the Christ he believed was foretold in the Old Testament, especially in the tenderness and in the suffering of the Psalms. When you are afraid of sin, cling to Christ. When the enemy comes in like a flood, Christ will raise up a standard against him. Faith is the presence of Christ in the midst of life and at the hour of death. Christ makes up for the corruption of human nature. Luther found Christ as a living person, speaking to him directly from Scripture as if the words had been preserved for centuries for just this moment in the life of a monk under attack for seeking the truth.

Perhaps we might infer from all this that Luther's own stress through the indulgence controversy brought on the inner crisis that made him discover faith. Writing long afterward, he attributed his discovery to seeking in Scripture, and he tended to relate it to a long and anguished period in the monastery when he had tried to please God. But he also wrote frequently of the dreadful question that assailed him as the ties binding him to the institution of the Catholic Church slipped loose: Can you alone be right and all these centuries wrong?

We have so completely lost the experience of corporate identity that we can hardly imagine what it was like for anyone to come into conflict with the Catholic Church of the sixteenth century. The Church was the umbrella of civilization and the fabric of the common life. To be expelled from it was to be cast out of humanity itself, and to attack it was to suffer the guilt of assaulting the dearest and best possession of humankind. Luther had begun with an act of devotion—an attempt to cleanse his beloved Church of an evil soiling its hands and its head. Almost before he could understand what had happened, he found himself an outcast, threatened with the fiery stake, accused of every abomination, confronted by powers of entrenched evil now drawing together to destroy him. He must have gone through days of absorbing loneliness and nights of terrifying solitude.

So he turned all the more vigorously to the person of Christ, for if Christ were for him, who could be against him? He tracked Christ through Scripture and read every word as though it had been a message sent directly from God to himself. Finally he fell on the passage that was his redemption: "For therein is the righteousness of

God revealed from faith to faith: as it is written, The just shall live by faith." And what Luther discovered sometime in 1518 and 1519 was simply this—that he had faith. So he could enter the fight that was coming to him in the assurance that Christ stood for him even if the world raged against him.

Such indomitable faith can make men heroes or fanatics, builders or destroyers, leaders of men or profaners of civilization. Faith made Martin Luther all these things.

11

In the wake of the Leipzig debate, Luther burned and brooded while his enemies strutted about, crowing like cocks. A swarm of little men flew up to stab him with their pens, and the papal bureaucracy went grinding on like a blind machine in motion, to end with an official condemnation for heresy.

The papacy could afford to give time to Luther now. The imperial election was over. Charles of Hapsburg was Emperor. Perhaps Leo X was smarting with his own fears and defeat as he contemplated the gloomy prospect of dealing with young Charles. The Pope would certainly want to rid himself of the Luther question as a preliminary to the struggle looming between Empire and papacy. Like men from time immemorial addicted to the orderly routines of bureaucracy, Leo thought that the matter could be resolved by throwing paper at it. In this case he would hurl pronouncements and bulls of excommunication at Luther's head and at all who hesitated in their steadfast obedience to the Roman See.

Meanwhile at Wittenberg Luther was teaching, preaching, writing, and studying the works of John Huss. He was amazed at how many places he found himself in agreement with Huss, especially on the matter of the Church. The Church was not an institution with its head in Rome and its feet in all the world. It was the community of Christian believers, a spontaneous fellowship, a union formed not on the dry bones of an institution but on faith in Christ. Akin to this conviction about the Church was Luther's growing certainty that the Pope was the Antichrist.

The Antichrist in Christian mythology had a shadowy existence all the way back to the New Testament. The idea had a certain logic to it. If Christ was the Incarnation of God among men, and if the world was a battleground in a cosmic struggle between God and Satan, Satan should have his incarnation, too. And if the Church was, in some sense, a continuation of the Incarnation, Satan must also possess some sort of continuing incarnation to be present in the midst of the people of God, playing his great role as adversary.

The world in Luther's thought abounded in paradox and mystery. Things were not what they seemed; on the contrary, both the works of God and the works of Satan were veiled in seeming opposites. What was more unlikely than that the cross should be the miracle of God's redemption or that the life of God's people on earth should be suffering, persecution, shame, and death? And so it was in keeping with this inverted order of expectations that the Antichrist should be found where most Christians least expected him to be. And what was more unexpected than that Satan should infest the papacy and become the prince of the Church? The high priests in the Temple at Jerusalem had been the adversaries of Jesus. The high priest of the Catholic Church had become the enemy of the gospel in Luther's time.

The notion grew and filled Luther's teeming mind as it became clear that the Pope was not going to listen to him and was not going to change. To Luther the conflict had now become a cosmic battle, not a mere quarrel over indulgences. His use of the figure of Antichrist to describe the papacy was a sign that he expected the world to end soon. The Antichrist had always been expected shortly before the return of Christ. Luther was never a fanatic who rushed out every morning to see if the sky was yet cracked by the blast of the concluding trumpet; but he did not expect Christ to defer his coming for long, and much of his thought is unsatisfactory to Christians today for that reason. His aim was not to change the world but to show Christians how to endure it. The changes would be made by Christ. In anticipation of his coming, Christians should be watchful, and they should wait.

Now began Luther's astonishing literary production that was to continue for the rest of his days. He wrote more in his lifetime than most men can read in theirs. He published something on the average of about once every two weeks. One of the hardships in Luther research nowadays is that to study Luther's life is to give up one's own. And one of the consequences of that fact has been that most historians who have written about him have had some confessional lens to grind, making Luther the glass with which to see a religious world deeply important to themselves. It is quite difficult to spend years studying a man's thought if one believes that the content of that thought has no truly meaningful place in the modern world.

Through all this enormity of writing, several themes remain constant for Luther. God's Word is the final source of all authority for the Christian. God's Word is not quite the same thing as Scripture. Luther often uses "Word of God" and "Scripture" in the same sentence to describe distinct things. Scripture is the written record of the acts of God from Creation to redemption. God's Word is the guiding principle that holds that written record together and makes it meaningful. Scripture tells us of Moses, who went up on Mount Sinai and brought the tablets of the law down to Israel, and Scripture tells us that Christ lived, died, and rose from the dead. God's Word tells us that man could not fulfill the law, that the law was given to show man the magnitude of sin, and that God Himself made the law perfect in Jesus Christ, who fulfilled the law and redeemed Christians. At times the name of Jesus is a synonym to the Word in Luther's thought, for Jesus most completely spoke God's Word to mankind. And at other times he uses the word "gospel" in the same sense, for the gospel is the message that Christ has done what no man can do for himself. Christ has fulfilled the law.

At times Luther uses the phrase "Word of God" almost as an incantation. Here he reminds me a little of those protagonists of the occult today who believe that if they repeat a certain magical phrase again and again, they will absorb and concentrate in themselves the creative power of the universe. When Luther speaks of the Word of God, there is something in him akin to the mentality which held that vampires must flee at the sight of the cross or that devils could not bear the sound of Mass bells. To speak the Word of God, to claim the promises of Christ aloud, is always much more to Luther than to make a statement declaring factual knowledge. It is to speak a sacred sign; it is to call on God to be present, to keep His word. It is to throw oneself upon the power by which God Himself works in the world. The Word strengthens the Christian, fights against evil, and makes the demons themselves tremble when it is spoken. The Word comes to man from God, and it has an independent existence and a sovereign power apart from man. But when the Christian speaks the Word, that power is in some way appropriated by himself, so that when he claims it he has a weapon against the powers of darkness. Christ is the power that makes good the law, redeems the Christian, vanquishes the demons, and treads Satan's head under his heel. When the Christian calls on the Word of God, Christ does again all his great deeds that are comprised in that word.

Most of us cannot truly recapture Luther's sense of the living Word of God. The popular mind nowadays has tended to equate the Word of God with Scripture, for that is all we really know to do with words—put them in books which can be shut and called on only when we need them.

But Luther's sense of the Word of God goes back to the primitive notion that the invisible, fleeting, spoken Word was the most powerful sign of the genius of the individual—the invincible, uncontrollable expression of true life and being—and that sacred words associated with the gods should be pronounced with reverent care, for these words were agents of both blessing and destruction. For Luther the Word of God is dynamic, irresistible, mysterious, and uncontained. It is God's promise; it is God's breath! It is the light shining on man out of God's unfathomable darkness. For Luther that Word had burst around him with vivid clarity. He was sure that it lighted his way and dazzled the eyes of his enemies so that they stumbled blindly into destruction.

Scripture was useless without the Word. Though Luther did not use this image, I think that for him God's Word was a sun, and Scripture was a vast and complex landscape, supremely beautiful and rich beyond description. Here were rivers; here were green and grassy plains. Here were wooded hills and naked mountains. Here were tangled wildernesses where no one could find the way, and yet one could perceive that the wilderness with its impassable regions had a fitting place with the whole. Without God's Word, all this scene was plunged into the blackness of night where even the wisest of travelers would be lost. But with God's Word, the Scriptural landscape became a haven for the soul and a place where the Christian mind and heart could find rest and comfort and wisdom. To leave Scripture was to tunnel underground, to forsake both the sun and the bright vision. But to read Scripture without the Word of God was to become hopelessly mired in a landscape that, in the invincible dark, became incomprehensible, tortuous, and full of danger.

So Luther could explain easily enough why so many people disagreed with him so profoundly on what Scripture meant. False interpreters, he thought, did not possess the Word of God. And without the Word, they must be on the side of the devil. There was little room here for an honest misunderstanding or an honest difference of opinion. If people did not understand Scripture, it was because they did not possess the Word; and without the Word they must be the agents of Satan, no matter how innocent they might appear.

Luther was always to judge others on how they understood Scripture, and the hostility of his judgments increased as they varied further from his own. He was to say with grim resignation that he and Ulrich Zwingli were possessed by different spirits. The remark was not mere allegory. He thought that Zwingli was possessed of the devil. To the younger John Calvin, who frankly acknowledged his debt to Luther, the German reformer was still obstinate beyond belief. Philipp Melanchthon, who came to Wittenberg in 1519 as a professor of Greek and theology, was to be Luther's right-hand man for nearly three decades, yet he experienced Luther's dangerous wrath. Erasmus was condemned by Luther as a pagan and not a Christian—though Erasmus had given Europe the printed Greek New Testament Luther studied so avidly. Kaspar Schwenkfeld was a spiritualist who believed that possessing the love of Christ in one's heart was more important than understanding the literal word of Scripture, and Luther sent him word to go to hell. The "table talk" Luther's students wrote down at dinner is filled with hatred not only for people in the present who differed with Luther but also for people in the past whose interpretations of the Bible had been different from his.

We may recoil at this vehemence, especially when we try to make moral sense out of the diversity and contradictions of the Bible. It is not our temper to wax wroth over interpretations of the most widely sold unread book in our times. But to Luther there was simply nothing unfitting about a mixture of hatred and piety. It was piety to interpret the "divine Scripture" as the Word of God. Only servants of Satan did otherwise. And since God did not love Satan, Luther felt no compulsion at all to love Satan's disciples.

12

*D*URING THE YEAR 1520, Luther published four great tractates that stand out as promontories from the flood of his works, and here historians have generally stood to take a look at his developing thought.

The first of these was called *On the Papacy in Rome*. It was a resounding blast against papal pretensions. Luther did not come out with his private thought that the Pope was the Antichrist. But he did say that most of the popes had acted like Antichrist, and his description has become standard in Protestant thought. The papacy was used by unscrupulous men in their drive for worldly gain. Popes greedily wanted to subjugate the governments of Europe. Because the popes were such evil and malicious men, the entire Church was poisoned by their insidious schemes and immoral deeds.

But Luther's most important argument was not about the evil of popes but rather about the nature of the Church. Here the studies inaugurated by the Leipzig debate showed their effect. The popes ruled over an external body made up of offices, buildings, and a constitution called the canon law. By human decision they were indeed heads in succession of that earthly enterprise. But this visible institution was not the true Church.

The true Church was something spiritual. It was an affair of the heart of man and the spirit of God, and its true head was not the Pope but Christ. It had some visible features. Baptism, the Mass, and the preaching of God's Word are all signs that the Church is present. These are the marks of the true Church in Scripture. Rome or any other place that may claim some geographical or traditional authority has nothing to do with defining what the true Church is and what it is not.

He implies that the true Church is made up only of faithful Christians. These are people who have the proper faith in Christ. They are sinners in that their nature remains corrupt for as long as they are in this world. But they are sinners in faith, redeemed sinners, into whose hearts Christ has come.

What Luther is rejecting here is extremely important. It is the notion that the Church is a great earthly institution possessing a nature somewhat similar to the Incarnation of Christ—a visible body of external laws and offices (a personality, if you will) and an invisible nature of a Holy Spirit operating within human spirits to animate that visible body, leading it into all truth. Tradition is a part of the visibility of the Church. One can point to saintly men who have held correct doctrine through the centuries, and one can ask the standard Catholic question: How could God have allowed so many good men to err? But Luther rejected this defense. He was always to hold that no Christian could know for sure whether any other man was truly redeemed. Later he was to say that even if the Apostle Peter appeared among Christians, no one could know whether he was redeemed or not. Only God knew the elect; hence, the Church was invisible to mankind and visible only to God. And so one simply could not argue that doctrines were good because good men had held them for so long. Only God knew who was redeemed; thus, Christians could not point to "saints" and hold that their consensus in matters of doctrine made that doctrine true. The argument from tradition as most Catholics expressed it was in a sense an argument for the value of goodness in the world, goodness certified by long endurance in time. Luther pointed out that Turks, Persians, and the wicked world itself have endured for ages. Consequently, mere survival in time could not be considered as a sign of God's favor. So the Church's role as a visible institution in history did not have any truly determining force in deciding what the ecclesiastical institution must always be. The consequence of this view on Luther's part is, as I have said, to make history a realm of darkness—even chaos—insofar as human reason is concerned. We may observe the past, but we cannot know what the details mean in the divine ordering of things. We must assume that God has a purpose in all that He does. But we cannot find any continuing thread to tell us what that purpose is except in the general moralizing truism that the proud are often brought low and the humble exalted. And we need have no respect for any tradition that is not sanctioned by the clear word of Scripture—as Luther understood Scripture. Old practices are not good because they are old.

In this cavalier attitude toward tradition, Luther was again unconsciously preparing the way for the modern age he would have detested. Both Renaissance and Reformation tended to look back in history, finding some kind of golden age gleaming in a roseate dawn of yesteryear. The typical Renaissance humanist tended to find in classical Greece, and to a lesser extent in classical Rome, the best possible achievement of man. Imitation of classical styles, classical science, classical rhetoric, classical history, and so forth became a fetish among many. The reformers, including Luther, tended to see the early history of the Christian Church as an ideal time, though Luther never believed that the Christian was obligated to slavish imitation of the New Testament or the age of the early Fathers.

The modern temper has been, until recently, to find the golden age not in the past but in the future. We have accepted the idea of progress, and most people in our society tend to think that the newer something is, the better it is. Luther obviously had no intention of formulating a doctrine of progress; the very notion that human beings could better themselves was not congenial to his spirit. But by attacking the sacred character of the past, by refusing to accept the old merely because of its antiquity, he was helping to remove some of the blocks standing in the way of freeing man from slavish devotion to tradition.

The visible Church, according to Catholic thought, was a very special agent of salvation. Catholics had often echoed the sentiment of Cyprian, "Outside the church there is no salvation." The motto came to mean that, apart from the Pope and the visible institution the Pope headed, there could be no Christians. All Catholics would agree that the Church on earth contained members who were both good and bad. The Ark of Noah had contained both clean and unclean beasts. In the Gospels, Christ told of the separation of the sheep from the goats in the last day, and in the parable of the net he spoke of the good and bad fish that were drawn into the boat by the fishermen. The Church on earth was the Church militant, a body in conflict with the powers of darkness, and here many children of Satan hid themselves among the children of God. But in the great day of doom, Christ would judge the good and the bad; then the good would be rewarded and the bad cast into an eternal hell. And in heaven the Church would be triumphant and pure. On earth the Church was pure only in its teaching. It never called bad doctrine good, and it never excused evil living. The Church was a pillar of truth, the vehicle of salvation—not a perfect community where everyone who belonged was pure. The Church told bad and good alike what God required, and bad and good alike would be judged by how they responded to the revelation the Church proclaimed.

Luther's Church was only in a very secondary sense an agent of salvation. It was, rather, the consequence of a salvation worked out by God. Membership in Luther's Church was, for the Christian, much like Luther's conception of the place of good works in the Christian life. It was something that came as a result of salvation. The people chosen by God to have faith were made to be members of the Church.

So the essence of the true Church was not to be found in any institutional expression. It was a fellowship, an invisible bond. The Church did have its external manifestations, but they were only the right use of the sacraments and the right preaching of the Word. They did not include popes, bishops, elaborate ritual, or whatever else might be dictated by tradition. Christian organization and Christian ritual should express love, but this expression might differ from place to place, just as the ways families show love often differ according to custom and geography. Consequently, the speaking of an institution could never be equated with the voice of God, even if that institution had a long history, even if its spokesman happened to be the Pope, who traced his historical lineage all the way back to the Apostle Peter himself.

Catholics argued that invisible relationships are vital and that without them no one could be saved. But they also said that the external expression of these invisible affections could be made perfect only by the Church of Rome, defined by its tradition and ordered by its officers. Otherwise, the unity of the Church would break down, and no one could tell for certain what was sound doctrine and what was not. The Pope existed as the arch that upheld the unity of Christian fellowship and Christian teaching. Luther was confident in 1520 that the Spirit of God itself could preserve unity among true Christians. He did not believe that they needed any worldwide institution to hold them together under one head. Sacraments, Word, love! With them no pope was necessary.

I have paraphrased much of Luther's thought in this tractate, and I have freely combined his thought in this attack on the papacy with other works of his done in later years. I believe that I have reflected the spirit of his opinions quite accurately, and again I must note an impulse toward modern individualism that Luther never intended. He truly believed in the living power of the Spirit of God, unseen but overwhelming, and he expected all true Christians to be brought into concord by that spirit. No institution such as the papacy was needed to whip them into line. But the effect of his teaching was to force people (or else their governments) to make up their own minds about what they learned from the Spirit of God. Christians did not agree with each other. And the vain hope that they would led in fact to a diversity of opinion and an individualism that Luther would have thought blasphemous.

In this vitriolic tractate we find another essential thought that was to assume vast proportions—the priesthood of all believers. Since the Church is a community united by invisible bonds not requiring a hierarchy, the Christian layman is just as close to God as is the Catholic priest. The priest was considered, in Latin, the *pontifex,* the builder of the bridge from man to God. In Catholic thought, from early times the priest had stood apart from the lay people of the Church. He held a status signified by special dress, by special privileges under the law, by special restrictions such as that against sexual intercourse, and, above all, by holding the special power to perform the sacraments, those channels of grace necessary for the good Christian life.

But in Luther's thought, God Himself builds the bridge to every Christian. No priest need stand between. And so it seemed that the ancient division between clergy and laity was about to fall to nothing, especially since Luther saw priestcraft as the foundation of the papal tyranny. He had to return later on to a redefinition of the clerical status. But in the meantime his idea of perfect Christian equality was fascinating to many of Luther's contemporaries. It was to lead to glory and scandal, both to the Quakers and the quiet dignity of the inner light shining in every man and to the ranters under whatever name who have preached the blessings of ignorance and extolled the wisdom of the unlearned and the unwashed.

Luther always held that man is a whole being, not a composite of body and soul. He was deeply hostile to the Platonic attitude, so frequent in Christian mysticism, that the soul was superior and good while the body was inferior and bad. For him soul and body are so indissolubly connected that for most of his life he seems to have believed in "soul sleep," the doctrine that the soul was not conscious between death and the day of resurrection. That notion would be in keeping with the Jewish belief that man was not man except insofar as he had a body to express his being, and it makes sense out of the Christian doctrine of the resurrection of the body that is in direct opposition to the Greek idea of the immortality of the soul.

But throughout this tractate Luther expresses a tremendous confidence in the power of the invisible. It is a function of faith to be invisible. Faith is the invisible presence of the Christ whom we shall someday see face to face. The true Church is not visible. The Spirit of God is not visible. Invisible love, not a visible institution, holds the Church together. And the grand purpose of God for the ages is alike invisible. Why does the Pope rule over the Church? Luther holds that the papacy is the sign of God's wrath, and Christians must endure it just as they must endure rule by the Turks if that should be their fate.

But the invisible in Luther's thought always has some kind of visible wrapping. One sees Christians. One sees the working of the Spirit of God. One feels in one's own heart the working of Christ. The papacy, the Turks, and the other terrors to Christian life are abroad in the earth as a demonstration of the wrath of God, and wrath is a mark of God's presence in the world. What the Christian cannot clearly see is the way all this fits together in God's grand design. To believe that there is a purpose to the Creation requires faith. The natural man, unenlightened by faith and the Word of God, must see the world as chaos—or else he must impose upon the world an artificial order conjured up by the illusions of frail human reason. Reason, operating by itself, will see the Pope to be the head of the Church, and reason will base that belief on externals such as tradition. But the true Christian sees the Pope as the enemy to God, and he sees his loathsome presence in the chair of Peter as yet another sign of the divine mystery that permeates the universe.

Throughout this work and nearly everything else Luther wrote, one thought reigns. God is in charge of the world. That being so, all the apparent evil we perceive must have a place in His divine plan. If anything escapes God's control, then God is not God. And so Luther must reconcile his experience and the experience of mankind with the doctrine of providence. Nothing can be left out. But the consequence of bringing everything together under the command of God is to force the humble Christian to confess that he cannot understand how these things can be. Luther confronting the papacy is like Job suffering his afflictions. He cannot understand why he suffers, and when he goes to God for an answer, God only speaks to him out of the whirlwind and shows him the greater mysteries of the universe itself, leaving him understanding nothing except that God rules over all.

13

*L*UTHER'S SECOND GREAT BLAST of 1520 was his
Address to the Christian Nobility of the German Nation.

In many ways it was a much more sweeping and radical document than anything he had written before. Now he was bolder in his public affirmation that the Pope was Antichrist. "The pope almost seems to be the adversary of Christ called in scripture the antichrist." The Pope's claims to authority over territories in Italy are put in contrast with the spirit of Christ, who would not allow his followers to make him a judge over worldly affairs. Likewise, the humility of Christ is compared with the arrogance of the Pope, who is carried about Rome in a litter like an idol—the Pope who requires cardinals to kneel to him, and other Christians to kiss his feet. "Truly," Luther wrote, "I am afraid that we can call the pope the 'man of sin.'" "Man of sin" was the title the writer of Second Thessalonians had given the Antichrist.

Luther sought to destroy the authority of the papal monarchy in Europe. No taxes should be paid to Rome. No case should be tried in an ecclesiastical court. No bishop should receive his office from the Pope, and so no bishop could pay the Pope a fee for episcopal appointment. No one should go on pilgrimage to Rome. Since all these matters involved money, one can almost hear the leather in the Pope's purse shrinking under the flood of Luther's attack.

Yet the most radical proposal in the *Address* lay in Luther's sweeping development of his conviction that all Christians are priests. He argued his point in detail and reached some revolutionary conclusions.

Luther claimed that there was no Christian priesthood in the New Testament, and his idea is at least plausible. The early disciples of Christ constituted a movement rather than an institution, and leaders seemed to arise rather spontaneously, assuming such offices as overseer, elder, presbyter, deacon, and shepherd in the disorganized way any movement is likely to cast up leaders in the midst of turbulent times.

But if priesthood did not originate in the New Testament, it nevertheless came very early in the Christian Church. There are always a few who pretend to special knowledge of the secrets of existence and claim a special status. And there are always many others who long to find somebody who will pretend to show them the way to the dawn.

The Christian Church developed its priesthood like every other religion of antiquity, and the process of priestefaction was obviously accelerated when Jesus did not return in clouds of glory as he had apparently promised. The Church did not suffer as much as the common traditions about persecutions and martyrs claim, but still Christians were outcasts and targets of violence in the Roman Empire, and even as early as the two epistles attributed to "Peter" in the New Testament, there is evidence that some were doubting that Jesus was going to come back to redeem his people. To ward off the unthinkable proposition that Jesus might simply be dead, the Church replaced expectation of the imminent end of time with ceremonies that would fill the minds of Christians with symbols pointing to a reality that had been mysteriously deferred. And so the Church passed swiftly from being a movement to becoming an institution, and priests multiplied in the Church in the way worms will grow in dogs.

The special knowledge and special place of the priesthood must have some visible signs. After the orgies of sensuality that had marked Roman culture, the world passed into a time of troubles, and some turned to chastity for relief from the dissatisfactions of the cycle of lust and orgasm. To many sexuality became something nasty, and the Catholic priesthood was caught up in a thickening mood of religious distaste for sex and so was condemned to abstinence from sexual intercourse.

Three hundred years after Christ a few Christians were still pointing out that the Apostle Peter had been married. There is no word from Christ in the New Testament condemning marriage. He is said to have healed Peter's mother-in-law of disease without then warning his disciples not to have mothers-in-law in the future if they intended to be priests of his. But Paul the Apostle held that it was better to remain unmarried because the world was a troublesome place and wives only added to the troubles. Soon the Church had converted Paul's advice into a universal law for the clergy.

Tied up with the priesthood were vows in which the young priest swore to remain poor, chaste, and obedient. Hands were laid on his bowed head by a bishop or two, and so an apostolic authority was thought to be passed on to him. The tradition of the laying on of hands went back to the New Testament. Christ had laid his hands on the sick to heal them, and it was assumed that a special divine power passed from the hands of Christ to his apostles and from them to their successors, priests and bishops. (There is no evidence in the New Testament that Jesus *ordained* anybody.)

We have forgotten how important vows are, for our society considers them to be only the pious intention of the moment, subject to the change of circumstance. But in the New Testament and in the Middle Ages, the vow made God a witness to the proceedings to see that they were properly done. To take a vow in God's name was to make a promise not only to men but to God Himself. To break a vow was to take the name of God in vain—as a mere word, empty of power. Such vanity was the most horrible blasphemy anybody could imagine short of denouncing Christ. And in a way the two blasphemies amounted to the same thing. They treated God with disrespect, as if He were a weakling unable to punish anyone who broke a promise to Him. The mythologies of the world are filled with tales of woe that have come on the unwary from that presumption. Cassandra promised Apollo to lie with him in exchange for the gift of divination; but when he had done what she asked, she would not yield to him her body as she had promised. He thereupon kissed her mouth and made all her words such that she could not persuade anyone that they were true.

In Christianity the vow-breaker was subject to the awful penalty of being considered unfit for the human community. In the Middle Ages, the terror of his vow probably lay on the average priest with a much more compelling weight than the burdens of chastity itself. To turn from priesthood once it had been assumed was to turn away from God and man, to be an exile in the midst of the earth; and among the Fathers of the Church in the first six centuries of Christianity, vow-breakers were considered to be committing adultery against God. Such was the rule of the canon law, and such people were regularly consigned to hell by the Church. This mentality lingered, so that pious Catholics were horrified in the days ahead when Luther told clergymen that they could marry and set them an example by marrying a runaway nun. Luther came to consider the vow as an attempt to earn salvation, and so he thought it was not binding. But his opponents took him to mean that promises made to God could be disdained. Thus he was seen as a dangerous blasphemer.

At any rate ordination set the priest apart from the common run of Christians. We have seen that he alone had the power to administer the sacraments (though in an emergency anyone could administer baptism).

The stature of the priest was powerfully enhanced in the evolution of doctrine about the Mass. The thought that Christ was really present in the meal of bread and wine converted it into a potent ritual, and we have noted that within three centuries after Christ, only priests were partaking of the wine, the blood of Christ, and that even the lay people who were allowed the bread were not allowed to touch it with their hands lest they defile it. The priest put it on their tongues. In some sense the formulation of the doctrine of transubstantiation in 1215 was in response to a liturgical habit well established by then; namely, the habit of priestcraft. Transubstantiation not only magnified the Mass, but it enormously increased the standing of the priest who was granted such incredible power in his ordination. For now he had the authority to perform a miracle that was in many ways more awesome than the Incarnation itself. Jesus had been a historical person, limited to a certain time and place, but the priest possessed the power to bring the physical presence of Christ anywhere the Mass was observed.

We should also note the immeasurable authority gained by the priest by hearing confessions. He was the one who announced forgiveness. And like Congressmen who announce government benefits to their constituencies, the priest received credit for something that was in fact given by the authority of the Church as a whole.

In Chaucer's "povre Persoun of a toun," we see the medieval priesthood at its best. Here is a man conscious of his superior status and the obligations that go with it. He tries to do his duty, striving to live a pure life as an example before his lowly flock. For, as he says, "If gold rusts, what shal iren do?" Yet at best he seems to us to be a drab figure amid those brighter souls in Chaucer's company. In spite of Chaucer's praise, the good parson seems to be yet another example of that decline in respect toward priests that we have seen already.

We may suppose that the priest had been a sort of scapegoat to medieval men. In a barbarous and violent age, some sort of vicarious satisfaction must have been consoling to a society where a special class was set aside to live up to a morality and purity that few others could possess. It must have been somewhat akin to the pleasure dull people mired in dull lives get today when they see interesting people living interesting lives on television. And we can scarcely imagine a duller life than that lived out by the average man in the agrarian Middle Ages, when isolated people endured a monotonous and backbreaking routine interrupted only by the excitement of religious ceremonies, the passing of kings, or the onslaughts of violent death.

But by the end of the Middle Ages there were flourishing towns, and there was wealth enough to allow a life of leisure to a few. Society became ever more complicated and various, at least among the more wealthy. Some people of verve and intelligence found a thousand pleasant things to do with their time. And priests lost their hold on the popular imagination. They were like the hunger artist in Franz Kafka's story. A busy world ignored their ideals even when they practiced them, and after a while many priests ceased to practice virtue.

The decline in priestly morality was probably exaggerated by the literature of the time. Thomas More said that human nature did not take note of the good priest. But when one priest did sin, the self-righteous were likely to say, "See how bad all priests are!" Modern studies tend to support More's view. And yet many priests were ignorant. Many lived openly with concubines and so exposed themselves to that ridicule society is always eager to heap on idealists who fail. Most priests were poor in an age when a few wealthy merchants and bankers in every town were introducing Europeans to the delights of conspicuous consumption. Many swarmed into the priesthood without any dedication in the way the failures of society are likely to gravitate to a peacetime army, seeking a living that, while not being sumptuous, is at least adequate, requiring neither hard work nor special intelligence. And if More was right about the good living of most priests, he was also right in his judgment that all clergymen were scorned for the sins of a few.

Luther spoke to this situation by abolishing priesthood as a class. All that was legal for any Christian was also lawful to the priest. He told those priests who had been living with concubines to consider themselves married and to assume their rightful responsibilities to their families. And yet Luther's mentality was such that he could never consider human beings to be capable of functioning in an orderly way in associations unless they had some official leader. Abilities differed; some had a gift for leadership that was needed for the good of the Church.

So in place of the priest, Luther proposed the pastor to preside over the spiritual affairs of the local Christian congregation. The pastor should be learned and devout. He should be chosen by Christians who know him. And he should be supported by gifts from the congregation so that he might do his duties without the burden of abject poverty. But again we find one of those consistencies in Luther's thought that appear under the occasional contradictions like ribs of steel. Faith comes before works; the inner reality always comes before the external form. The pastor does not receive his power as a consequence of the rite of ordination. He is ordained only after he has shown the gifts and powers a good minister should have. In Luther's thought ordination was always important because it allowed the congregation to preserve an orderly ministry in the Church; however, the ceremony was always only a recognition of gifts and not their real cause.

Most important of all the pastoral gifts was always the power to preach the Word of God as it was reflected in Scripture. If the Catholic priest demonstrated his status by administering the sacraments, the Protestant pastor has always shown his authority by preaching the rousing and eloquent sermon from a Scriptural text.

In the *Address* Luther had a special reason for his doctrine of the priesthood of all believers. He wanted to persuade the German princes to take the lead in reforming the Church. To do so he sought to prove that the lay status of princes did not make them inferior to priests. Indeed, by proving that priesthood was a Catholic deceit, Luther wanted to show the princes that they exercised a legitimate, divinely ordained power against the Pope and all his clerical subordinates, who had no true authority at all.

In this endeavor Luther was going against Catholic thought as it had stood for several hundred years. In the investiture controversy of the eleventh century, the popes had battled to free themselves from the control of the emperors, who pretended to rule Germany and Italy alike under the guise of a Roman Empire restored in the West. From Charlemagne on, emperors had claimed the right to regulate the papacy, to assure themselves of the good morals of popes, to appoint bishops in their lands, and either to appoint the Pope himself or else have the right to confirm a pope chosen by the Church in Rome. Popes fought for their independence with many weapons. Legates of Pope Leo IX excommunicated the Patriarch of Constantinople in 1054. Since the excommunication implied that anyone who supported the Patriarch was also banned from the Catholic Church, later popes considered that the Emperor of the Eastern Empire had also been cast out of true Christendom. Any lingering legal authority that the Emperor at Constantinople might have claimed over Rome was thereby eliminated forever, at least in the eyes of the popes.

In 1059 Pope Nicholas II established the college of cardinals. From that time on only popes have been able to create cardinals, and only cardinals have been allowed to elect popes. This step was to assure the freedom of papal selection from imperial control exercised from north of the Alps. After that, Pope Gregory VII tried to end the practice that allowed governments to appoint the bishops of the Church in Europe.

Naturally the emperors resisted these measures, and the popes and writers sympathetic to their cause launched a theological attack to demean government itself. Government was necessary, they said, but only to control the effects of man's sin. In the Garden of Eden there had been no need for compulsion. Therefore, government, which existed to compel men to be orderly, was one of the consequences of the fall of man. Princes were men with bloody hands. Pope Gregory VII also considered the sort of people princes were. In general he found them proud, vainglorious, ambitious, greedy, and possessed with a fever to rule over their fellows. Their pride was in direct opposition to the humility of Christ Gregory proudly claimed to represent. His point was that they were unfit both by the nature of their job and by the nefarious quality of their persons to handle the spiritual affairs of the Church. Rulers, being impure, could not make a pure bishop; bishops could be made and invested with their episcopal authority only by the Pope, the successor of Peter, the vicar of Christ. Only the unstained priestly authority that came from Christ could handle any spiritual affair. Princes began not with Christ but with Adam, and they ruled over this world, whose real prince was the devil. The Pope ruled over the Church, whose captain was Christ. The Church was superior to government in the way eternity is superior to time. And the Pope was superior to all secular rulers in any matter where man's sinfulness might be involved. Since rulers were also sinners in need of the sacraments of the Church, the Pope was claiming a vast power to meddle in their affairs. In asserting the incapacity of princes to rule over the papacy, the Pope came to declare his right to rule over them.

The medieval controversy over investing bishops is of monumental importance in our history. It was one of the many steps teaching us that government is not divine, that rulers are human beings who can err, and that they may be reasonably opposed by men who may be right when government is wrong. God is not present in the person of the ruler. The fact that the autocracy of the Russian czars has always seemed monstrous to most Westerners is in some sense a legacy from the medieval papacy, which vigorously asserted that rulers were sinners like everyone else. But at the time, the papacy pushed its victory to extremes, holding that insofar as spiritual affairs were concerned, princes should be seen and not heard—except in confession.

Luther held in the *Address* that this division between secular authority and spiritual power was a wall blocking true reform in the Church. There was no distinct priesthood, he said. Princes possessed the same gifts as do all Christians, for all Christians were priests and on the same level before God. Princes did possess an important authority. That authority came from God, who had ordained government. It was the Christian duty of every man to use any authority he possessed in the service of God. And what better service could a prince do than to lead in the reform of the Church?

Luther was far from asserting any quality of special divinity for princes. (There was at least one Council in the Eastern Church where the Emperor residing at Constantinople was said to be inspired by the same spirit that had moved the apostles to write Scripture.) For Luther princes had no right to define doctrine merely because they were princes. In good Western fashion he always made a distinction between the man and the job, holding that a bad man could occupy a good office. In the *Address* he was simply saying that the world runs by various orders, all of them necessary, all of them good, and that princes with their secular authority should use their legitimate power to do what was good for the Church. Luther assumed that, in reforming the Church, the princes and all other Christians would be guided by the Word of God, as clearly understood by them as it was by him.

What is perhaps most astounding is that Luther sincerely expected that motley herd of licentious, gluttonous, quarreling drunks who were the German princes to reform the Church. He lost his wild hope soon enough. Yet the hope requires some attention, for it provides a sign of Luther's temper in this exuberant year.

Certainly he shared the hopes of most prophets who begin popular movements, hopes that the exploding enthusiasm they see generated among multitudes will go on and on until the old order has been swept away and a new world born. Luther's confidence in 1520 is like the thrill of Lenin in 1917 or the excitement of the French national assembly in 1789 or the mood of Jefferson in 1776. He felt the earth shaking under his feet from the power of God, and he saw his enemies in retreat before God's victorious majesty.

In the fire of such bliss, all who are not in active opposition to the movement are likely to seem its friends, at least for a few happy moments. In 1520 the princes were not yet acquainted with their new Emperor, who had not yet come to the German lands. They were suspicious of him, and they were largely uninterested in the fine points of theology. They felt themselves abused by the papacy, and they had many obvious reasons to oppose the rich papal monarchy with its base in distant Italy. So it seemed to Luther that the princes had every reason to stand with him against the Pope.

As far as I can tell, Luther had seen only two German princes by the time he wrote his *Address*. He had seen Duke George at Leipzig, and Duke George was to become his bitter enemy. But though Duke George was a curmudgeon, he was a religious curmudgeon, needing perhaps only the proper guidance and the proper spirit, and in 1520 Luther still had hopes for him.

The other prince Luther had seen with his own eyes was Prince William of Anhalt, whom he had observed in his student days—the prince begging his bread like a pauper in the streets, emaciated and in rags, having renounced all earthly glory to seek salvation. This noble young man, stooped, starved, and probably unbalanced by the terror of death, was hardly typical of his class.

Luther was always quite medieval in his notion of the relation of heaven to earth. Earth was a part of a great cosmic drama that rolled through the universe. In that realm God possessed absolute authority, and it was by this authority that He kept order against the legions of demons and Satan himself, who were the agents of chaos. The Pope represented chaos in what Luther saw as the persistent papal conspiracy to subvert government and to institute the papal tyranny in its place. The Pope had insisted on his right to make kings and emperors and to depose them by excommunication. As William Tyndale said later on, the Venetians had long since discovered that papal excommunication did not disturb their digestion. But most simple people still trembled before that official condemnation to hell, and a prince who was excommunicated ruled with difficulty. So in Luther's mind the papacy represented a demonic confusion in the realm of politics.

But he lived at a time when men looked to authority to settle most questions. And so he might be expected to see the authority of princes as in some sense representing the authority of God. For both prince and God, the emblem of rule was order. He saw the German princes as the natural agents of reform in a great battle to determine the fate of Christianity. The princes could use their authority to restore order in the Church. What was to be the first step in such reform? Luther thought that the princes should call a Council of the Church.

It may seem strange that Luther could speak so positively about Councils after he had rejected their binding authority in the debate at Leipzig. But at Leipzig Luther had especially condemned Constance for sending John Huss to the stake. And what he condemned most of all was the notion that only the Pope could call a Council, that a Council was valid only because the Pope said it was, and that a Council could deliberate only with the Pope as the presiding officer. Such Councils, like the Fourth Lateran of 1215, Luther found to be contrary to the Word of God.

But for years he retained the conviction that a Council based on Scripture and attended by honest and learned Christians would assert the truth of Christian doctrine. He thought that some Councils had done just that. He prized the Council of Nicaea that in 325 had proclaimed God the Father and Christ the Son to be of one substance and coeternal. That Council had been called by the Emperor Constantine, not by the Pope; and the Pope, the Bishop of Rome, does not even seem to have attended it. Luther was convinced that Nicaea had defended the old faith, clearly set down in Scripture, against the "novelty" of those who held that Christ was somehow less than God. Since the Christian prince could have no more competence in reading the Bible than could any honest and studious Christian, the Council would not be a meeting like the German Diet. The Council would be called by the princes and defended by them, but its deliberations would be carried out among equals, led by the Word of God. And the decision of the Council would vindicate the true faith—Luther's faith. It would possess authority in Christendom by the eminence of its doctors and by its affirmation of the Word of God.

Such a Council was never to be held. Yet Luther kept talking about it for decades. In his mind that imagined Council came to assume a mythological status that reminds us of the great general strike in the thought of the labor movement of a few generations ago. It provided an object of hope and a rhetorical assurance of eventual vindication—a vindication that in prospect conferred authority on present actions. The fact that such a Council was never called was probably better for Luther than if it had come to pass. It would not have been what he hoped for because Christians never demonstrated the agreement about Scripture and the Word that he anticipated. The general strike that was never called kept trade union leaders unaware of their weakness, but by dangling the supposed consequence of that strike before the eyes of ordinary workers, the indispensable importance and the dignity of labor were affirmed to the world. And Luther's Council that never happened helped assure his followers that Scripture was as clear as he said it was and that good men brought together in a free assembly would agree that Luther's gospel was the same that Christ came to teach.

14

*L*UTHER'S MOST INFLUENTIAL AND HATED TRAC-
TATE of 1520 was his *Babylonian Captivity
of the Church,* published in the late summer of that year. This was to
be one of the most debated documents of the Protestant Reformation.
Luther's foes regularly quoted from it to show how far he had departed from the faith of the Catholic Church. Even some people
who had been well disposed toward Luther were now turned against
him. Erasmus read the *Babylonica,* as it was popularly called, and pronounced the breach of Christendom irreparable. Other humanists who
had been striving for reform in the Church made haste to declare that
they had no part with Martin Luther, and the impulse toward any
reform at all now seemed likely to be associated with heresy.

Henry VIII of England felt compelled to answer the *Babylonica*
with a royal theological effort in Latin. His work was called *The
Assertion of the Seven Sacraments.* With it he won the papal title
"Defender of the Faith," still worn by the sovereigns of England.
Henry also enlisted the aid of Thomas More, knight, in a theological
controversy that would lead to More's martyrdom at the command of
Henry himself.

Luther said that there was nothing really new in the *Babylonica,*
and his judgment was true. Everything that he wrote here might have
been inferred from what he had written already, especially about the
primacy of Scripture as a norm for doctrine and the universal priesthood of all believers.

But the *Babylonica* was such a bold assertion of Luther's principles that nothing was left to inference. And those people who in every age see only what they want in any man's thought had their liberty sharply reduced because now they could no longer make Luther say what they thought he should be saying. This was the predicament of Erasmus, who always believed that theological disagreement should be patched up in generalities, leaving Christians to their real task in life, the cultivation of an inner and personal piety.

The *Babylonica* treats the seven sacraments of the Church. Luther makes three major points about them: (1) All sacraments should originate with a command of Christ in the New Testament for reasons unique to the Christian faith. (2) The sacraments should be an aid and sign of the direct communion between the Christian and God. (3) The sacraments should be freed from all those ties that enslave the Christian to the corrupt tyranny of the Pope at Rome.

Luther found only three sacraments in the New Testament that fitted his first rubric: baptism, the Mass, and penance. Thus he rejected four sacraments practiced by the Church for many centuries: confirmation, ordination, marriage, and extreme unction. (Within a year or so he was to reject penance, too.) He argued that the sacraments he dismissed possessed neither Scriptural authority nor great antiquity. By this rejection he was attacking the very heart of the Catholic doctrine of tradition, the faith that God would not let all his Church err for so long about something so essential for salvation. For at least since the days of Peter the Lombard in the twelfth century the Church had agreed on the validity of seven sacraments. But to Luther's mind the word of Scripture prevailed over any tradition, no matter how sacrosanct, and because he found only three sacraments in Scripture, he was willing to cancel the faith of centuries and of millions.

To his enemies, Luther's most outrageous comments in the *Babylonica* were on the Mass. He was angry at the way the Church had employed the language of Aristotle to express the doctrine of transubstantiation. Luther always regarded Aristotle as Satan's henchman in matters of faith. Aristotle had divided all things into "essence" or "substance" and "accidents." The essence made a thing what it truly was. The accidents were those sensual qualities available to human perception. Modern science has junked both essence and accidents. The terms are worthless to physics, chemistry, and any other experimental science. But for Aristotle the essence of bread was the quality that makes bread what it is and not merely flour and water and salt or whatever. The accidents of bread are those several qualities we can perceive by our senses—its taste, its appearance, its texture, its smell, and the sound it would make if we dropped it on the floor. The doctrine of transubstantiation held that in the Mass the essence of the bread and the wine are miraculously changed to the body and blood of Christ, while the accidents remain those of bread and wine.

Luther saw these philosophical terms as a conspiracy on the part of the papacy to enslave Christians to idolatry—the worship of bread and wine instead of God. His view of the Mass included a real presence of the body and blood of Christ in the bread and the wine. Christ had declared, "This is my body. . . . This is my blood." Luther had probably been overwhelmed more than just once by the majesty of the Sacrament. And here he was the supreme literalist in the interpretation of Scripture. The joining of body and blood to the bread and the wine, he said, was like the joining of heat to iron, an unseen and felt quality that added to what was there already, not the replacement of one thing by another. Thus one adored not the bread and the wine but the body and the blood of Christ in the bread and the wine. This doctrine of the Mass has been accurately enough labeled "consubstantiation," though Luther did not himself use that term. The importance for liturgy in Luther's doctrine was that the worshiper could come to the Mass believing that Christ was present in a comforting and physical way, abiding in the same bodily world where the Christian must live. Yet he was not required to rationalize the process by an elaborate and unscriptural theory based on Aristotle. In fact, Luther's analogy of the heated iron to describe the presence of the body and blood in the Mass was an attempt to do precisely what the Aristotelian theologians of the Middle Ages wanted. That was to make the doctrine of the presence of Christ comprehensible to people who wondered how these things can be. Luther's heated iron is no more to be found in the New Testament than is Aristotle's essence. In using the analogy of iron, he was trying to think clearly about a murky doctrinal issue by moving from the imprecise language of the New Testament into another realm of language where people explained the common life to themselves and one another. People had had experience with heated irons, but they had also had experience with the common human perception that the definition of an object is usually somehow more than the mere sum of its parts. Philosophy is the persistent effort on the part of man to think clearly about his experience, and so Luther's image of the heated iron is a sort of philosophy. But he thought his position was self-evident in Scripture.

Luther also held that laymen should partake of both the bread and the wine in the Mass. This view had been advanced by John Huss. It exalted the lay status, and it was for Luther an outgrowth of his doctrine that every believer was a priest.

His view on baptism seems to be in contradiction to the rest of his thought. Everywhere he stresses the need for personal faith when we approach the ceremonies of the Church. The Mass testifies to our faith in the Incarnation of Christ, his Passion, and the bloody victory of the cross. Baptism testifies to the redemption we receive in faith from the curse passed on to us from Adam. Faith, says Luther, cannot be transferred from one person to another. He likes immersion as a mode of baptism because it is most like the death, burial, and Resurrection of Christ. Yet he insists that newborn infants be baptized! He even speculates about the validity of baptizing a child only partly born—with a foot or a hand sticking out of the mother's womb!

Why Luther took this position has always been hotly debated. The so-called "Anabaptists" of the Reformation quickly went beyond him and held that only people who could testify to their faith could be baptized. That usually meant that baptism could be administered only about the same age at which a Catholic received the sacrament of confirmation. The Anabaptists excluded infant baptism as a relic of popery. They claimed Scriptural authority on the simple fact that no instance of infant baptism is recorded in the New Testament. And Luther turned on them all the vehemence and slander of his furious pen and tongue in a hatred as seething as that which he directed against the papacy.

Luther strained to refute the Anabaptists. He said that no one can prove that children do not have faith. Here he sounds just a little like the Platonists he usually despised. Some Platonists taught that the child's soul comes into the world still conscious of the divine realm whence it sprang. As the child grows older, it slowly forgets that other world. William Wordsworth entertained such notions, and he implied them when he wrote, "The Child is father of the Man." Luther could not bear to think of the human soul as eternal. Yet he longed to posit some sort of consciousness in the infant to justify infant baptism. The yowling baby protesting the water dribbled on his head by the minister should be, within his infant heart, consenting to the faith symbolized by baptism.

Luther also justified child baptism on grounds that have become more traditional in Protestantism. These involve inferences that may be made from Scripture, though they are not clearly stated in Scripture itself. In the New Testament entire households were baptized; these households must have included children. Baptism is the sign of the covenant with God in the New Testament just as circumcision is the sign of the covenant in the Old. Since circumcision was done to children, baptism ought to be done to them, too. Luther also held that since infant baptism had been a part of tradition for many, many centuries, no one should go against this Christian consensus unless he had clear Scriptural grounds for doing so. There was embedded in this thought a doctrine that was later to distinguish Luther from more radical reformers such as Ulrich Zwingli of Zurich, who were to hold that unless Scripture directly supported the tradition of the Church, that tradition was to be abolished. Luther always was more likely to hold that a tradition might be followed if it did not directly contradict Scripture.

There were so many contradictions involved in Luther's position on baptism that no one should be surprised that the *Babylonica* was greeted by Catholic theologians with a mixture of horror and disdain, contempt and ridicule. Here is Luther at odds with his own assertions about the need for personal faith, and at odds, too, with his claim to found his doctrine only on the clear word of Scripture.

Yet we should probably see Luther's position on infant baptism in much the same way that we might view the earlier development of a Catholic tradition. Here was a liturgical ceremony that possessed great emotional appeal to the people who engaged in it. Baptism was the Christian rite of purification, originating in the same world of thought that provided a sacred bath for the initiate in many religions of the Mediterranean world. For Christians it was the most potent sacrament in that it freed them from the hereditary curse of Adam. Children are weak and defenseless, and even in the warped mentality of Luther's age, so callous to childhood, parents did love their offspring and cherished the best for them. Baptism was the only way anyone could imagine to extend to children the benefits of Christ. Little children in that evil time were more than likely to cough themselves to death in the middle of the damp night or else to burn out their insides with some nameless fever or else to die some languid death like a frail white candle burning to a soft end without a sound. And so good parents longed to see their children baptized to protect them against the dark world of death. As we have seen, the Church from a very early time accommodated itself to this desire, and Martin Luther agreed with the Church.

To Luther the ceremony of baptism was always profoundly moving. It was the perfect symbol of the Christian life. He believed that it was not only a symbol but a means of communicating the power of God to the Christian. He thought that anyone who was baptized should live out the rest of his days with a fervent consciousness of the death, burial, and Resurrection of Christ. Luther never saw religion as some strictly psychological impulse akin to the "inner light" of the much later Quakers or the nonritual piety of a Ralph Waldo Emerson; rather, he always saw God's work with men in a way much akin to the standard Catholic view of that divine process. Man was a unified nature of soul and body; God worked in the world by means corresponding to man's nature, invisible power wrapped in a cloak of the physical. Creation was good because God had made it, and only the improper use of created things was wrong—not the things in themselves. Therefore, there was no contradiction involved if God wished to translate His almighty force, His grace and power, to the Christian by means of the water of baptism. The Christian must receive that grace in faith just as the impulse of trust in our hearts must be there before we can put out our hands to receive any gift. But the means God uses to convey His grace is through a physical wrapping, and so it is with baptism, the Mass, and Scripture itself. In baptism we have a rite Luther could not reject for little children because the feeling he had for it was overpowering.

We may note in passing that many of his thoughts about baptism do not seem to be in keeping with the rest of his theology, and we may make the point once again that Luther was far from being the Scriptural literalist he claimed to be. We may judge him because of his bitter hostility toward the defenseless Anabaptists who disagreed with him. But then Emerson wrote that a foolish consistency is the hobgoblin of little minds, and Luther's was no little mind. He felt passionately about most things, including the baptism of children. His theology was not, as he thought, a straight exegesis from Scripture; it was, rather, an attempt to reconcile his various passions with the Bible. We are engaged always in a similar attempt at fitting our impulses to our supposed authorities. Some succeed completely in this endeavor, but they usually turn out to have minds as sterile as plastic. Still, the ambition to reconcile our passions with our idols and our ideals goes on in any thinking mind.

I have mentioned that Luther still believed in 1520 that penance was a sacrament, though he soon discarded it. Confession to him meant that one Christian should contritely confess his sins to another. The hearing Christian should then console the penitent by speaking the forgiveness open to all who acknowledge their sins to God. Luther knew that though we may tell ourselves that we are forgiven for our misdeeds, the comfort we receive is much greater if someone else assures us that we need have no further reason to feel guilty. He found abundant sanction for such oral confession in Scripture, especially in the Psalms and in the stories of the New Testament. Again the doctrine of the priesthood of all believers was crucial here. Luther broke the clerical monopoly on confession. By stressing the value of simple verbal confession and the verbal assurance of forgiveness, he also eliminated the multitude of liturgical practices by which Christians had sought to perform their satisfactions—the pilgrimage, the relic, the fast, the vigil, the funerary bequest to the Church, the vow of service to God for oneself or for one's children.

His enemies said that he made confession easy and that therefore sin was now easy. But he believed that confession was for those people (admittedly few) who were true Christians. And a true Christian lived with a genuine abhorrence of sin and could take the comfort of forgiveness without any sense that he was getting away with anything. There was no place in Luther's view for any suggestion that a sinner could work off a penalty for sin by some sterling work of satisfaction. Pilgrimages and all the rest smacked of works-righteousness. Christ had already won the battle against sin. Righteousness was faith in Christ. That faith was planted by God, and no power on earth could root it out once God had placed it in the heart of his elect. That was the absolution that one Christian could use to comfort another in the hour when sinful human nature outraged the pious heart of the one who possessed it.

So if we take liturgy to be the set of rituals and ceremonies and other acts by which Christians seek to worship God, Luther's radical redefinition of the sacrament of penance became the most important single liturgical event of the Reformation. It made more visible changes in formal Christian practice than any other reform he made. Indeed, he made confession so informal that it became less than a sacrament in his own thought, and it has dropped out of most Protestant sects.

We can pass over Luther's dismissal of the other sacraments in some haste. Since they were not Scriptural, he regarded them as various perversions in spite of their long tradition in the Catholic Church. We have already mentioned his rejection of ordination. Confirmation was only a sacrament, said Luther, because it gave lazy bishops something to do. Confirmation was generally administered by the bishop rather than by the local parish priest. Extreme unction might indeed be valuable to comfort the dying Christian, Luther thought, but it was not a sacrament, and most of the time it was improperly used as a part of the tyranny of the clergy over laymen.

He did not believe that marriage was a sacrament, and he rejected the provisions of the canon law for matrimony. These legal articles, mostly about blood relationships within which marriage was forbidden, rules for divorce or annulment, definitions of betrothal, and so forth, made marriage into a Gordian knot of regulations where lawyers, theologians, and keepers of genealogical tables swarmed among the threads like vermin. For many centuries Church rules would not let two people marry if they shared an ancestor seven generations back. After the Fourth Lateran Council of 1215, marriage was permitted if the couple had no common ancestor earlier than four generations back. The change was not much of an improvement. Even today we have trouble discovering who our great-great-grandfathers might have been. Since every one of us has eight such ancestors, the problem of keeping up with all their descendants is formidable. It was nearly impossible in the Middle Ages, when all records were scanty. The canon law complicated things even more by holding that anyone who stood as the godparent of a child at baptism became spiritually related to that child's family. Since the Church regarded this spiritual kinship as being as important as blood, godparents became members of the family in the definition of the canon law. That meant that their relations might never marry. Naturally enough, if a man got tired of his wife, the surest way to be rid of her was to discover that he and she had a common great-grandfather. Such a crusty old ancestor, immobile in the grave for decades (or perhaps even nonexistent), might thus be summoned up to cut those marriage ties that had been supposed to bind till death. Or an unhappy husband might learn that his grandfather had served as godfather to his wife's mother—a relationship that made his marriage invalid. It was all a sleazy, impossible business made to order for the purveyor of false genealogies, who could manufacture a common ancestor with a flourish of his pen, a wink of the eye, and a clink of the proper coin.

Luther wanted to get rid of all the sterile rules that hindered warm human relationships. He wanted genuine affection between husband and wife, unbound by the rigidities of ossified custom. To him marriage was a relationship between two people, marked by love, sexual intercourse, publicly assumed obligations, and a shared life. Husband and wife had certain human responsibilities toward each other, but these did not require the definitions of the canon law. They were matters of common sense. So the canon law should melt away. But in this melting, the power of the institutional Church over marriage was also washed away.

Some of Luther's thoughts on marriage sound radical to many even today. Certainly one is not likely to hear them proclaimed from the bashful Protestant pulpit, where sound and fury generally signify nothing very much. But all of them arise from Luther's desire to make marriage a humane institution.

Suppose a man is impotent, says Luther, and unable to have sexual intercourse with his wife. He might give his wife her freedom to marry another—a divorce, in other words. But at the very least he should grant her the liberty to have sexual intercourse with somebody else. And if she has children from such a union, the impotent husband should happily bring them up as his own. Luther, always conscious of appearances, suggested that in such cases the intimate arrangements be kept from the public at large.

His point is commendable. Marriage is not an institution where the husband owns the wife as though she were a slave. She is a person. She has certain rights. If the husband truly loves her, he should be willing to let someone else supply her needs if he cannot. Here Luther not only exalted women relative to their lowly medieval status (chivalry only pretended to exalt women), but he also departed from the medieval Catholic view that sex is nasty, something that must be tolerated because the world depends on it, but something always to be regarded with aversion and engaged in dispassionately for the propagation of the race.

For Luther sexuality is as much a part of life as eating. He did share a common prejudice of his day: He believed that women, the weaker sex, craved sex more than heroic men did. Yet he knew the power of the sexual drive himself. He confessed openly in a sermon of 1519 that his own sexual desire was intense and painful. He spoke very frankly in lectures to students of the problems of nocturnal emission and lust, all with the candor of a man who knows these to be part of the common male experience. And when he made these rather jarring proposals in the *Babylonica,* he was carrying on that healthful propensity of his to see the biology of humankind as something natural. Sin for him never lay in the mere act of anything. Nature required its due. Sexual intercourse was a part of the creation that God had made. And so he could hold that an impotent man should supply a sexual partner for his wife. He could make this suggestion without even a shade of that jeering hilarity that would be provoked by such a notion today among those new puritans among us whose world is the body, whose scripture is *Playboy,* and whose gospel is orgasm.

Luther touched briefly on the issue of divorce. He hated divorce so much that he would prefer bigamy, he said, though he was not sure that bigamy was right. The notion was not farfetched to one as steeped in Scripture as Luther was. Nowhere in the Bible is polygamy condemned. The devout patriarchs and kings of the Old Testament had many wives. Paul, in the New Testament, said that an "overseer" should be the husband of one wife, but he never suggested that the ordinary Christian had to be so limited. Monogamy is probably a legacy from the Greeks and the Romans. By approving of bigamy, Luther was concerned to protect a wife from being discarded in a world where a woman required a man to protect her. But bigamy seemed radical at the time, and much later on, when Luther advised Philip of Hesse to commit bigamy rather than to put aside his first wife for another, the result was scandal. Philip took Luther's advice. The public found out, and Luther and Philip were both humiliated. And although the notion of bigamy does not upset many of us today, we have but to recall the tribulations of the Mormons in our own mottled history to see how polygamy made them fair game for any pious Christian with a gun in his hand and murder in his heart.

But though Scripture made Luther sound radical in some ways, his notion of consensus kept him rather conservative in most beliefs and practices. At least he is conservative when he is compared with many Protestants who came after him. For example, in his *Babylonica* he was silent on the matter of foot washing. The very mention of foot washing is likely to call up in our minds an illiterate congregation of primitive Baptists in the mountains of eastern Tennessee, earnestly scrubbing the needy feet of one another in that special humility that looks proudly down on the rest of the world—especially on other Baptists—for not possessing it.

But the Gospel called "John" tells the story of Jesus' washing the feet of his disciples. Not only did he wash their feet, but he commanded them to wash the feet of one another. So the ritual of foot washing possessed every criterion Luther used to justify a sacrament. And there had been times during the Middle Ages when the rite was revived here and there in Europe. Luther's enemies, such as Thomas More, suggested that if he remained true to his own principle of Scripture alone, he would have to advise his followers to wash feet.

Luther seems never to have thought much about the question. It was not part of his religious experience. He had grown up with a very deep commitment to the religious customs of his time. He was a man of powerful feeling—almighty hatreds and devoted attachments. As his life developed, he performed a stupendous task. He looked at the commonly accepted religious life of his time in a critical and inventive way. (Not many of us are able to do the same.) And though he formulated a so-called Scriptural principle for liturgy and doctrine, he did not really begin with Scripture. He started with his own experience. He used a very selective interpretation of Scripture to refine that experience in a way that brought a more spontaneous liberty to the Christian life.

We must always think of Luther in terms of the way he spent his days. Luther at prayer. Luther at the Mass. Luther at confession. Luther preaching. Luther at study. Luther the pastor. Luther writing with furious energy. To all these activities he brought Scripture. And always his aim was to reform the old, to make it more viable, more meaningful. He never tried to sweep everything away and begin anew with Christian teaching and practice drawn out of Scripture alone like some Red Guardsman willing to destroy all the past in the name of cultural revolution and strict orthodoxy.

His attitude may be compared to that of the Anabaptists who swarmed up in southern Germany after Luther. Here were small groups of true radicals. They looked on the New Testament as a law to be followed in every particular. Were only adults baptized in the New Testament? Then they would baptize only adults. Was there no instrumental music in the New Testament? Then they would not use organs to accompany their hymns. Did the New Testament Christians practice a form of Communism? Then some Anabaptists would flee society, set up communes in the wilderness, and live unto themselves. Did Jesus forbid his disciples to swear? Then the Anabaptists would take no oaths; and by that fact they would exclude themselves from public life, where oath taking was one of the official rites of society. Did Jesus forbid his followers to kill? Then the Anabaptists would not be soldiers. And did Jesus command the washing of feet? Well then, some of the Anabaptists would resurrect the practice from the dead. And so it went.

My point is that the Anabaptists and others were the ones who sat down with a book and tried to generate a whole new world of experience out of that book. Ulrich Zwingli and John Calvin, both much more conservative than the Anabaptists, still were more bookish than Luther was in their attitudes toward Scripture. Luther only sought to redefine the old, not to create something entirely new. And so he remained essentially conservative, a sort of Edmund Burke of the sixteenth century, by no means opposed to change but unable to sympathize with those dangerous men he thought to be interested in revolution only out of a lust for novelty and pride in their own daring.

The pity is that Luther's experience was so intense that he could never detach himself from it enough to see that people might differ from him and still be honest. He read his experience back into Scripture, freely discarding those parts of Scripture that did not fit his thought, and never understanding that others might not see things as clearly as he did. He put out the *Babylonica* to show how Scripture judged the sacraments. It is really a tractate on how Luther understood Scripture to apply to his own experience of the sacraments. Though Luther expressed humility again and again, though he always made a difference between divine Scripture and the fallible word of interpreters such as Augustine, Jerome, and himself, his rhetoric was such that when he explained Scripture, he never made the slightest difference between his explanation and the supposed divinity of the sacred text.

15

THE MOST ENDURING of Luther's 1520 tractates was his *Freedom of a Christian*, which appeared in the late autumn. Luther had heard a rumor that the Pope's attitude was softening toward him. Many Christians were urging compromise. Some suggested to Luther that he make one last attempt to win the Pope to his side. It is possible that Frederick the Wise was worried and did not want to be placed in the embarrassing position of being the only princely champion of a totally obdurate monk. Some gesture on Luther's part would be welcomed as a sign of Christian charity and Catholic concern.

And so Luther began with what purported to be a friendly, open letter to Pope Leo X. Luther's partisans have always wanted to see this letter as conciliatory, evidence of the graciousness of their hero and his willingness to compromise, and they have used it to make the Pope seem obstinate and wicked. It was the effect Luther probably intended. In fact his letter is about as conciliatory as a knife in the ribs. True, Luther professed his willingness to make amends, claiming that he had never spoken evil of Leo as a man, praising his innocence, blaming bad counselors around the Pope for the troubles of the Church, and begging for a hearing where the two of them might get their minds together. The attack on evil counselors was standard in the rebellions of the Middle Ages. A rebellion was seldom said to be against the king himself. On the contrary "loyal servants" of the king felt compelled to take up arms to free him from his wicked advisers. At least that is what rebels claimed time and again. So Luther's ploy was ancient and threadbare at the start.

Luther never had much talent for making apologies. Now he addressed Leo in the firm tones of a good German schoolmaster. Though he had not attacked the person of Leo, he nevertheless declared unremitting war against the papacy itself. Leo was counseled to give up his "glory"—that is, his title of Pope—to retire to the parish and live on the income of a simple priest, and to accept all the doctrinal definitions Luther had proposed. As a very obedient and secondary servant, Leo could then help Luther reform the Church. In effect, Luther told Leo that there could be peace between them if Leo would help destroy the papacy.

The letter was probably a calculated insult on Luther's part to convince friends and enemies alike that no compromise was possible between true Christians and the Antichrist at Rome. Or it might be that Luther was so swept up in the righteousness of his cause that the arrogance of his letter to the Pope seemed to him only a statement of obvious fact to a world in danger. Rome, he said, was Sodom and Babylon. It was a brothel and the sink of iniquity. Leo was a lamb in the midst of wolves, and Satan himself should be Pope in Rome.

Leo was not converted. He probably never took time off from his amusements to read it.

Yet the major part of this tractate is one of Luther's finest pieces of writing. Here he proposes his famous paradox: A Christian is utterly free, master of all, slave to none; a Christian is the willing slave of all, commanded by all.

The freedom of the Christian resides in the fact that Christ has done all the work to earn salvation and there is nothing left for the Christian to do himself. The Christian is thus freed from the law and freed also from the tyranny of good works. He knows that the commands of God are given so that men may try to accomplish them and in the trying discover that no one can obey them completely. So the commandments humiliate man's pride, and it is pride that makes man turn himself into a god, the center of the universe, the object of his real adoration. Only in humiliation does man perceive that he is not divine, and only then can he be truly willing to let God be God. Then he recognizes the truth of the universe, and only then can he be saved. For only when man despairs of himself can God's grace be given to him. Freedom thus consists in the knowledge that one has already been released from the bondage of sin and that one need not suffer anguish trying to win something he already possesses.

It seems to me that Luther's intent may be fairly expressed by an analogy drawn from common experience. If I love someone, I do not have to go to a rule book to see what bargain I must strike, what deeds I must perform, what gifts I must bring, what dragons I must slay to get my beloved to love me. Those relationships where someone says, "Do this, and I will love you," are cold and mechanical. And under conditions of trade and bargain, one can never be certain of love at all.

But if I already know that someone loves me, I can enter a warm relationship where I have real freedom. I do not have to prove my love by constant strain. Yet what sort of freedom is it? It is obviously not a freedom to do anything contrary to the nature of love itself. I am not free to slash my beloved's tires, to beat his children, to poison his dog, or to burn his house down. I am thus bound by love, but it is a bondage that I do not feel as bondage. Luther's view is that the cross has demonstrated for all time how much God loves us. And because he is assured of that love, the true Christian spontaneously acts in immeasurable gratitude to the Christ who has redeemed him. Christ loves all mankind, and the Christian will reciprocate by sharing the love of Christ for his fellows.

This tractate is enough to dispel a popular misconception about Luther's justification by faith, a misconception that we have already discussed: that his doctrine meant that the Christian could believe in the propositions of the gospel and still live like the devil. For Luther faith was the presence of Christ in the heart, and it required the Christian to have the same selfless attitude toward the world that Christ had possessed. Luther expected discipline, love, and service from everyone who bore the name of Christ. But the motives of this life were not to be selfish. The Christian did not love his neighbor out of some slavish lust for reward; rather, he loved other people because Christ had already loved him. Good works did not make a man good; Christ made the Christian good, and so the Christian did good works out of gratitude.

Karl Marx had a certain spiritual affinity with Luther. Marx saw the capitalist world as a place where human life and every other value were measured in hard coin, a feverishly grasping realm where the merciless competition of capitalism had destroyed every spiritual relation among men. Luther, like Marx, saw selfish calculation as the sickness that sapped virtue and made humanity unsound. Both of them wanted to change human relationships to spontaneous and selfless generosity, something like what Jonathan Edwards called "disinterested benevolence."

But are such relationships ever truly possible among the generality of humankind? Marx had to impose a dictatorship of the proletariat, and he could not predict how long it would be needed to force people to be selfless. Luther fell increasingly onto the notion that if few could be found like the Christian he described, it meant that there were few Christians in the world. But then God ran the world in a mysterious way and never depended on majorities. Only a remnant had been left faithful in the Old Testament. The disciples of Christ had been a small and hunted band in their day. True Christians had obviously not been a majority during the long years of papal tyranny. So Luther was content to let God make few Christians, but for those few the motive for life was to be the warm and spontaneous generosity that was the true freedom of the Christian.

The tone of this tractate does not comfort those leaders of government who believe that they should support religion as a means of upholding the civil order. The freedom of a Christian as Luther interprets it does not lend itself to stress on the political usefulness of Christian faith. Political religion is always pleased with the mechanical observation of forms. The forms serve to keep populations obedient, and they provide an outlet for the frustrations and the quiet despair of the ordinary citizen, who cannot think in abstractions but whose loyalty is necessary for any established order. Luther's religion in this tractate demands a complete obedience to the demands of love, even to the point of indifference to all the comfortable old forms of religious expression.

Such freedom proved to be completely unacceptable to those princes who adopted Lutheranism and so became the real apostles of the sect. For they wanted the same undeviating loyalty from their populations that had been the desire of every Christian prince from the time of Constantine. And Luther himself, battered in later years by onslaughts from the right and the left, was to settle back onto the reliable old forms of religious expression like a sea lion finding a rock in the storming ocean, where he might sit and roar back at the tempest. Already in this tractate he was saying that Christianity could not get along without ministers, and so he was on his way back to making the distinction between clergy and laity that had originally created a special class of priests in the Catholic Church. This in spite of the fact that in the *Freedom of a Christian* Luther once again makes one of his thundering affirmations of the priesthood of all believers. The theory proved to be somewhat different from the practice. For the rest of his life Luther was to develop catechisms, write Biblical commentaries, approve confessions, give advice, and perform all the other services of a spiritual monarch, and his followers were to translate his teachings into iron laws binding on all the faithful. And so this work became a dead letter almost at once. Its spirit was devoured by the ravenous hunger in man to fix upon the outward forms of religion and to harden them into institutions that can be controlled by the decent and reliable elements of society; namely, the rich, the powerful, and the self-righteous. In this tractate Luther taught that the Christian should be willing to suffer, that he should be obedient to secular authority, and that he should expect the worst from the world. From this notion it was easy to pass into a mentality that regarded any attempt by ordinary men to improve their lot as an incitement to rebellion not only against the laws of men but against the purposes of God. Luther was to make this transition during the peasants' rebellion a few years later. And so from his brief, giddy flirtation with spontaneity, Luther and his sect were to pass into an institutional and dogmatic hardness as unyielding as any granite formed in the bowels of the earth by the cooling of rock that had once been molten and volcanic.

From the standpoint of the history of religions, Luther's tractate is interesting because of the many primitive notions it embodies. Christ enters the soul invisibly through faith and absorbs the deficiencies of the Christian. He communicates all his goodness in the process, and there is between Christ and the Christian a true marriage. Faith is the wedding ring, and Christ devours the sin in his bride, the soul of the Christian. It all sounds very much like the cult of Dionysus or the other mystery religions of the classical Mediterranean. Salvation comes through a mystic joining of the initiate to the god, an interchange that is invisible, though it may be helped along by physical objects and ritual forms such as the elaborate and still largely unknown rites at Eleusis where ancient Athenians joined themselves to Persephone and hoped to share in her triumph over the underworld.

Luther also uses the notion of the Savior who descends into the underworld to win a duel against the powers of darkness on their own ground. Death and hell try to swallow up Christ; but Christ ends by swallowing them both, and so he is able to translate his victory to his adherents, who are joined to him by faith. Here we have Christ entering the underworld like Persephone or Orpheus or Hermes or Dionysus, who journeyed into the realm of Hades to redeem his mother, Semele. There are, to be sure, echoes of this idea in the New Testament, as when Paul speaks of Christ, who "descended first into the lower parts of the earth" so that he might later ascend to lead "captivity captive."

In resurrecting these ancient conceptions as to the meaning of the work of Christ, Luther was turning away from a theory dear to medieval theologians. What exactly had Christ done? Why was an incarnation of God in man necessary? Why the death of the cross?

Near the beginning of the twelfth century Anselm of Canterbury had formulated a doctrine of "satisfaction" to explain the atonement. He said that God is a God of absolute justice, and such a God requires satisfaction for every injustice committed in the universe. Otherwise sin would escape retribution, and in an orderly cosmos such an evasion was impossible. Indeed, it was chaos itself and therefore unthinkable. Sin is to be judged not according to the standing of the person who commits it but according to the status of the person against whom the sin is committed. A serf who is disrespectful to another serf has not really done something very offensive in feudal custom, but a serf who shows disrespect to a king deserves to die. Consequently, when Adam sinned, his sin took on an infinite guilt because it was committed against an infinite God. That being so, satisfaction had to be infinite. And God's sense of justice could be assuaged only by the satisfaction done by a God-man, one who shared human nature so that he could make satisfaction on behalf of the human race. But the God-man must also share the nature of God, who alone is infinite, so that the satisfaction would be infinite. The atonement thus became something God had demanded for Himself so that His own sense of justice would not be outraged. This explanation is obviously quite mechanical. But it preserves the power of monotheism, making the Almighty God to be in complete control of all things at all times. God does not have to wrestle or fight with some darker force, and He does not buy off the devil. The atonement is completely His own affair. There is something serenely rational about all this that mightily appealed to a medieval mentality craving to find a meticulous order in all the works of God.

But Luther's view of the atonement, like the more primitive notions of the New Testament itself, goes back to the ancient belief in a conflict between gods of goodness and order and gods of evil and chaos. By consenting to sin, Adam aligned himself with the powers of darkness and gave them the right to claim him as their own. Christ entered the world as the champion of God's purpose, and he defeated Satan and all his minions, including death and hell, on their own ground. Some partisans of this line of thought in the earlier Middle Ages believed that Satan was deceived by the humanity of Christ. Thus Satan inflicted death on Christ, claiming him as one of Adam's children and therefore rightfully enslaved by the powers of darkness. But when Satan had dragged Christ down to the underworld, he discovered the unquenchable divinity of his captive and learned that he had been tricked into attacking one he had no right to attack. That violation of his limitations opened the way for God to redeem from Satan everyone who adhered to Christ. From this view we get the "fishhook" or the "mousetrap" analogies for the atonement. The humanity of Christ serves as bait. But when Satan lunges greedily for that humanity, he finds himself impaled on the hidden divinity. And so he is helpless as Christ redeems Christians who join themselves to the Captain of their salvation by their faith. Echoes of these perceptions resound in the tractate on the freedom of the Christian man, and they predominate in Luther whenever he discusses the atonement.

This is hardly the stuff of which philosophy is made, and even under Christian assumptions there are difficulties here. The atonement becomes necessary because Satan has the power to withstand God, and in some sense Satan has a legal right to mankind. To speak of giving the devil his due is very nice as a proverb, but it causes some perplexity to Christians who believe in an Almighty God. Luther always tried to make the devil God's devil; that is, strictly limited by God. And he believed that God would plunge Satan into eternal torments in the end. But this is more theory than anything else for Luther. In a practical way he experienced the warfare between God and Satan as a deadly conflict. God will win, but as yet the conflict rages and the battle is unresolved. We do not know why it is unresolved; but we experience the fact that it is so, and Luther warns in nearly every sermon against the wiles of the devil. He usually sees the Passion of Christ as a cosmic victory over the powers of darkness, and he nearly always ignores the nicely rational view that God demanded the cross as a satisfaction to Himself. Normally for Luther the cross is the weapon that skewered Satan and loosened his grim power over mankind. That idea is in keeping with the imagery of the *Freedom of a Christian.*

The purported aim of the *Freedom of a Christian* was dead even as Luther wrote. There was to be no sweet reconciliation between him and the Pope. By the time Luther took up his pen to write his open letter to Leo X, the papal declaration *Exurge Domine* had already arrived in Wittenberg. Leo X, taking a short vacation from hunting, wrote, "Arise, O Lord. . . . Foxes have risen to destroy thy vineyard. . . . A bellowing boar from the forest is trying to demolish this vineyard. . . . A wild beast. . . . Arise, O Peter. . . . Arise, O Paul. . . . Arise, all saints. . . ." Many of Luther's beliefs were listed and condemned as heresy. Luther was commanded to remain silent from then on. His books were to be burned, and no Catholic was to read them on pain of excommunication. No one was allowed to praise anything Luther had written. And Luther himself was ordered to recant within sixty days or be excommunicated from the Church.

Luther could speculate that the papal pronouncement was a forgery long enough to write the *Freedom of a Christian.* But the authenticity of the bull was soon evident. (A papal "bull" was so named because of its seal or *bulla,* not because of its content.) The bull was published all over Germany. To many it seemed to be the coal implanted at the foot of a stake that would soon set Luther's funeral pyre ablaze.

Luther responded in a characteristic way. During a great student revel in December, he burned the papal bull in a great bonfire. Some books that supported the Pope and the canon law were also burned. He cast the bull into the flames in a moment of sudden resolution; it does not seem to have been a premeditated act.

There would be many another fire before the Reformation burned itself out in ashes of religious indifference. In the flames, men, churches, cities, governments, and an old order would vanish in smoke. For three years the conflict had been smoldering and spreading through the rickety old barn that was Catholic Christendom. Argument had not cooled passions; argument had only convinced everyone that people on the other side would not listen to reason. Now the Pope's bull and Luther's act of incineration constituted an exchange of declarations of war. The conflict was to be longer, greater, and more disastrous than either side could imagine on that wintry morning when students sang merrily around a bonfire at the gates of Wittenberg and dancing flames went spurting up into the cold and infinite sky.

16

ERE, at the outbreak of open war between Rome and Luther, we might pause to take a look at Luther's thought about himself.

We have seen that by 1518 he had arrived at several convictions dangerous to Catholic orthodoxy. Salvation was a free gift of God, and no man could do a thing to merit it. Even good works were sin if they were done to earn salvation. And even in the heart of the righteous, sin was always present in this world. Faith was the presence of Christ in the Christian's heart, conquering sin, making the Christian take Christ at his word; that is, faith was the assurance of the forgiveness Christ offered his people. The Christian life was to be a process of warm and spontaneous gratitude to God. Good works came out of a good heart just as a good carpenter would build a good house. They were a result of salvation and not a cause.

By 1520 one of the most striking things about Luther's statements about himself is his certainty that God's grace had been granted to him. Gone completely was the late medieval notion that it was good to be unsure of one's salvation. Luther taught that the Christian should be triumphant and confident in his faith. Christ promised redemption from hell. It became a sin to doubt one's own salvation, though no one could ever be sure about the salvation of others. Even if the Apostle Peter himself were to appear before us, only God and Peter would know if he were to be saved. It was all God's work, of course, and Luther's rhetoric is always filled with humility. Yet it is a terrible humility, for it made Luther believe that God had chosen him personally to hew down the forests of iniquity.

Certainty about redemption did not mean that Christians would have good comfort in the earthly life. Luther thought that Christians were always suffering, always dying. He expected to die the horrible death of a heretic. He admonished his followers to prepare for the worst. The Christian would have rest only in heaven.

But in spite of his forebodings, he attacked his mission in life with furious energy. Willing to put himself in mortal danger anytime, he flung himself recklessly into any place he thought God wanted him to be. Whatever else we may think of him, Luther was surely one of the bravest men who ever lived.

The modern student often asks why Luther worked so hard. He believed in predestination. Why not leave God to work things out by Himself? Why not be passive and comfortable?

At times Luther seemed to take such an attitude. Once he said that while he and his friends Nikolaus von Amsdorf and Philipp Melanchthon were drinking their good beer in Wittenberg, the Word of God was destroying the papacy in Rome. Aside from the rather premature estimate of the fate of the papacy, the comment shows a willingness to stand aside while God did the work. And Luther often said that he did nothing himself. But such an attitude was not really his, no matter how he might sometimes pretend that it was. He worked with the fury of genius all his life on behalf of the God who had already worked out the destiny of the world. Why did Luther feel compelled to strive so hard?

The question shows how alien to us is the very notion of providence. But one may ask the same question of the dedicated Marxist. He works and often dies for the triumph of a socialist heaven on earth. But Marx taught that such a triumph was inevitable, predestined by history itself. And if nothing can halt that victory, why bother to sacrifice for it? Luther's headlong bravery, the martyrs among his followers, and the heroic deaths of Marxists all over the world counsel us to pause a moment. In some perplexity we note that the idea of predestination often makes spiritual athletes out of simple men.

Luther and Marx alike believed that the destiny of history would be accomplished by men. Men were tools in the hand of an unseen power. Luther did not believe that God worked in miracles any more. He thought that miracles had stopped when the New Testament was confirmed as Scripture. The Catholics claimed that miracles went on all the time at their shrines. Luther did not deny that something wonderful took place there; but he said that these were false miracles, perpetrated by the devil to deceive the ungodly. The magicians of Egypt had done as much. Their wonders deluded Pharaoh and hardened his heart. God worked through His majestic Word. He worked through the Scripture that proclaimed that Word. And He worked through the preachers, gifted men, who spoke that Word aloud so the world could hear. What more joyful thing could anyone imagine than to be God's servant in such an enterprise?

Luther's example helps explain the old riddle noted earlier in this book. Why are believers in predestination often such great exhorters? Why did Luther and Marx spend so much time writing books urging their views on the world? The core of their thought was the belief that no individual could of himself change history one jot from its ordained destiny. And why do behavioral psychologists such as B. F. Skinner spend so much time begging us to change things when they believe that we live in a world governed by inflexible chains of circumstance?

Partly the reason must be the pleasure men always get when they are sure of a future that is an opaque mystery to most. Hardly anyone can be immune from the grand sense of authority that comes from secret knowledge. But beyond mere pride is the satisfaction of being a cog in the machinery of the universe, machinery that drives all men toward a great goal. If we stand too close to it, it may appear to be a chaos of spinning wheels and dancing light. But it does make sense, and what a sublime thing it is to be a tiny part of the whole! What a terror it must be to believe that there is a destiny and not to believe that you are a part of it! It is as though chaff or sawdust were granted self-consciousness of rejection.

Luther believed that God would use him to death. But beyond death was glory. He was delighted in his own role in bringing God's Word to the world. He spoke of restoring the gospel. It was a burdensome task, and he often complained about the demands on his inner and outer man. Death threatened him. Some friends became enemies. He was depressed. He was smitten by a dozen illnesses. He was constipated. The devil assaulted him, haunted his nights, tempted him to doubt. But always his faith came back. Enemies might threaten him. Some friends were worse than enemies, for they urged him to be cautious. And yet he kept furiously on. He lived a life less fettered than most men, less chained to the demands of self-preservation. In our own time, when we are all at a loss to decipher official pronouncements and political jargon, Luther's boldness is refreshing. He sounds like William Lloyd Garrison: "I am in earnest—I will not equivocate—I will not excuse—I will not retreat a single inch—and *I will be heard!*"

But there is an insidious side to such heroic confidence. It crops out among most men who consider themselves as God's tools. Luther was always likely to believe that anyone who disagreed with him was malicious, an agent of Satan, not worthy to be considered a Christian. "They know they are wrong!" Such was to be his judgment again and again of those who remained loyal to the old Church. He was a complete ideologue, judging people always in terms of their doctrines rather than on the grounds of a larger humanity. There is hardly a shred of sustenance in Luther for those who believe in a human brotherhood based on the toleration of diversity. Diversity to him was akin to disorder—and disorder was Satanic.

To be sure, Luther was more sinned against than sinning. John Eck, his opponent at Leipzig, took it as his special mission in life to damn Luther's name and destroy his body. Luther called him a "little glory-hungry beast." It is hard to fault his estimate of the man. Others accused Luther of attacking indulgences because he had been denied a commission to sell them himself. He was accused of lust and perversion. And of course he was accused of being possessed by demons. His doctrines were villainously distorted. Even a man as upright and brave as Thomas More saw in Luther's teachings only a summons to incest and rebellion.

The problem was that all sides believed that heaven and hell hung on doctrine. If anyone considers Satan as the captain of his enemies, it is blasphemous to give dissenters any measure of toleration. To be tolerant is always to confess uncertainty. Luther's Catholic adversaries were as certain of their traditions as Luther was certain of Scripture. They hounded him with the relentless and bloodthirsty pursuit of wolves in a pack, snapping at a prey whose death is necessary for their lives.

In these circumstances it would have taken a bloodless saint to remain calm. Luther was possessed of a boundless and furious passion. He wrote to an old friend, "I cannot restrain myself; I want to be serene, but I am propelled into tumult." So it was all his life.

His celebrated appearance at the Diet of Worms in 1521 shows his heroic self-confidence. His friends feared for his life if he went. He said he would go if there were as many devils in Worms as there were tiles on the rooftops of the city. Such was his conviction that God had given him a mission. Better to perish in that mission than to live in a cowardly and useless peace!

He went to Worms to take his stand against an ancient order. The symbolic importance of his appearance there before the Emperor and the estates of the Empire can hardly be overemphasized. It has always been remembered in our history. And for once the popular imagination has correctly fixed upon a great dramatic moment as decisive to our civilization.

Yet the most important thing about Luther's appearance was not what he said at Worms. Everyone knows that he stood on his conscience. He refused to recant his beliefs, and he would not disown his books. He stood boldly against the accumulated tradition of fifteen hundred years, one man against the multitude of the living and the dead. He looked the Emperor himself in the eye and did not blink, and he refused aloud the desire of the Emperor's heart. All important enough. The stuff of good theater, the substance of legends. But the extraordinary fact was that Luther was invited to appear before the Emperor at all.

In *Exurge Domine* Leo X ordered Luther to recant within sixty days. The sixty days had passed. Rome had taken a very deep breath and had spoken again. Luther was excommunicated in January. In the old days, when Rome spoke the case was finished. A heretic excommunicated was exiled from the human race. And had Luther lived a century before, the papal edict against him would have made his fate as predictable as an eclipse of the sun.

John Huss, in 1414, was tricked into coming to Constance, and there, the following year, he was burned. Charles V might well lure the notorious Dr. Luther to Worms, seize him, and burn him alive. Rome had spoken. Even emperors could go to hell if they resisted the word of popes. So the popes had decreed again and again in the Middle Ages, and the decrees stood yet in 1521. Indeed, if one is to believe the doctrine of papal infallibility, they stand today. Papal diplomats at Worms exerted all the pressure at their command to keep young Charles V from giving Luther a hearing. Rome had decided the case. It was sacrilegious for a mere emperor to go about making his own decisions in matters like this. The Emperor should now do his duty: destroy the heretic.

Yet Luther went to Worms and stood before the Emperor and departed safely. There is little evidence to suggest that he was ever in danger of being taken and burned. Charles later regretted that he had allowed Luther to escape. But this was the rumination of an old man, out of power and far removed from the events he longed to have changed. In 1521, when all that would come was not yet clear, Luther stood at Worms and respectfully defied the will of the Emperor, scorned the edict of the Pope, and rejected centuries of custom as of no account. And no one dared to touch him.

One can adduce many reasons for this remarkable event. The drone of insurrection was in the air. Luther was a national hero by now. Many thought that if any harm came to him, the German lands would burst into civil war. When Luther rolled into Worms in a cart in April, he was greeted with wild enthusiasm by the populace. Someone said that nine out of ten Germans were shouting the praises of Luther and the tenth was crying, "Death to the Pope." Before that vehemence princes walked lightly.

Then, too, Charles was making his first appearance in the German lands. The princes of the Empire were getting their first good look at him. When he was elected, he had promised to condemn no German without a hearing. And if he went back on his word now, if he allowed an Italian pope to damn a German professor without giving Germans a chance to speak for themselves about one of their own kind, Charles was bound to be in trouble at the beginning of his reign. A little over a century before, the German princes had banded together and had thrown Wenceslaus, "King of the Romans," out of office. ("King of the Romans" was the title given to an emperor who had not yet been crowned by the Pope.) "Good King Wenceslaus" was a drunk and perhaps a little crazy as well, but the princes of his day had made a point, and the memory of it endured in 1521. Even emperors could be removed if they violated the laws and customs of the German lands.

Behind all these practical reasons of politics was the fracture of an old order. What had been happening for a long time in Europe was that government was slowly declaring its independence from the papacy in ecclesiastical affairs. No longer could the Pope merely pronounce a man to be a heretic and expect governments to put the heretic to death. Luther was a heretic, but he was also a German. The Pope was Italian. The Germans hated the Italians. And before any German could be put to death or even made an outlaw, he must be heard by Germans on German soil. Once he was heard, some political decision could then be made about him. The demands of politics and the demands of religion might coincide—or they might not. Such was the new world. And so it was at Worms.

Luther was not heard very much. He appeared late in the day of April 17, 1521, before the Emperor and a grand assembly of other notables in the bishop's palace at Worms. His books—so many that they astounded people who saw them all together in one place—were heaped up on a table in the middle of the room. An official from the entourage of the Archbishop of Trier acted as spokesman for the Diet. He bellowed only two questions at Luther: Were the books his? Would he recant their heresies?

The answer to the first question came directly. Yes, the books were all his, Luther said. Indeed, he had written more. But in response to the second question, he asked for another day to consider.

This unexpected request for more time disappointed the large crowd breathlessly awaiting his response on that spring evening. It has baffled biographers of Luther ever since, pleased as they have always been to record the thundering affirmations of their hero. Did he suddenly lose his nerve? Was he afraid? Did he abruptly stumble into doubt? Was he so moved by his sense of the holy that he could not speak, feeling himself not only in the eye of the Emperor but under the finger of God? We can never know for sure.

The explanation for his hesitation may be simple enough. He came to Worms expecting to argue his case before the Emperor. There were rumors afloat that he would not be able to debate. The papal diplomats seem to have wrung this concession from Charles. The "hearing" was only to be an occasion for the Emperor to echo the Pope. Luther would be asked to recant, and if he refused everyone was supposed to see that he was indeed a heretic. The Pope had not lied. But if he heard these rumors, Luther did not believe them. All his life he shared the almost pathetic trust common people placed in their sovereigns until assassination and revolution swept the old charms of authority away. Luther always believed that if right-minded people in high places heard his arguments, the good would triumph and his doctrines would prevail.

So it was at Worms. The Emperor was young. Youth in exalted position has always filled some people with a boundless and foolish hope for the renovation of the social order. Luther seems to have expected that he would have a grand opportunity to vindicate himself, to lead young Charles and the whole Empire with him in the paths of righteousness. Instead, he was presented only with the harsh and inflexible demand that he recant! So he asked for delay.

He knew that he would have only a limited time to speak. He would be cut off in a moment if he tried to argue his doctrines in detail. He knew that he must study to make every word count. For here was the only chance he would ever have to address the Emperor face to face. And here was the only audience he would ever have that would represent all the ruling classes of the Empire.

So the stage was set for his magnificent appearance before a grand and hushed throng in the hot early evening of April 18, 1521. When he stepped forward to speak in the torchlit gloom, the question was again posed. Would he renounce his books? Here his deliberations through the night were rewarded. He deftly turned his answer into a speech, and it was unforgettable.

He could not renounce all his works because they were not all of one kind, said he. Some dealt with the Christian life in terms that even his enemies accepted. If he were to condemn them, he would be condemning accepted Christian doctrine. That was unthinkable. (It was the same issue he had raised at Leipzig. Constance had condemned all the works of John Huss. But in some of his works Huss had affirmed the doctrine of the Trinity, the articles of the Apostles' Creed, and other doctrines that Christians were supposed to believe. By issuing a blanket condemnation of the works of Huss, said Luther, Constance had in fact condemned sound doctrine.)

A second group of his works, he stated, was directed against the evil living and foul doctrine of the papists. Here the young Emperor broke in with a ringing "No!" It is difficult to know what he meant. Luther was speaking German, and Charles, who had been raised in Burgundy, where the chief language was French, understood hardly any German at all. But Luther would not be stopped, even by the shout of an emperor. He went on to accuse the papacy of holding a tyranny over the Germans, and because of that tyranny he could not take back the accusations he had made against the Italian Pope.

He was on sure ground here. For months before he came to the Reichstag the princes and representatives of the great towns had debated what they called the "complaint of the hard-pressed German people." They had attacked many papal practices in Germany. Taxes that drained money off to Rome, absentee bishops, the abuses of the ecclesiastical courts, the miserable condition of the parish clergy, and many other matters were attacked, and remedies were demanded. Many of the most devout Catholic princes were angry with the Pope. Among the leaders in protest was Duke George of Saxony, who hated Luther like the plague.

Charles might well have objected to any denunciation of the papacy. His reason might seem strange and confusing to us. He had come to all his grandiloquent titles with his young brain teeming with the romance of chivalry. Chivalry reeked like the heavy perfume of funeral flowers in the Burgundian courts where Charles had grown up. Chivalry was a mirage of illusion and pretense for an idle nobility that no longer served any useful purpose. It was a mixture of coarse lust and holy idealism. It was loudly espoused by flamboyant fraternities such as the Order of the Garter in England or the Order of the Golden Fleece in Burgundy. Here would-be warriors dedicated themselves to the exaltation of fair women and mother Church. In practice these same men often contributed to the degradation of both. In the fifteenth century one Renaud of Agincourt was a member of one of the great "courts of love" sponsored by the Marshal Boucicaut. Here the praises of honor and love were sung in touching ballads and signaled in dazzling ceremony, and every member vowed "to practice humility and loyalty to the honor, praise, protection and service of every matron and maid." Renaud was also prosecuted for attempted rape against the widow of a jeweler.

Yet chivalry remained as the ideal code for the fighting man. Its rhetoric was filled with exhortations to personal honor and Christian devotion, and its partisans listened in tearful rapture to stories of King Arthur and the Round Table or to the wandering gallantry of Amadis of Gaul or to the instructions for chivalrous conduct contained in the romance called *Le Petit Jehan de Saintré*.

Braggarts who imagined themselves to be the very model of knighthood were habitually arising after spectacular and gargantuan meals to swear drunken oaths that they would forsake all to go on Crusade. The Turks had long since recaptured Jerusalem from the Christian Crusaders of the Middle Ages. All the holy places where Jesus had walked and died lay under the dominion of the crescent and the scimitar. The Sultan and his immense harem occupied Constantinople, and his castrated slave administrators ruled the bureaucracy of a vast empire. The island of Rhodes in the Mediterranean was under siege. And while Luther stood before the Emperor, the Turkish army besieged Belgrade. Within a few months the Christian defenders of that ancient and isolated city would enter the long night of Turkish indolence and barbarism. The ruthless and seemingly invincible advance of the Turks was enough to inspire in noble Europeans terror, rhetoric, and the bravery that swims in wine. In the gaudy and unreal world of Burgundian spectacle and romance, the Pope was still the captain of Christendom. To serve the Pope remained the supreme duty of every Christian knight. Or at least it seemed so when these noble warriors were well drunk, when minstrels sang in quavering voices of the afflictions of Christians groaning under the infidel, and the sad, liquid notes of the lute resounded in full hearts and tipsy brains.

Charles still nourished that dream at Worms. He was inspired by his chancellor and confidant, the aging Mercurino di Gattinara. Gattinara, like so many of the real mischief-makers of history, was possessed by a sublime vision. Charles was to restore all the imagined glories of the Christian Roman Empire. Italy, Spain, Germany, and Burgundy were to serve one master. France would become a client. And all Christians were to recognize the Emperor as their head, the political vicar of God on earth.

Gattinara seems in retrospect to have been a silly old man drunk on an impossible vision. But he may have been a prophet of sorts. His dream of world government still entrances some. Whatever he was, Gattinara's voice was insistent. He tempted Charles into that sin history never forgives its lords—the sin of trying to do more than a single man can do and to rule more than any hand can hold. Charles, a frail-looking lad with an undershot jaw that left his wide mouth perpetually agape, was eager to dream, and honor required him to rebuke anyone who would call the dream a lie. So he shouted "No!" to Luther.

Luther, sweating profusely now in the crowded and stuffy hall, went on to describe a third group of his works. These included attacks on private persons. Here he admitted to being rough and immoderate. But if he had not attacked these people, he said, tyranny would have increased. Impiety would have grown worse. So he could not retract these works either.

He concluded with an earnest appeal to the Emperor and to the Reichstag. They should not condemn him out of hand. They should prove him wrong from the prophets and the Gospels. If they should do so, he would be the first to cast his books into the fire. And then he said:

So it is that because of my teaching danger, dissension, and conflicts have risen in the world. So yesterday I was admonished about them in the strongest terms. But I have seen what has happened and what is happening. And I must say that for me it is a joyful spectacle to see that passions and conflicts arise over the word of God. For that is the way the word of God works! As the Lord Jesus said, 'I came not to send peace, but a sword. For I am come to set a man at variance against his father, and the daughter against her mother, and the daughter-in-law against her mother-in-law.' And so we must weigh carefully how wonderful and how awful our Lord is in his secret counsels. We must be sure that those things we do to banish strife (if in so doing we undertake to condemn the word of God) do not rather lead to a flood of unbearable evil. Then it might be that the government of this young, noble prince Charles (on whom next to God we hope for so much) would become sick unto death. I could call on many examples from scripture—pharaoh, the king of Babylon, the kings of Israel—that would show how they were brought utterly to earth when they tried to free their kingdoms from strife by means of their own wisdom. For God traps the wise in their own cunning and turns the mountains upside down in a moment. Such are the requirements of reverence towards God! I say this not because such exalted men need my teaching and my warning but because I must not shun the duty I owe my Germany. And so I commit myself to your majesty and to your lordships. I humbly beg you not to condemn me without reason because of the passions of my enemies. I have spoken!

And here he stopped. Now the great, listening, silent hall must have burst into a murmur of confusion. Luther had talked for about ten minutes. Like so many great speeches in history, his oration left those who heard it debating about what he meant.

John von der Ecken (not John Eck of the Leipzig debate!) was in charge of the proceedings. Now he thought that things had gotten out of hand. He found himself in debate in spite of the careful plans to keep such a thing from happening. But he also found an eloquence to match Luther's. Heretics had always claimed Scripture against the Church, he said. The worst heresies were those in which a little error was mixed in with a lot of true doctrine. Scripture cannot be understood out of the head of one man. Some things have been decided for all time.

> We cannot draw things into doubt and dispute that the Catholic Church has judged already, things that have passed into usage, rite, and observance, things our fathers held onto with firm faith, for which they suffered pain and torture, for which even thousands suffered death rather than reject a one of them! And now you want to seduce us from the way to which our fathers were true! And what would the Jews and Turks and Saracens and the other enemies of our faith say when they heard about it? Why, they would burst into scornful laughter! Here are we Christians beginning to argue whether we have believed correctly until now! Do not deceive yourself, Martin. You are not the only one who knows the scripture, not the only one who has struggled to convey the true meaning of holy scripture—not after so many holy doctors have worked day and night to explain holy writ! Do not set your judgment over that of so many famous men. Do not imagine you know more than all of them. Do not throw the most sacred orthodox faith into doubt, the faith that Christ the most perfect lawgiver ordained, the faith that the apostles spread over the world, the faith confirmed by miracles, the faith that martyrs strengthened with their red blood. . . . You wait in vain, Martin, for a disputation over things that you are obligated to believe with certain and professing faith!

Again Luther faced the question: How can one man dare to set himself against history?

That question, so foreign to a world like our own where nothing is venerated for its age, always stung Luther to the heart. Perhaps its force explains his passionate outburst when the official again asked him to recant without "horns or teeth"—which is to say, without equivocation. "Since then your majesty and your lordships desire a simple reply, I will answer without horns or teeth. Unless I am convicted by scripture and by plain reason (I do not accept the authority of popes and councils because they have contradicted each other; my conscience is captive to the word of God), I cannot, and

154

I will not, recant anything, for to go against conscience is neither right nor safe. God help me. Amen."

Later on the words "Here I stand; I can do no other" were inserted before "God help me" in printed editions of this speech. They do not appear in the extensive stenographic accounts taken down as Luther spoke. But they do express his conviction.

Words change their meaning in time. Luther's thumping declaration of his obligation to his conscience has made him seem to some to be a spokesman for liberalism and individualism. But we must recall that these ideas imply a certain autonomy of man under the umbrella of reason. I decide by reason and by experience what convictions I must hold. No one else must make me go against my conscience in these matters. But it is assumed that if I demand liberty of conscience for myself, I must grant an equal liberty to those who oppose my views. This was not in any way Luther's definition of conscience.

For Luther conscience was the inner conviction that was kindled in the heart of the Christian by the grace of God. Nobody arrived at conscience on his own. Conscience was a firm, inner assent to the gospel, and God gave conscience as He gave faith. Conscience could not really be diverse, being one thing in one person and something else in another. God was one. Truth was one. Consequently, all good consciences had to be joined in perfect agreement. It would have made no sense to Luther to say, "Your conscience tells you to rebel against the Pope, but my conscience tells me to remain loyal to him." Luther would answer that such an addiction to Rome was the act of a knave or a fool. The gospel was enough to rid the mind of ignorance. And if one still held to papal authority after hearing the gospel preached, Luther must then wash his hands of that person and condemn his invincible bad will. We have already seen how he responded to the attacks of his enemies. They knew better, he said. And so their damnation would be all the more terrible because they had gone against their own consciences.

Luther's stand before the Emperor did mean a rejection of the claim that truth was the property of a historical institution. The Church of the popes had been wrong for centuries. Yet Luther was utterly convinced that a common truth was held by all true Christians. It was a truth implanted in their hearts by the Holy Spirit. If anyone deviated from that truth, he was seduced by Satan. True Christians could get along with many different institutional forms, and the Holy Spirit would see to keeping doctrine pure. Luther's later disciples could not cope with this view of the truth freely and unanimously held by all true Christians. The Lutheran Church quickly became even more hidebound and ossified than the Catholic Church had ever been. Luther felt gloomy and mistrustful as he saw formalism growing up in his own movement. He longed for the joyful spontaneity of the spirit that never seemed to come bringing unity to Christians.

His vision of the Christian conscience, so stoutly defended at Worms, soon proved to be sheer illusion. Agreement on the meaning of Scripture was impossible even among those Christians who were meek and mild. Yet Luther clung to his conviction that true Christians must see things in the same light. Increasingly as old age and disappointment came on him, he was likely to hold that even the slightest disagreement with himself was a sign that the person at variance was not a true Christian. His anger at these dissidents knew no bounds. His furious capacity for hatred, directed at first against the papal Church, was now turned increasingly against those who should have been his fellows.

Here again he resembles Karl Marx. Marx spent his later years in conflict with people such as the socialists and the anarchists who had been inspired by him. They thought that they could correct his doctrine. Marx said that it was not *his* doctrine; it was a scientific description of an inevitable process of history. Anyone with eyes to see could see it. Those who could not see were knaves or fools. Perhaps the prophet must always smite hardest against his own disagreeing disciples. They are the chorus singing the antiphon to his lead, and if there is discord in their song, his own voice is likely to sound cracked and off-key, a disruption in the splendid harmony of things, and he may waver and fall silent in confusion.

Luther could speak in ringing tones of conscience when he stood bravely at Worms. And he could spend the rest of his life damning anyone who stood on a conscience different from his own. The backside of his sort of courage is almost always hatred for anyone who does not share the cause for which the courage is expended.

17

FTER LUTHER WAS DONE speaking for the last time, the meeting broke up in confusion. Luther himself was hurried out of the hall. As he departed, he lifted a hand high above his head—the sign of triumph of a knight who has struck a good blow against an adversary in a tournament. Spanish soldiers in the Emperor's entourage greeted him with cries, "To the fire! To the fire!" as he passed by. But in the streets of Worms he was a hero to the German people, who in their confused but prodigious sense of injury believed that they had found in him a champion.

The next day the young Emperor handed down his own verdict in the Luther affair. It came in the form of a letter written in French. His decision was to stand by the faith of his ancestors, "the most Christian emperors of the renowned German people, the Catholic kings of Spain, the archdukes of Austria, and the dukes of Burgundy, who were all till death itself loyal sons of the Church of Rome."

The appeal to history, so vigorously made by the Catholic side, had won the Emperor to a lifelong obedience to the old Church. Perhaps rulers are especially susceptible to this kind of argument. If what we have been doing for so long is wrong, then nothing we do now will make any sense. Most wars have been prolonged by a secular appeal to this sort of logic. So many men cannot have died in vain; we must keep fighting to prove that their deaths meant something. The argument for the righteousness of past deeds is always likely to appeal to the person who, feeling the frailty of the moment, holds the strings of power in his hand and senses in a vague and terrible way how feeble that power is and how weak are the hands confronting destiny. The ideals Charles held for Europe came to him from a sense of a glorious past, and, like John Henry Newman centuries later, he could not trust the judgment of a single man against the testimony of generations.

In May 1521, Charles issued an edict approved by those princes who had lingered at Worms. (Luther's own prince, Frederick the Wise, had departed and so did not join in a condemnation of his professor.) Here he called up the grand theme of German history as he imagined it—the great German nation celebrated for ages as the destroyer of heresy. He pronounced Luther an outlaw of the Empire, to be seized on sight. No one was to give Luther or any friend of his any aid. Anyone who helped the outlaw was to become an outlaw himself.

But by May Luther was safely in hiding. After his appearance before the Reichstag, he had engaged in several fruitless conferences with Catholic representatives panting with diplomacy. Diplomacy is the art of hiding disagreement in ambiguous language exchanged between those who have some real reason for getting along. Unity in the Church and public calm seemed to be compelling reasons for compromise. Politically minded Catholics and some earnest contenders for the old faith joined in an effort to find some formula Luther could accept. But Luther was a true believer in his cause, expert in language, a monk locked up for years with his convictions and unaccustomed to that grinning world where men let no principles stand in the way of their interests. He always mistrusted lawyers and diplomats and others whose profession was to use words to deceive. So all the attempts at saving compromise fell to powder against his granite conviction about his mission in the world.

Luther was spirited away into hiding on his way home to Wittenberg. Trusted servants of the elector Frederick the Wise took Luther to the isolated Wartburg castle in the wild Thuringian Forest. They did not even tell the elector himself where Luther was. In that way, Frederick could claim perfect ignorance as to the outlaw's whereabouts. Soon rumors were circulating that Luther was dead.

The action was taken to protect Luther. But it also had an effect that the elector Frederick must have relished. Luther was out of the way. For the moment Frederick did not have to think about him. But the courage of Frederick's act was real enough. The edict of Worms called on Catholics to fall on the property of heretics or of their friends. Religious convictions reinforced by the promise of loot have often inspired faithful Christians with murderous zeal. In theory

Frederick could have been the object of a Crusade. Pope Julius II had preached a Crusade against Venice a few years before on a purely political matter. How much more justified would have been a holy war against the defender of a notorious heretic! Frederick's lands might have been taken by plundering armies under the red banner of the cross. His title might have been given over to someone whose orthodoxy was more certain and whose ambitions to shed blood were stronger.

Only in retrospect do the dangers Frederick faced seem less important than they did at the time. Wars, even holy wars, were financed by hard cash. Cash was one commodity no prince in the German lands had in abundance. To raise an army of mercenaries to fight an enemy was a little like assembling a colony of rattlesnakes in your house to kill mice. The mercenaries were always likely to strike the towns and castles of the prince who hired their services. And if the prince could not pay the wages he had promised, and if his lands were fair, mercenaries could enjoy the pleasures of righteous indignation while they raped and burned and stole everything they could carry off. The geographical location of Wittenberg and electoral Saxony offered Frederick some protection. Electoral Saxony was then on the eastern fringe of Germany. It was not wealthy. An invading army would not find much worth risking life and limb to have. Luther found himself defended by geography in much the same way Utah was to defend the Mormons in nineteenth-century America.

Then, too, there was a sort of clubbiness among the German princes that made them reluctant to fight one another. It was not quite the loyalty between the "old boys" that later gave such solidarity to the British ruling classes. And it was to vanish soon enough in the German lands under the remorseless grinding of religious passions. But it was still a class sentiment of real power while Luther lived. Everywhere there were lethal enemies to threaten all princes. The lower nobility, endowed with small plots of land and vainglorious titles—men who were poor, envious, and incredibly stupid—regarded the princes as the undeserving possessors of good luck. Any effort to bring princely power down would win the devout commitment of these lesser nobles who were called *Ritter* ("knights" or "riders"). In 1523 many of them did go to war against some of the princes. It was a petty conflict that led to the speedy humiliation of the knights. But class hatred smoldered on, and the princes felt uncomfortable about it. The peasants, too, hated the princes. The economic condition of the peasantry was slowly improving in the southern parts of the Empire; but like all improving classes from time immemorial, the peasants found that a taste of good fortune gave them a prodigious appetite for more. They saw the princes as obstacles in this upward surge and hated them.

The prosperous and cultivated burghers of the German towns looked on the princes as boors and sots. And the princes were always gloomily afraid of a strong emperor who might try to make the Empire a government in fact as well as in name. In the increase of imperial power, they saw a lethal threat to their own.

So the baffled princes, like dinosaurs in a changing climate, found themselves attacked on every hand by foes their tiny brains could hardly fathom. They did not feel that the moment had come for civil war among themselves. In only a few years they would be making leagues with each other, and they would find themselves strangely warmed by divine rhetoric exhorting them to sacred violence. They would be inspired by greed, and they would be manipulated by clever foreigners such as the King of France. Then the Germans would fight each other with the terrible ferocity that marks all civil wars. But that time was not yet come in 1521. For the moment Luther and his elector were left alone.

Luther sat out his exile in the Wartburg with restless impatience. And he was often plunged into deep melancholy. From about this time onward he suffered repeated attacks of horrendous depression. Naturally enough he ascribed these assaults to the devil, for in his world the devil was everywhere. During all his time in the Wartburg he heard the crackling and thumping noises the demons made as they haunted the castle both by night and by day.

By now he was convinced that an illusion of the devil had tricked him into the monastery. Satan, he said, had been after him since childhood. It was the natural assumption of one who believed so fiercely in his divine mission. What was more to be expected than that Satan should attempt to thwart the career of the one who would wound him in his dragon's head? Satan had tempted Christ. Satan, Luther thought, brooded over Germany, plotting some dreadful calamity for the German people. And there were terrible periods when Luther thought that the power of Satan was about to burst out and overwhelm him.

Luther was frightfully constipated. Sometimes he went for five or six days without a bowel movement. Then he defecated at last with such frightful and harrowing pain that he nearly fainted. Like hypochrondriacs of all ages, he assumed that his friends at home impatiently awaited the most minute details of his symptoms. He regularly wrote back to Wittenberg, giving a box score on his stools and the agonies they cost him.

He was offended and disgruntled with the unbelief he thought ruled in the court of Frederick the Wise. By "unbelief" Luther meant a lack of conviction that everything was in God's hands. Such unbelief made Frederick cautious. Luther believed that all Christians should always fling themselves headlong into their convictions. Sometimes he thought that even his friends had turned against him.

His gloom in the Wartburg is open to a few observations from mere common sense.

He had entered the monastery out of deep piety, and he had been a good monk. He had labored in good faith to reform abuses obvious to any good man. He had uncovered the meaning of Scripture that he sincerely thought to be self-evident truth. And because of all this he had come down to infamy and exile, out of control of events, neglected by his own friends, apparently relegated to unending safekeeping by the prince who was his patron but now also his jailer. His lonely evenings must have been excruciating. He was always a gregarious companion, eager to drink beer with his friends, to talk, to sing, to laugh. But now he was surrounded by crude men who could think of nothing better to do with their charge than to take him hunting—a sport Luther regarded as barbarous.

In his solitude he did what men like himself have often done. He set to writing.

He turned out a multitude of works—pamphlets, books, letters. One of the most interesting was a booklet simply called *Against Latomus*. Latomus was a theologian of the University of Louvain, a bastion of Catholic orthodoxy, who had written against Luther. Later on Luther was to say that Latomus was the best of all his opponents, though that respect scarcely shows through in the blast Luther fired off at him. Yet there is no better place in all Luther's works to gain an understanding of his mature position on justification by faith. The Pope is the Antichrist. No hesitation about that any more! No one can force God to give him grace by doing the best he can. The law cannot give us righteousness. All men are sinners, even after baptism. Luther's point here is to argue that though sin is forgiven by the act of baptism, sin remains. Forgiveness does not take sin away as long as we are in this life. Consequently, every good work done in this world is sin. Luther means that since man is completely sinful, all his works must have sin in them even if the work is outwardly good. The law is death without faith. Only God's mercy permits us to be considered righteous. Without mercy, we would be swept away like the wind. The only assurance we have lies not in our righteousness but in God's merciful grace. The difference between the true Christian and the condemned sinner is that the Christian never consents to sin but fights against it even when it overwhelms him. The Christian acts daily in the expectation that sin will be annihilated in him, and he lives with all his heart directed to the great day of the Lord. Thus the Christian lives with his flesh mired in this world but with his heart set on the world to come. Why did he, Luther, insist on causing trouble? He insisted on drinking from the spring and not from the creek. He would take only Scripture, unfouled by any man even if that man happened to be a saint. The Catholics have covered Scripture with human interpretations. But, said Luther, he would not eat bread covered with shit. He spoke harshly of Jerome, disparagingly of Augustine. They were Fathers of the Church, but they had been wrong in some things, and Jerome had been blasphemous to say that God did not command what man could not obey. None of the law can be obeyed. The law is to condemn us and to humiliate us. And once the law has shown us our evil, we are prepared for the coming of Christ to our hearts, and Christ in us is the good that allows us to stand before God. Young men should avoid scholastic philosophy and theology like the death of the soul itself. Luther suspects that Thomas Aquinas might be among the damned. Only Christ is to be taught and heard; only the Scripture should reign above all other books. Such is the work *Against Latomus;* and if anyone wants one short book that will capture the essence of Luther's thought, this is the one to read.

Yet by far his most significant work done in his captivity in the Wartburg was his translation of the New Testament from Greek to German. He accomplished the work with astounding speed. Naturally he used the text of the Greek New Testament published by Erasmus in 1516. And he used his own superb gift for language to put the words of Christ and the apostles into a rich and flowing German that has profoundly influenced the evolution of the German language.

Later on he was to translate the Old Testament from Hebrew, and he was to attach a preface to each book of the Bible. Here he briefly expounded his sense of what the books meant. This was something of a contradiction. He always held that the ordinary man of good sense could understand the naked text of Scripture alone without any commentaries. But in these prefaces his eloquence is grand. Of his beloved book of Romans he wrote:

This epistle is the true masterpiece of the New Testament and the most limpid gospel, so excellent that the Christian man should not only know it word for word by heart but every day haunt it as though it were the daily bread for the soul, for it can never be read too much or studied too well.

Yet these prefaces also reveal how difficult it is for anyone to build a consistent and honest theology out of the contradictions of the Bible. Luther did not like the Book of Esther. A ringing tale of sex, conspiracy, and slaughter, it recounts a great massacre of the enemies of the Jews in the Persian Empire; but it does not once mention the name of God, and in it one looks in vain for the quality of mercy. Luther called Esther "cloudy Jewishness." He disliked the book of James with its thumping affirmation of the place of works in the Christian life. In his preface to the work he expressed doubts that James the Apostle had written it. He called it a "right strawy epistle." He was mystified with the stupendous and arcane visions of the book of Revelation. He was content to leave its glittering symbols alone.

He dropped altogether from the canon the so-called Apocrypha, books dealing with the history of the Jews between the Old Testament and the New, books that were not a part of the Hebrew Bible and had to be translated from the Greek. This step was not so radical as it might seem. These works had never been secure in the Catholic canon anyway, and theologians usually disdained arguments based on them.

Luther did not consider his difficulties with Scripture truly important. His experience told him that the Bible was one grand unity no matter what the objective evidence suggested. Everything should be interpreted by the Word of God. By the light of that word he found Christ all through the Old Testament. Christ spoke directly in the Psalms. He was being continually foreshadowed in the history of the acts of God among His people. As I have said, this does not sound like literal interpretation to us. But it had been the constant practice of the writers of the New Testament to interpret Christ in terms of the messianic expectations of the Old Testament. Luther could claim with some justice that he was looking at the Bible as any Christian must. For clearly if the New Testament is misguided in its citations of the Old, the cosmic significance of Christianity falls utterly to pieces.

We must defer until later the way his attitude toward the Old Testament influenced Luther to hate the Jews.

He wrote other things in his exile. One of his most important works was called *On Monastic Vows*. It was dedicated to his father, and it was an apology of sorts. Old Hans had been right all along It was the devil that had seduced Martin into the monastery.

The conclusions of this work follow naturally from Luther's earlier development. Still they cost him much pain. He had been a monk for all his adult life. He had never imagined that he could be anything else. To do away with monastic vows was a kind of divorce, a death. And in his correspondence when he was first secluded in the Wartburg, he argued the issue with friends such as Philipp Melanchthon back in Wittenberg. They were ready to dispose of vows before he was, and when he finally did his little tractate on the subject, it was a sign that his friends had persuaded him that his own theology of grace made vows superfluous.

Now he said that the vows a monk took could be broken without sin. Vows were only outward forms. What mattered was the inner condition of the heart. Vows were symbols of man's persistent and fatal attempt to earn salvation, so they must go. Monks could marry. Monkery helped no one to gain salvation. If one wanted to live as a monk, that was a matter of taste. No special value was to be placed on such living by others. Here Luther was one with the new spirit of the age. Better the active life of humble service to the neighbor than the selfish isolation of the monastery that engendered pride and sloth. Monks had nothing more to do. The printing press ended forever their function of copying manuscripts. And they had become parasites on a society less and less patient with their pretensions.

It would be wrong to claim that *On Monastic Vows* ended an age. And yet in reading it, one can almost hear an old world slipping and falling, a world of isolated and serene monasteries on green hills amid prosperous and bountiful lands where life went on to the musical chiming of bells and devout men spent their days in hourly rhythms that prepared them for a good death and the life everlasting. The Fathers of the Church held that to break the vow of chastity was to condemn the soul to hell. Now Luther held that to make vows might be a sign of damnation and that monasticism was a peril to the soul. After him the ancient institution went into a decline even in the most devoutly Catholic lands. Here again he was not so much the cause as he was a sign that the world was changing.

18

THE ELECTOR FREDERICK probably would have been content to let Luther spend the rest of his life in the Wartburg. But as Luther's exile was prolonged, other leaders rushed in to take charge of what he had begun. The consequence was disarray in religion and dangerous tumult in Wittenberg.

Foremost among the usurpers was Karlstadt, whom we have already met during the Leipzig debate of 1519.

Karlstadt seems always to have thought that he deserved much more credit than he had received for being a chief of the Reformation. In Luther's absence, he appears to have been driven by a frantic desire to prove his own importance to the movement. In similar cases, second-rate revolutionaries have always fallen on the device of becoming ever more radical, accepting as true the ancient fallacy that if a little is good, more must be better.

Karlstadt's way was to take the Reformation to the common people. Perhaps we should say to the mob: He got married. His bride was a girl of fifteen. He threw away his clerical garb and served the Lord's Supper in the clothing of an ordinary town citizen. He preached railing sermons, telling the uneducated that their opinions were better than the thought of scholars. God supposedly moved directly in the hearts of the ignorant, unhampered by the pride of those who were learned. And with the true zeal of a fanatic, Karlstadt urged the extirpation of the last sign of popery from Wittenberg. There are always people around who love to break things. Karlstadt provided the Wittenberg representatives of this class with a dizzy promise: to break things is to glorify God. And so things were broken —especially images, forms of the crucifix, and the windows of churches and monasteries. Monks and nuns who had not yet been convinced that their old ways were wrong were terrorized.

Behind Karlstadt's iconoclasm was a growing theological conviction that was to assume terrific importance. This was the notion that body and spirit were antagonistic to each other. It was not a new belief, for there had always been a strong impulse among some Christians to discipline and minimize the body so that the soul might profit. In Matthew 19:12 Jesus mentioned without condemnation some who had castrated themselves for the Kingdom of Heaven. He may have been speaking of some radical ascetic group of his time. But, as we have seen, the prevailing Christian sentiment had been based on the belief that one God was creator of both body and soul. That being so, body and soul, the physical and the spiritual, could exist in harmony together. Karlstadt and many others, however, took up the belief that the physical is a deadly menace to the spiritual; therefore, the physical aspects of worship must be limited in every possible way. Simplicity became the rule, and everything that pertained to the senses should be controlled in the way one might chain up a very large, vicious, and aggressive dog.

Along with his hostility to the physical, Karlstadt held the equally radical conviction that the aim of the Reformation was to restore the Church to exactly the condition it possessed at the time of the New Testament. This was to lead to a vain attempt to remake one time into another as if there had been no intervening history. And it was also to make the impossible assumption that we can know what the New Testament Church was really like. The modern Amish, who will not use automobiles because Henry Ford arrived on the scene long after Jesus but will use the horse collar invented centuries after Christ, exhibit some of the hardships of converting an irrecoverable era of history into a model of life. But it is always an attractive position for those who hunger to be rid of their own complex and dangerous times and to return into an imagined golden age of yesteryear.

The New Testament made no mention of images, of stained glass, of crucifixes, of saints, of special garb for the clergy, of elaborate ceremony in worship, of monks or nuns, of organ music or of chants sung for the dead. The New Testament showed Jesus confuting the learned rabbis without, apparently, any formal education of his own. Jesus looks to be the master of simple common sense (though in fact we have no earthly idea of what Jesus was doing during the thirty or so years of his life before he comes on the scene in the Gospels). The Mass did not seem to Karlstadt and to his crowd to be that solemn ceremony whereby God Himself became physically present on the altar and in the hands of a priest. There was no real, physical presence of Christ in the Sacrament at all. The Mass became only a physical symbol of an invisible reality that lay beyond all expression available to human senses.

Karlstadt shared abundantly in the febrile enthusiasm that made the Reformation such a horrible age. If people could not see the truth, they should be forced to see it. Everything that stood in the way of true religion was to be rooted out. In the words of a later English fanatic, Karlstadt's Reformation was Reformation without tarrying for any.

Other notions came from Karlstadt and were later taken up by radicals in the Reformation. (Knowing exactly when Karlstadt held this or that doctrine is a little difficult, and it is not certain that he espoused all these ideas while Luther was at the Wartburg.) He thought that some books in the Bible were worth much more than others, and he seems to have been willing to say that some were not divinely inspired at all. Only a few years later some who shared Karlstadt's abhorrence of the physical were holding that the Bible itself was a physical thing, full of confusion and therefore a detriment to the devout and holy life.

Karlstadt did not reject the New Testament, but there were others in Wittenberg who called themselves the "heavenly prophets." They were either comrades or rivals of Karlstadt's—it is hard at this remove to say which. They believed that God directly inspired the faithful. And that could mean that all ceremonies, all institutions, and the Bible itself were unimportant.

One might argue that the heavenly prophets took God's personality seriously. If I wish to communicate with another person, the easiest way is not to write him a letter or to send him some symbol of my intentions. No, my best means of communication is usually by direct speaking, and the heavenly prophets thought that they talked to God and He talked back to them as easily as do friends in conversation.

Maybe that is why Luther hated the heavenly prophets so much. Their ideas about how God and man got together assumed that God was not so exalted that He and man could not communicate with each other directly. In their view the holiness of God vanished away. He was accessible and completely comprehensible to anyone who had the faith to speak with Him. In some respects the heavenly prophets bore an affinity to the people who write testimonials nowadays with such titles as *God Was in My Corner* or *God Was My Co-Pilot* or *My Pal God.* They made community with the divine so easy that it became almost silly.

While Luther was wrestling in the Wartburg with his bowels, his solitude, and his pen, Wittenberg was in tumult. Tumult was not only a sign of the devil; it was also a grave political threat. Rulers in the sixteenth century were not hospitable to doctrines that upset the public order, and if Wittenberg roiled with riot and confusion, princes might decide that all the new doctrines—Luther's included—had to be stamped out.

Luther's doctrine of Christian freedom was also under attack in these radical gospelers. For if the New Testament became a new law, demanding absolute imitation of a bygone time, what would become of the joyful spontaneity Luther wanted for the Christian? He loved music, and he saw no harm to anything that genuinely aided the Christian to feel his faith piously and with reverence. Karlstadt and his crew were ready to rip the organs out of churches because there was no evidence that Peter, Paul, and the Virgin Mary ever gathered around an instrument to sing hymns. A crucifix or an image might not be necessary to all Christians, but Luther would not coerce anyone who found such helps to worship valuable. He was convinced that the Word of God would gradually lead the faithful to agreement on such things without the necessity of force.

Most important of all, Luther was threatened in his conception that God used means to work in the world. Here again he was formed by the old dichotomy between the absolute power of God and the ordained power, what God could do and what He has actually done. God could indeed inspire hearts as the heavenly prophets claimed, for nothing was impossible to God. But in fact God has chosen to work through Word and Sacrament. To renounce these tools of God would be to turn religion into rampant individualism, with every man proclaiming his special revelation as absolute. And Luther was always a believer in the corporate communion of Christians within the word of Scripture, the Spirit of Christ, the observance of the sacraments, and the Word of God.

By March 1522 Luther could bear his long isolation from events no longer. He went back to Wittenberg to restore order. The elector Frederick did not want him to return, but typically Frederick did not feel moved to send him away again. So Luther remained on the scene to preach his people back into submission.

The sermons he preached at this time constituted Luther's finest hour. He treated his misguided people as children who had gone astray. He argued humility, restraint, forbearance, and brotherly love.

Two thoughts dominate. Christians do not have to take the responsibility to do everything under their own power. God's Word will do the work. As I have said, Luther did not practice such passivity himself, but the idea makes a good and comforting sermon, and he preached it well.

Alas, it was not entirely the Word of God that whipped Luther's opponents into submission. He was supported by the force of the elector. And as Luther preached the power of the Word of God, the elector used the power of the sword to drive into exile or silence all those who had led the disorders. Luther was left in the position he was to occupy for the rest of his life—chief pastor in Wittenberg, leading lecturer at the University, unofficial head of the developing Lutheran Church. And the Reformation had had a taste of what was to come. By making an alliance with princely power, the Lutheran faith was on its way to becoming as stultifying and narrow-minded as the Catholic Church ever had been.

19

Richard Friedenthal has called this period in Luther's life the "false spring." It is an apt term. The Word of God seemed to be carrying the day. The spread of the Lutheran gospel seemed invincible. Yet within a year the mood had changed, and Lutheranism had begun the spiritual retreat so common to revolutionary idealisms that lower their hands from climbing and begin to protect their behinds.

The forces against Luther began to prove more powerful, more resilient, more aggressive than had been thought. The new movement began to divide, each faction showing the deep and invincible hatred for the others that is the special affliction of ideological civil war. Jacobins and Girondists, Bolsheviks and Mensheviks, Federalists and Democrats never hated each other any more than Luther hated these dissenters who would not follow his leadership. And they hated him in return.

While Luther was in the Wartburg, Henry VIII of England had written *The Assertion of the Seven Sacraments*. Henry defended the sacraments vigorously, claiming that all seven were certified by both Scripture and tradition. He also made a strong case for the divine institution of the papacy—a fact that was to prove embarrassing later on when he was wrenching England away from papal authority. And he said that Luther's doctrines would lead inevitably to violence and sedition—a royal prophecy that must have been uncomfortable indeed to Luther, coming as it did just at a time when tumult was breaking out in Wittenberg. Until now Luther had expected monarchs to follow his lead; they seemed to be natural allies to his cause. He even yet held out hope for the Emperor. Henry's regal assertions may have taken Luther by surprise.

Perhaps his shock stung him to reply as quickly and as angrily as he did. In June 1522 Jerome Emser, an untalented Catholic sycophant, translated the *Assertion* into German at the request of Luther's redoubtable antagonist, Duke George. By July 15, only eighteen days after Emser's translation came from the press, Luther's answer was in the streets. The assault on Henry, done first in German and then in Latin, was the sort of polemic that was to mark Luther's works against his foes for the rest of his life. Probably no more vulgar and vicious tractate had ever before been written against a Christian king. Luther ridiculed Henry's learning, his pretensions, and his arguments. He did so in such obscene and irreverent words that Henry never forgave him. Henry was an idolater and a dunce, and his *Assertion* was a product of the royal bowels rather than the kingly brain. Whatever Henry might do later on, this railing tractate was enough to assure the fact that neither he nor his realm would ever be Lutheran. Here Luther's own views seemed so arrogant and so furious that men of calmer temperament in all countries could see him as an obstinate and reckless personality, intolerable as a leader to other men equally sure of their standing with the Lord. This tractate marks the beginning of Luther's descent into being not the leader of an international movement but of a German sect—a large and important sect, to be sure, but nevertheless a sect.

Henry had quoted Jerome, Augustine, and Cyprian against Luther. Luther roared back, "I care not for a hundred Jeromes, a hundred Cyprians, a hundred Augustines!" All he cared for was Scripture and the Word of God. The outburst may sound like the courageous decision of a man to put his own assurance before all time. But alas! Luther was not some modern microbe hunter, expressing his findings about germs to a world convinced that disease was caused by bad humors in the body. The "truth" he professed is not verifiable under any canons of reason. Religious truth finally stands or falls in history on the stature of those who embrace it. Luther's blast against the Fathers, before there were any noteworthy Lutherans besides himself, was shocking to his age. The Fathers were revered as the best men who had ever lived after the apostles themselves. Their virtues and their goodness, their learning and their superhuman understanding of Scripture, were nearly articles of faith among Catholics. For Luther to denounce them created in the minds of his readers a revulsion that we might expect today if an American political candidate should declare that he cared not for a hundred George Washingtons, a hundred Thomas Jeffersons, or a hundred Ben Franklins.

Luther's anger was partly frustration. In January 1523, there would come a bitter letter from Henry VIII to the princes of Saxony, Frederick and George, demanding that the Lutheran sect be crushed in blood. In England old Bishop Warham on another occasion muttered fearfully, "The wrath of the king is death!" In Germany Luther could see that it was so.

His ire was perhaps also raised by his study of the Fathers of the Church. He had begun by assuming that the deviations from Scripture had come about in fairly recent times under the nefarious seductions of the papacy. He had asserted his willingness to be convinced of his errors from the Fathers and from Scripture. But as he began looking into the Fathers, he had to discover that Jerome and Origen differed profoundly from him in their approach to the Bible. For them the sacred text was a tissue of allegory. The Greek Fathers all disagreed with him in the definition of faith. And even Augustine, Luther's favorite, revered vows, virginity, and prayers for the dead. Augustine believed in predestination, and Luther loved him for that. But the great African saint also sent people to the tombs of martyrs, there to await a miraculous answer from God to settle a dispute. And he was such an ardent believer in the corporate and institutional unity of the Catholic Church that he was the first of the Fathers to advocate bloody suppression of heresy by means of the secular sword. When the Donatists in North Africa attacked the Catholic priesthood, Augustine quoted Luke 14:23 to the Roman authorities in the province: "Go out into the highways and hedges, and compel them to come in, that my house may be filled." Compulsion meant forcing the Donatists to be Catholics or else!

Both Augustine and Cyprian had adhered to the famous proposition that outside the Church there was no salvation. It is clear beyond any reasonable doubt that the Church, for both of them, was not merely an invisible body held together in an invisible communion of God by preaching and by the sacraments. For them the Church was also and inseparably an institution with officers and offices, a body recognizable to common sense, spread throughout the inhabited world, and organized around its bishops, who possessed a divine spirit of authority going back to the apostles. Augustine was appalled at any schism within the Church, and there is little in his immense work to suggest that he would have been anything other than horrified at Luther's revolt.

And Luther himself, while continually calling on Augustine as a witness to the doctrine of predestination, still had to recognize that in a host of other important issues, Augustine differed from him profoundly. Luther then said that he would accept Augustine only in those places where Augustine's teachings were in harmony with Scripture. But that was really to say that he would accept Augustine only in those places where Augustine's interpretation of Scripture happened to match his own. And never in all his life was Martin Luther willing to admit that he could be as badly in error in doctrine as he claimed that the Fathers of the Church had been.

Luther must have felt himself increasingly isolated in both time and the world as 1523 drew on. And he must have been forced to call on every resource of personal conviction to assert his position. He *knew* the truth; yet he could not get others such as Henry VIII to see it. It is understandable that his rhetoric should have become ever more vehement and vicious in consequence.

On July 1, 1523, two monks who had gone over to Luther's faith were burned at the stake in Brussels in the Burgundian lands of Charles V. They were John van den Esschen and Henry Vos, young men, Augustinians like himself, and they were the first Lutheran martyrs. Christian legend and iconography have managed to convey an impression of firm resolution, calm, and dignity to the end among those witnesses to the faith whose bodies were destroyed by fire. But most martyrs died screaming in agony as the flames licked their bodies. Luther was horrified at the news from Brussels. He was always prepared to die himself, but he was unprepared to make others die in his stead, especially in such a savage way. Disheartening, too, was the fact that these burnings came at the order of the young Emperor Charles in whom Luther had placed such high hopes. It was clear that Charles intended to extirpate Lutheranism from the earth.

So it was in a mood of bitter disappointment and sober reflection that Luther wrote one of his greatest political tractates, *On Secular Authority and How Far It Should Be Obeyed.*

The work owed much to Paul's epistle to the Romans and to the political theory of Augustine. Government is a divine order, one of the ways God rules the world. Without government, human society would fall into chaos. Christians themselves do not need to be compelled by the power of government, for they are always seeking to do the good spontaneously, without the coercion of laws. But there are few Christians in the world. Without government to protect them, true Christians would quickly be devoured by the wolves who are always ready to rage against the innocent. Christians owe it to one another and to God Himself to serve government, for in so doing they are ministers of an order established by God. But though God rules over both the spiritual and the secular orders, Church and government are never identical. That means, of course, that the Pope or any other ecclesiastical official cannot arrogate to himself the powers of a worldly prince. But it also means that princes are not to be considered as authorities in religion merely because they are princes! A wise prince, says Luther, is a rare bird, and a righteous prince is even harder to find.

In this world the first duty of every Christian is to glorify God. Thus the Christian obeys government and serves it whenever he can because government is part of the created order, part of God's glory. But the Christian cannot obey his prince if the prince commands him to do something directly contrary to the Word of God. Here Luther was talking about those princes who commanded their people to follow the Church of Rome. Faith is a free act, he said. No one can be forced in matters of faith. Princes cannot force their subjects in affairs of religion. The Christian must stand on his conscience. The princes of several German territories had ordered their subjects to give up their copies of Luther's New Testament. But, says Luther, no one should give up so much as a single page on the pain of losing his very salvation. Here the evil prince is seen as a bad man corrupting a good office.

But even as he urged this passive resistance to the unjust demands of princes in matters of religion, Luther was firm in his conviction that rebellion is a grievous sin. The lives of princes are in the hand of God. To resist a prince by force is to try to take the place of God. If a subject is oppressed by a tyrant, he should pray to God for relief. He should also take care to amend his own ways, repenting of his sins with a contrite and humble heart, for an unjust ruler is often the demonstration of the wrath of God against sinful people. But if government should persecute the Christian for his convictions, he must suffer willingly. Only a tyrant would burn men at the stake for believing the true gospel. Yet the Christian must not resist tyranny. He must, rather, suffer burning patiently and hopefully with the steadfast faith and humble submission that must by its witness make an appeal to the righteous conscience of humanity, even as it glorifies God by accepting what is finally His mysterious will. Luther's spirit in all political and social questions is always that of Paul expressed in Romans 8:18: "For I reckon that the sufferings of this present time are not worthy to be compared with the glory which shall be revealed in us."

It is this tractate more than any other that formed the Lutheran and Prussian attitude of the Christian toward government. The Christian, in this view, should be thankful for authority. He should certainly keep his own conscience alive to judge the demands of the state. Luther himself was often vehement, and sometimes even insulting, in his many communications with princes, including his own long-suffering rulers in Saxony. He fearlessly told them what they should be doing about religion, trade, taxes, and anything else that came up. Yet he still leaves the Christian at sea when it comes to the task of organizing any movement for political change or active resistance to unjust authority. For him, God is the absolute ruler of all creation and in such almighty control of political matters that the average Christian remains a passive observer, tossing in an opinion here and there, but usually reduced to submission to whatever government demands in worldly affairs.

Luther sees only the two extremes: cooperating with government whenever cooperation is possible and suffering when the prince becomes an oppressor. What we call politics is nearly always for Luther an affair of princes, and princes were, in his mind, usually evil or misguided men, trying to serve themselves rather than realizing that they have a stewardship from God to be exercised for Him. It is not the role of citizens acting in groups or parties to initiate anything or to judge any political matters on their own unless religion is directly involved. If the prince says, "Go to war," the Christian must obey unless the war is unjust. Then the Christian may refuse to fight, but he must submit to being executed by the authorities if that is their will. If the prince says, "Pay taxes," the citizen must pay, even though he knows that the taxes are going to unjust enterprises. To Luther politics always seems to be authority and obedience, and our own view of politics—that it is the science of compromise among conflicting groups that bring their various pressures to bear against government—seems totally alien to his thought.

This Lutheran proclivity for prayer and passivity was dreadfully illustrated in the so-called German resistance to Adolf Hitler, especially in the group that included Dietrich Bonhoeffer. These people were bungling and incompetent conspirators, mired in theory and in unreal plans for the future like oxen belly-deep in wet sand. Their pitiful efforts to assassinate Hitler would be ludicrous performed on a stage against a paper villain with a painted mustache, who might allow us the detachment of laughter.

And yet these men proved to be glorious martyrs. Bonhoeffer's most noble writing was the collection of letters he wrote from prison while he awaited a terrible death. In the end martyrdom was the vocation that suited him best. We might wish that he and his crowd had been better with pistol, bomb, or poison than they were with words and suffering. But Luther would have been proud of them. Yet had deliverance from Hitler been left to Bonhoeffer and others like him in Germany during that dreadful time, the entire world would now lie prostrate under Nazi barbarism. If one considers that this world is the only world we have and that human life is precious because it is so limited by time and that in the active labor to destroy tyranny by force the human spirit may achieve its most noble expression, then neither Martin Luther nor his tradition has anything to give us for help.

20

Not only did the period after 1522 bring Luther problems with secular authority, but he also now lost the support of many Christian humanists who had been ardently working for reform in Church and society long before he came on the scene. Thomas More in England, whose *Utopia* of 1516 was a powerful critique of secular and religious life, detested Luther almost as soon as he heard of him. Willibald Pirkheimer, a somewhat shallow but well-known spokesman for learning and reform in Nuremberg, was excommunicated in the same papal bull that blasted Luther from the Catholic Church. Pirkheimer quickly made his peace with Rome, and though he tried to mediate between the contending factions, his heart remained with the old Church, and he was no real help to Luther. Johann Reuchlin, the great German scholar of Hebrew, never had any real sympathy for Luther. Albrecht Dürer, the most renowned German painter of the Renaissance, was a warmhearted advocate of Luther's gospel even after the Diet of Worms; but with Luther's return to Wittenberg and his descent into nearly perpetual polemic and vehemence, Dürer apparently turned back to the Catholic Church, and he probably died a loyal subject of the papacy. Though the question is still debated by scholars of Dürer's life and work, there is no doubt that his support of Luther became dim and muted after 1522, if indeed it were support at all.

The most important humanist of all was Erasmus, and in 1524 he came out firmly against Luther.

Erasmus was a name nearly synonymous with criticism of the

Church and pleas for reform. His own ideal of piety was inward devotion to the simple Christ of the Gospels. He had attacked vain ceremonies and outward religion based on forms and show. Some think that Erasmus is the real father of the puritanical spirit so visible in Karlstadt and others. One can find in his thought a consistent disdain for the bodily and the ceremonial that is quite different from the sensual Christian piety of most medieval people. Always in his view physical usages tend to corrupt true religion, which for him is an affair of the heart. He had been a monk, but he had managed to escape the monastery with the permission of the authorities. First he was a bishop's secretary, then briefly a student at Paris, then a tutor, and finally he became the first author after the invention of the printing press whose works could be counted on to make a profit as they issued from the publisher into the hands of an eagerly expectant public. He detested monkery and blistered the monkish piety that seemed to be a way to win heaven by outward works, abstinence, and uncomfortable dress. Erasmus had a gift for mockery, satire, and irony. And he assaulted in print those superstitious people who bargained with saints, bishops who were more interested in wealth than in overseeing their flocks, and theologians who cared more for games of theological trivia than for the love of God and man. Perhaps most amusing of all to his age were his attacks on popes who made war and lived in luxury. He was almost certainly the author of a little tractate called *Julius Exclusus*, in which crusty old Pope Julius II is shown ascending drunkenly to heaven after his death only to be met at the gates by his supposed spiritual ancestor, the Apostle Peter, who did not recognize the Pope at all. One might even argue that in Erasmus's account, Saint Peter does not recognize the papacy itself. No wonder he put the work out anonymously!

Erasmus exalted the personality of women in a day when most men viewed them as sexual objects and obedient mothers. Erasmus held that a layman who had children and carried on his life according to Christian principles was serving God as well as the priest who served the sacraments and lived alone. So he exalted the common life. He was always on the side of the young woman who chose pure marriage over the lifelong virginity of the nunnery. And so he held that while the body was a threat to worship, physical nature must still be given its due.

His great motives were simplicity, inwardness, and scholarship. He thought that if men read the New Testament, they would be inspired to follow the examples of Christ and the apostles and other good men. The difficult passages of the Bible that he could not understand he was content to leave alone or else to make them types and allegories according to the ancient dictum of Paul that the letter kills but the spirit gives life. He loved the work of Origen, the great Greek commentator who died in the third century after Christ. Origen had taught that the aim of Biblical exposition was to get under the surface of difficult passages—such as accounts of holy war—to find the spiritual truth hidden there. As I pointed out earlier, such allegorical exposition was a very convenient way of eliminating those aspects of the Bible that are bloodthirsty, superstitious, and cruel or even savage. So the Biblicism of Erasmus was not medieval because he treated the Bible as much more than a mere assortment of proof texts, and he was utterly hostile to the medieval tendency to sew an elaborate panoply of philosophy onto Scripture. He also differed from the medieval expositor in that he wanted to read the New Testament, at least, with careful attention to the history of its times and to the historical development of the Greek language in which it was written. And yet his conclusions from Scripture were not always strictly literal, for they were always humane and gentle. And one can say truly enough that Erasmus looked into Scripture and found what he wanted to find; namely, admonitions and examples he thought taught men how to live a simple and devout life of reverence and brotherly love.

When Luther first came into the public eye, Erasmus was mildly encouraging, and he advised tolerance and forbearance on all sides. Probably most intellectuals tended to link the two men together in the same cause, for it is easy to think that if men share the same enemies, they must be friends. But they were cut from different timbers. Erasmus was made of the hard and graceful wood that flourishes in the temperate zones and floats in powerful serenity on the surface of the flood. Luther was made of ebony, a creature of tropical power, too heavy to float on any stream or to be carried by any current of compromise, calculation, or caution.

Erasmus was shocked and dismayed by Luther's *Babylonian Captivity of the Church*. It was far too radical in doctrine and much too vehement in tone for his peaceful temper. Friends who knew his reputation begged him to attack Luther. He was accused of being a Lutheran himself, and some were muttering that Luther had only hatched the egg that Erasmus laid. Yet Erasmus hated controversy, and he could see that the Reformation was shaping up into a brawl likely to shatter Christendom. Erasmus was a man of libraries and Latinity, of solitary studies and occasional gaiety with a few intellectual friends. The Reformation had become an affair of crowds and streets and blistering sermons in the vernacular, politics and blood, smoke and fire. Erasmus longed to abstain. Yet his friends and some threatening men of power who could become dangerous enemies if they chose kept pushing him to enter the fray.

In 1523 he wrote to Henry VIII that he was meditating about an attack on the new doctrines. But he held off. In February, still yearning for a peaceful resolution to this crisis in Christendom, Erasmus wrote to Lorenzo Campeggio, papal ambassador at a diet held at Nuremberg, urging him to find ways of resolving the Lutheran tragedy. But in vain.

In April Luther wrote to Erasmus, begging him to remain silent. "Let us not devour one another," he wrote. But throughout the letter Luther took a supercilious and arrogant tone, implying that Erasmus was a weakling and a coward and not fit to meddle in controversy. On the other hand, a close friend to Erasmus, Luis Vives, confidant to Henry VIII's Queen Catherine, wrote him not to count on returning to England without having written against Luther. And so in August 1524, there came from the press of Johannes Froben in Basel the long-awaited statement of Erasmus on Luther's Reformation. It was called *A Declaration on the Free Will*. Erasmus, who courted favors from the powerful and rewarded his friends by dedicating books to them, dedicated this little tractate to no one. He flung it into the arena of controversy like a man shaking his hands to clear them of mud.

It is significant that Erasmus did not attack Luther for his views on the sacraments, the Pope, vows, monks, Councils, or for his notions about the priesthood of all believers. Neither did he attack Luther for the German reformer's definition of the Church. Erasmus perceived that the fundamental issue in the Reformation was the nature of man. Luther believed that man had no free will and that if anyone was saved for heaven, it was because God elected him, gave him faith freely, and granted him the power to persevere in this life as a Christian. From this followed an attack on all those means held out by the Church to help the Christian cooperate with God in the way of salvation.

To Erasmus such doctrines were dangerous to the common people and to Christian piety. His fears were unoriginal. They were the staple of theologians who had taught that man's safest moral situation was to live in a middle ground between presumption and despair. Why should one even try to do good if one thought one was predestined to be damned? And if one was predestined to be saved, why should one not indulge oneself with abandon? Better to leave predestination alone, Erasmus thought, for one could not talk about it without dipping into unfathomable perplexity.

Indeed, Erasmus found the entire question uncomfortable. He

did not like assertions, he said. In matters such as this he preferred to be a skeptic, suspending his judgment, leaving the matter to God, not rushing in to make firm and dangerous pronouncements in a realm known only to the divine wisdom. Erasmus was very close to saying something that the existentialists have said in various ways in our own time. Since we are always conscious of our freedom, we must act as if we were free. To do anything else is to make human life something very different in reality from what we experience it to be. To assume that we are always bound is to kill the inner demand on men that they do their duty and act responsibly. Whether we can fairly call his position existentialist or not, we can surely say that in his view of predestination, Erasmus was much like Ignatius of Loyola and John Wesley. Far better to assume freedom and to leave God's mystery to Himself.

Erasmus turned to Scripture to prove that man's freedom was to be assumed. Throughout Scripture there were commands issued by God to men. He gave numerous examples from both the Old and the New Testaments. His point was that God would not have given these commands if man did not have some power to obey them. God would then be acting deceitfully by giving the command in the first place.

We must not mistake Erasmus here. He makes no argument for man's autonomy, for any power on man's part to save himself. Sin has made man dreadfully weak. Without grace man would be nothing. But it is precisely the gift of God's grace that gives man a choice. Grace provides salvation by means of Christ, offers it to man, and gives man the strength to respond to that offer. But somewhere within himself, man must preserve a small place where he makes a decision, where he says either yes or no, and that very limited power is all Erasmus means by free will. I may be in a burning building high above the street, in a room filling with suffocating smoke. It is not by my power that a ladder is hoisted up to me and a brave fireman climbs into the inferno to share my predicament for a moment so that he may bring me safely down. And yet, limited though it may be, I still have a certain choice. I can fight the fireman off and run back into the smoke and flame to die. Or I can summon all my remaining, feeble strength and cooperate with him as best I can in the task of getting me down that ladder to the cool and solid earth. Something like this is what Erasmus means by man's free will.

The tone of the work is sometimes sharp. Erasmus notes that Luther and his followers have come claiming that they are reforming the Church in the way Christ and the apostles came to reform the synagogue of the Jews. He notes that the apostles were believed only because they did miracles. They shook poisonous snakes off their hands without harm to themselves. They healed the sick. They raised the dead. They gave men the gift of tongues. Even so, many who saw their miracles did not believe the apostles because their doctrines were so difficult.

Now come these new men whose teachings are even more difficult. But not one among them has arisen who could so much as cure a lame horse! The demand for some confirming miracle here is not likely to appeal to moderns, who have learned to be religious without requiring God to act in any supernatural way in the world. But in the sixteenth century nearly everybody expected God to be active in His world all the time. Catholics believed that miracles went on every day at their shrines in answer to the prayers of the godly (and sometimes even in response to the prayers of the ungodly who in a moment of repentance lifted their hands and begged for divine aid). On one side Luther was saying that God was active in the world by means of the Word. But on the other hand he denied miracles, and certainly never claimed to do any. Everybody believed, as Erasmus did, that the apostles had done miracles. And why was it that God was now making such a tremendous change from the old faith without giving Luther the power to do at least a few paltry wonders? If Luther had changed a little water into wine, even the Pope might have been converted, though for the German princes beer would have been more enticing. Considering their capacity for drink, a Luther-thaumaturge might have had to work his fermenting charms on an entire German lake, perhaps on the Baltic Sea itself.

The point is that Erasmus was telling Luther that if the Christian religion was God's most important gift to man, and if God was alive and active among men, surely He would not let that faith be changed as Luther wanted it changed without giving some unmistakable sign that Luther was God's prophet. If an anonymous stranger were to wander into my graduate seminar some evening and announce that I had been fired and that the president of the university had designated him to take my place, the least I might expect would be some unequivocal personal word from the president himself that the stranger was telling the truth—something more than the stranger's bare word that he was more qualified to teach Luther than I. And lacking that unmistakable official word ending my authority, I should feel quite justified in tossing the interloper out of the door and down the stairs and returning to my students to resume my teaching. Erasmus was not the only one who asked Luther ironically for a miracle to confirm the authority of the Reformation. In a world where, for the most reasonable men, the line between natural and supernatural was so blurred that it could not be located or defined, the request for a miraculous sign from a living God appeared to many to be perfectly just.

I see two fundamental aims in this tractate. One was to assert a view of man that would allow religion to be a cement in the social order. Erasmus feared the masses. The masses were subject not to reason but to unthinking prejudice and violent passion. Passion was always likely to make the mob run riot. Religion was one of the checks that kept the masses still. But to operate as a check, religion had to be truly accessible to the people. They had to feel that they had something to win or lose by their own acts.

It did not matter to Erasmus that in his sermons Luther was always exhorting the common people to do better and that he was continually threatening them with the loss of their salvation if they did not improve their living—a pastoral position seemingly in conflict with the notion of predestination. Erasmus was not sitting in an audience listening to Luther preach in the German language. And he could not foresee the stern and compulsive morality of later predestinarians who were always looking into their own lives for evidence of election. Nothing proved quite so conducive to rigorous discipline as the teaching that only a disciplined life was evidence that one had been predestined by God. Erasmus seemed to be seeing the logical effect of a doctrine of predestination on people who might read what they wanted into the teaching, and he thought that a belief in predestination would lead to the collapse of order. The fact that he was utterly wrong did not lessen his conviction up until the time that events had had time to disprove his fears. Nearly all Catholics agreed with him.

The position of Erasmus bears some similarity to that of people in the Enlightenment later on, who argued that religion with promises of blissful reward or ghastly punishment was necessary for the common people, for only striving to earn the reward and to avoid punishment could keep them quiet and in line. Most educated people could have a more tolerant and intellectual faith, and they could debate things among themselves that had better be concealed from the masses. The personal religion of Erasmus was one of warmhearted and genuine Christian piety; but he was no democrat, and his natural language—Latin—was incomprehensible to the common herd. By making the issue of the freedom of the will a subject of popular debate, Luther, so Erasmus believed, was stirring up boundless trouble. For to Erasmus, Luther's teaching must exclude most men from the communion of the Church with all its healthful restraints.

Erasmus not only underestimated the power of predestination to compel morality, but he also made a mistake that some intellectuals have always made about radical popular movements. This is the belief that such movements will remain radical. Erasmus could not understand that institutionalized radicalism always becomes the most conservative of creeds and that German Lutheranism (like Soviet Communism after it) would become so conservative that its impact on the world would never be riotous. It would, rather, become one of pervasive and stifling dullness, and the creativity of the movement would come only from the explosive relief of those who escaped its suffocating hold.

The other aim of Erasmus was to present his own views of the nature of man in a tone that would elevate the level of discourse in the controversy itself. Erasmus hated vehemence of any kind. He had always taught that Christians should not quarrel viciously with each other over theological issues. His attitude was taken to be cowardice by Luther and by others, but Erasmus was no coward. He was aware of how frail the bonds of human society are and how disputes in which the antagonists feel that they must win at any price are most likely to end by destroying the society itself. He was increasingly dismayed as the Reformation developed into a contest in vituperation. His own tractate was written with the sort of wry dispassion he wished others would use in religious discussion. He was convinced that the alternative to such moderation was the permanent rending of Christianity. And he was correct.

But Erasmus could not see how great was his disadvantage in an argument of this sort. His conviction was rather commonsensical. The question of predestination was something better left alone, something that could never be resolved by debate. And yet for Luther divine election was heart and soul of his conviction about the way God had chosen to work with mankind. And when one protagonist in an argument does not believe that the argument itself is very important, he is always likely to be overwhelmed in debate by an opponent who believes that the issue is one of life or death, heaven or hell.

Luther did not respond for over a year. It was a momentous and often terrible year for him, and there is some evidence that he considered not answering Erasmus at all. Yet everywhere Erasmus was being praised by Catholics who thought that he had spoken the last word on the matter. Luther's most bitter antagonists crowed at how soundly the greatest of the humanists had trounced the greatest heretic of them all.

Luther married in 1525. His wife was a runaway nun named Catherine von Bora, and he remained completely devoted to her for the rest of his life. It is the fashion of Luther biographers to praise her as Luther praised her for being such a good wife and for helping to found that important institution in Protestantism, the pastor's home.

I must say that on the same evidence others use to praise her, I find her to have been a miserly, greedy, and narrow woman, a typical German hausfrau of the time, without imagination, education, or beauty. There is something about her that has always reminded me of nagging Maggie in the old comic strip called "Bringing Up Father." She was pretentious, overbearing, and dictatorial, and she appears to have possessed in full measure the arrogance of the petty nobility from whence she sprang, a class which, having nothing but a long train of inglorious ancestors and miserable and impoverished land to give it place in the world, patched over the holes in its reputation by slavish attention to the rituals of pride. Luther claimed that Catherine made him answer Erasmus. The thought that she did so is fitting. In her circles men accepted the challenge to duel when it was flung down, and she probably could not bear to be married to a man who, so others were saying, was so vanquished that he had no defense to make.

Luther's work, *On the Bondage of the Will*, came off the press near the end of 1525. It was a smashing success, so much so that he and Erasmus were cut asunder for the rest of their lives, and the humanist reformers within the Catholic Church were shown to have no power to suppress heresy. After the failure of Erasmus, the Catholic Church had all the proof it needed to justify recourse to rack, stake, sword, and dungeon, and the faith rolled forward in baroque splendor and power, overwhelming opposition rather than arguing with it, leaving behind forever the clean, eloquent, rational simplicity that had been the mark of Erasmus and his age of humanism.

21

*L*UTHER'S TRACTATE on the bondage of the will was always one of his favorite works. His preference is easily understood. Here he treated in analytical detail the single most important issue of his theology, the nature of grace. And though it was in this work that he made a famous and redoubtable attack on human reason, he nevertheless worked out the implications of his doctrine with crushing logic, given certain assumptions of Christian faith that both he and his antagonists shared.

He attacked Erasmus along a wide front. Did Erasmus say that Scripture was unclear? Luther retorted that the fundamental message of Scripture was limpid. Though he granted that this or that passage might be unclear, he claimed that the few dark places could easily be illuminated by light cast upon them by those many other places that shone like the day. Thus he expressed his famous idea that Scripture was its own interpreter. His argument proceeded from an assumption that all Catholics made at the time. Scripture was inspired by God from Genesis to Revelation. God could not contradict Himself. So in spite of the apparent differences and difficulties within Scripture, God had provided the Bible with a consistency befitting His own nature. Catholics were willing to admit that they could not understand all Scripture just as they could not completely understand God. But to Luther Scripture was God's message to man, and it made no sense to send a message that was incomprehensible in parts to the ones who received it.

His view that Scripture was its own interpreter allowed him to simplify the approach to the Bible and to declare an independence from ecclesiastical tradition. Thomas Aquinas would not think of approaching the Bible without leaning heavily on earlier interpreters, including both the Fathers of the Church and medieval commentators. Sometimes, as in his commentary on the four Gospels, Thomas is maddeningly similar to the insecure and cautious scholar of today who spends so much time citing other scholars that no one ever catches an unequivocal glimpse of what the scholar himself may think. Such works are compilations rather than true commentaries, and they are always dull.

Luther could throw away the excess baggage of previous authority. (He would in fact always quote the Fathers or other writers when it suited him to do so.) The Bible became for him sufficient in itself. He prepared the way for the emphatic and significant gesture so peculiarly Protestant, the Bible uplifted like a torch in the hand of the preacher as though by upholding that single book he was doing enough to light the world.

From a practical point of view, his principle of interpretation freed Luther from many difficulties. If the Fathers rather unanimously disagreed with him about some interpretation, such as his view of vows, he could confute them by quoting Scripture at them. He could find in the amalgam of the Old and New Testaments suitably interpreted whatever he needed to buttress himself against later commentators.

I do not mean to imply for a minute that Luther was consciously dishonest in his approach to Scripture. On the contrary, his deep sincerity and conviction about the sufficiency of Scripture in itself were combined with an extraordinary linguistic understanding for his time. Yet the fact remains that he was able to see in Scripture pretty much what he wanted to see there and, believing that Scripture was sufficient in itself, he was unembarrassed by his disagreement with other interpreters. They were simply wrong. Quoting them at him did no good; he would not accept their authority.

He also flailed Erasmus because Erasmus had professed to dislike assertions. Christianity is filled with assertions, Luther said. Take away assertions, and you have no faith. A man must love assertions or else he can be no Christian.

It was a clever response, not entirely to the point, for what Erasmus meant was that he disliked assertions made about doubtful matters of faith. He would always accept the assertions of the great creeds of the Church. But he was unwilling to take assertions made by contentious authorities such as Luther in places where Scripture was dark or the faith undefined by Catholic consensus. Yet Luther won this rhetorical bout, for there is nothing the insecure human being loves more than ringing assertions about things important to him. And it is a simple historical fact that religion in the West has always attracted the crowd when it has made fervid announcements of certain authority about things that are not certain at all.

Erasmus had mentioned that he was a skeptic with much the same innocence that he had declared himself opposed to assertions. To be a skeptic is, in the Greek language Erasmus knew so well, to look at all sides of an issue. Hence a skeptic is one who does not accept dogmatic assertions without questioning them. But in the popular mind the skeptic is one who does not believe anything. Again Erasmus had opened himself for a pounding from Luther and got it. Luther called him more a disciple of Lucian than of Christ. Erasmus had translated many of the epigrams of Lucian, the great Greek satirist who lived two centuries after Christ. Lucian had poked fun at the ancient gods. A Christian could see him as a forerunner of worldwide acceptance of Christianity, for he had broken down the reverence due to the old divinities. Hence people were better able to accept Christ. That Lucian could be used by sincere Christians is proved well enough by the fact that Thomas More had collaborated with Erasmus in translating Lucian. And with his stern and completely uncompromising approach to Christian faith, More can hardly be called a skeptic.

But Luther fixed on Lucian's ribald skepticism and claimed that the skepticism of Erasmus was exactly the same thing, meaning that Erasmus did not seriously hold any religious belief. This was a tactic utterly unfair, but it was stunningly effective. Doubts had been previously expressed in high places as to the depth of the Christianity professed by Erasmus. He was always poking fun at the human condition, laughing in rapier thrusts of wit at the absurdities of his day, often expressing himself in ambiguities that left wounded men wondering if they had really been struck by his feathery blows. (Luther laughed, too, but his humor was coarse and blunt, and his polemical wit had all the delicacy of an executioner's two-headed ax.) Even today Joseph Lortz, a German Catholic historian of the Reformation, damns Erasmus for superficiality and mockery of the sacred. So Luther scored effectively against Erasmus in his introduction.

But all of this was only skirmishing. The burden of Luther's work was to affirm the bondage of the will and the predestinating grace of God.

Here he had Erasmus at a severe disadvantage. The assumption of all Christians is that man does not stand on his own. He needs God, and God must give him the grace to do good. Erasmus believed as much. But Erasmus also claimed, as we have seen, that divine commands would not have been given unless men had had some capacity to obey them.

Luther's notion of divine command was that it only made men aware of how helpless they were. He got this belief from the Apostle Paul, who had never known Jesus but who had spent his life telling the world what the significance of Jesus had been in much the same way Lenin had expounded the true meaning of Marx. Luther had apparently wrestled with himself, trying to do good and to be good against the impulses within his heart, and he had hit upon the idea that the commands of God had been but a schoolmaster to bring us to Christ. Failing to find in themselves any power to do good drove Christians humbly to understand God's free grace and to be thankful for it.

Now, Luther said, if Erasmus was correct, if commands meant that man could obey, then logically we should assume that man could obey all God's commands without any grace at all. This would mean that human beings could be good without any special help from God.

He had caught Erasmus in a dilemma. Erasmus certainly would not assert the modern existentialist view of freedom as expressed by Jean-Paul Sartre in one of his plays: "Si Dieu existe, l'homme est néant; si l'homme existe . . ." But on the other hand he had argued that the very existence of commands throughout the Bible meant that men could do something about obeying them. But what? Erasmus said, in effect, only enough to demonstrate a goodwill that would make grace effective.

But why did he not go on to say that the existence of a divine command meant that anyone could obey it in its entirety? God commands His people in the Bible, "Thou shalt love thy neighbour as thyself." Erasmus wants to believe that this command means that I can do something about loving my neighbor to prove my goodwill to God and to open myself to His grace and to help me love more. But on that logic, why should the command not mean that I can love my neighbor completely without any help from God at all? The same thing is true of the greatest command of all: "Thou shalt love the Lord thy God with all thy heart, and with all thy soul, and with all thy mind, and with all thy strength!" The logic of Erasmus, that command means the capacity to obey, could mean that someone could love God completely without the grace of God that helps that love along. But if that were so, why did Christ have to die on the cross? Over a millennium of tradition had held that grace, God's help, was necessary before that first love of God was possible. Yet what Erasmus was saying was that the command implied the power to obey. And if that were strictly so, grace might not be necessary at all. So Luther argued. And in his storming attack, he made the logic of Erasmus seem both rhetorically and Scripturally unsound.

For Luther the issue was simple, and in a very real sense he must be called one of the terrible simplifiers of our history. Man must let God be God. God must be the master of the cosmos and the master of man. God acts in evil men; He acts in Satan himself. God acts in all wills and in all events. Nothing happens that He does not will. Before that awful and stupendous power, it is simply ludicrous to assume that any man has any freedom at all.

Yet, as we have seen before, there remains a place for man's will in Luther's view of predestination, though we might call that place a sort of divine illusion. God does not pick any man up by the nape of the neck and fling him into heaven. The man God has predestined wills the godly way. His flesh may often fail him and prevent his will from enforcing its desires over the tumultuous capacity of man to sin. But the Christian's will always strives, hungers, and thirsts for God's will to be done. What Luther means is that goodwill is predestined, a product of grace, and the Christian can take no pride in it and make no boast about it, though the fact that a Christian possesses this will to do good is evidence that God has elected him.

On the other hand, the non-Christian has a bad will. He wills to be proud and malicious, a partisan of the flesh, an enemy of God. But here, too, that bad will is predestined. To us all of this may sound disturbingly like that psychological monstrosity who is currently a great terror in some science fiction, the man with electrodes in his brain that control his every impulse by making him want exactly what the person who controls his electrodes wants. God provides that Christians want to be Christians and that the damned want to be the sort of people who are justifiably damned.

The belief in predestination leaves most fair-minded men with serious qualms about the justice of God. How can God be righteous if he damns some men—most men, in fact—before they are born?

It is here that Luther made his celebrated attack on human reason, an attack often misunderstood. He objected to that reason by which men judge what God ought to be doing when they should be humbly accepting His own revelation of what He *is* doing. (Were Luther alive today he might say that human reason demands that God be dressed in a striped shirt, standing as an absolutely impartial referee on a playing field where men do battle with the powers of darkness.) It was frankly absurd to human reason that a good God should demand things impossible to men. How, reason asks, could a just God harden the heart of Pharaoh when Moses asked him to let Israel go and then damn Pharaoh for not granting the request

Moses made? Reason asks how a good God could have willed Judas to betray Christ. And how can reason accept the goodness of a God who wills to damn men as though He enjoyed their torments in hell? Luther, taking the side of human reason for the sake of argument, asked all these questions squarely.

But then, he said, reason has always been inept in eternal matters. The greatest philosophers have not arrived at Christian faith by reason. On the contrary, reason has always opposed the very articles Christians affirm to be necessary to their faith. All the great tenets of Christian doctrine are absurdity and foolishness when they are judged by reason alone. In religious matters, reason is only a whore. What is more absurd than that God in Christ should suffer the death of the cross? Philosophers have never arrived at the truth of the Christian faith on their own. So everyone must bow to the divine revelation that alone allows humankind to perceive something of the truth of creation. Confronted by what God reveals in the Word, reason can only bow in submission.

When properly informed by and subservient to faith, reason may aid in understanding the language of the Bible and in expressing the Christian message in a coherent and intelligible way. Reason can aid humanity in governing earthly things. Reason can determine the natural law. (The natural law in Luther seems to have been the set of reasonable assumptions people must share if they are to live together in an orderly society. He said that the Ten Commandments are a summary of the natural law. He meant that no society can survive that permits irreverence to God, a disregard for property, and so forth. All people must have a home where their rights are secure, and they have the right to expect honesty and compassion from their neighbors. Reason can affirm as much.)

But insofar as eternal salvation is concerned, reason can do absolutely nothing. Erasmus and most other humanists had a profound love for classical authors and an admiration for their learned virtues. In one of his little Latin colloquies, Erasmus had a character say, "Sometimes I am almost tempted to pray, 'Pray for us, Saint Socrates!'"

Luther vehemently rejected this attitude. The highest virtues of the pagans, the finest thoughts in the philosophers, the greatest human examples from antiquity were still, in the view of Almighty God, only flesh and slavery to the realm of Satan. For Luther there was only the gospel. All men—even the wisest and best—must be judged by the standard of the gospel, the Word of God. He would have agreed with Tertullian's ancient dictum, "What has Athens to do with Jerusalem?" And the pleasures of studying Plato or Aristotle would never seduce him into the facile notion that a sporting God would allow these fine fellows to enter the Kingdom of Heaven merely because they had been so wise.

Luther's condemnation of the pagan philosophers is a part of his general evaluation of mankind. Not for him was any flowery Renaissance notion of man's partial divinity. Men were all evil, so evil indeed that God could be considered gracious and just if He saved only a few. Luther was like Augustine here. Since all men deserved to be damned, no one could complain if God redeemed some for His own purposes.

Harsh as this doctrine may seem to us, we must recall Luther's motives in declaring it. For him and for all other Christians of his time, the doctrine of predestination was not something abstract, not a useless subject as Erasmus claimed that it was. The Apostle Paul did believe in predestination. The doctrine was a profound consolation not only for Paul but for all those who ever embraced it. No wonder Luther said at the end of his tractate that even could he have free choice he would not take it! On the one hand, free choice would leave him to face the demons alone, and they would surely overwhelm him. On the other, free choice would leave him in continual uncertainty about his own salvation, making his destiny depend on his own weak and frail human will. Luther found no peace in the idea that God stood by as a referee in a game between good and evil as liberal Christian theologians seemingly have always wanted a decent and gentlemanly God to do. If God is a mere referee, He is not in control of the action. Predestination is a joyful faith that God Himself is directing a baffling and darkling world to a triumphant destiny.

We must again reflect on Luther's situation in 1525. He felt himself alone in Europe with no strong human friend to depend on. By 1525 he had been preaching his version of the "gospel" for over seven years, but the overwhelming majority of Germans still remained content in the old faith, and only a handful of princes and cities had publicly espoused Luther's doctrines. And Luther was also feeling more and more isolated in history, attacking the Fathers of the Church more and more vehemently because their interpretations of Scripture were not his own. In his tractate *On the Bondage of the Will* he assaulted Jerome and Origen as though he had been a lapidary of invective, and they had been the foremost interpreters of Scripture to the late classical world.

In that prodigious loneliness, the notion of God's mystery, of which predestination was a part, gave him immense consolation. No one could understand why God did what He did, why He chose some and rejected others. And no one could understand why God did what He did in history. The Catholic appeal to tradition was, in Luther's view, an appeal to reason. "How could God have allowed so many centuries to be deceived? Why, sir, He could not! Indeed, He could not!" To Luther this argument, comfortable as it might be to some, was to demand that God be reasonable, that He do what ignorant men in their pitiful logic expected Him to do.

Luther *knew* the God of the Bible, and he *knew* that that same God stirred within his own heart. (Believers in predestination seldom assume that they are among the damned.) Firm in that knowledge, Luther could place all history in the bosom of God and know that, however nonsensical it seemed, God was still in it, still steadily working out a grand and eternal purpose, veiled to man's eyes in this life but someday to be revealed. No one could look at the past and understand how God had allowed so many centuries to err. No one could look at the present and understand how God could cause the just to suffer and the wicked to flourish. But every Christian could look to God and know that there was a meaning to everything, a purpose and destiny being fulfilled, even if that meaning was opaque to human reason. And so the Christian could be comforted. To believe in predestination is usually to say two things: No one can make sense out of the world the way we perceive it to be; however, there is sense there because God is in charge. Predestination commands us not to understand but to trust.

Luther's view of predestination in 1525 resembles the faith of Augustine, who in his *City of God* sought to make sense of the disaster that had befallen the Roman consciousness when Rome the Eternal fell to the Visigoths in 410. Augustine thought that he understood a lot more about God's workings in history than Luther ever pretended to know. But the confidence in each is the same: The world, swept by confused alarms of struggle and flight, is still directed by the divine intelligence to a good end.

Predestination did not make Martin Luther a heretic. But without the solace predestination gave him, he could not have had the strength to venture into the lonely solitude where heresy had led him by 1525.

22

*L*UTHER'S NEED for the consolations of predestination was acute in 1525, for that was the year of the great peasants' rebellion in Germany. It was the peasants' rebellion more than any other force that nearly destroyed Luther's Reformation.

The peasants' rebellion reinforced the notion assiduously spread by Catholic polemicists that heresy and sedition went hand in hand. Consequently, Catholic rulers became even more zealous in suppressing dissent in blood. Meanwhile, Luther became ever more conservative, more mistrustful of the people, more isolated from the masses, and the Reformation became cast in a rigidity and caution that were hostile to genuine social change. After the peasants' rebellion, the zeal of most leading reformers was to show governments what good citizens Lutherans or Calvinists or Zwinglians or Anglicans could be. The primary definition of good citizenship has always been to accept privilege as the divine order of creation. And so the churches of the Reformation lined up on the side of government to protect society from the wolves, the wolves being, by the usual definition, those classes wanting to change things. Luther himself was so tarnished by the peasants' rebellion that he became nothing more than the leader of a sect, and vigorous leadership passed to other reformers and to other movements.

The peasants who sprang to arms against the princes were, like most revolutionary classes, actually in a process of slow ascent. They were better off than their fathers had been. Many of them were literate. They had gained the special pride that comes from fighting in war. By now warfare was no longer the monopoly of the chivalrous knight in shining armor, charging on horseback. Indeed, the knight found his armor a lethal burden when his horse was shot out from under him, pitching him to earth, and a peasant soldier suddenly appeared above him with an upraised battle-ax. Many south German peasants had served as mercenaries in various armies. They had, in some cases, seen the glories of sunny Italy during the Italian Wars, and many of them had savored the special delight of beating out the brains of a gentleman who considered himself quite superior to the lout who killed him. Louts always thrive on the knowledge that they can kill gentlemen; and having tasted that pleasure once or twice, they are likely to fancy that it will always be easy.

Yet for all their newfound pride and sense of power, the peasants were still oppressed by the binding ties of ancient custom. They still paid rents to the nobles who owned title to the land, though the peasant family might have lived on that land and farmed it for generations. To many the nobleman appeared to be a lecherous sot who lived uselessly on the sweat of others. The hunting privileges of the noble class were especially obnoxious to the peasant. The peasant might laboriously till his ground and exact a crop from it, and just at harvesttime his fields might suddenly resound to the hollo of the hunting horn, the baying of hounds, and the thunderous gallop of fleet huntsmen pounding tantivy through the grain in pursuit of a wild boar. The passage of such a hunting party was likely to destroy an entire field of wheat or barley, and its flamboyant pageantry was not likely to soothe the peasant's temper as he stood by helplessly watching. Its memory would not inspire him when he ached with hunger during the following winter, nor would love for his lord ease his ears when he heard his children crying for bread in the long, starving time bound to come.

Perhaps worst of all was the humiliation of the peasant in every aspect of daily life. He was the nigger of his time, assumed to be less than human, a figure of remorseless ridicule, shamed by society at large into the persistent conviction that he was on the outside, eternally in the cold, never to be invited in to dine among men. When the peasant died, his corpse was subject to a death tax imposed by the lord—a good cow or a strong horse, a plow or a coat—something that offered a visible and devastating reminder that the peasant was not his own man, that he really belonged to another, that he must recompense his master for the inconvenience of his own death. And like the militant black of our own time, the peasant found in violence a means of affirming his manhood to a scornful world that wanted to treat him as an animal. Perhaps, too, violence was proof to himself that he was possessed of a dignity that enabled him to walk with his head erect.

The dying Middle Ages burst again and again with peasant rebellions throughout western Europe. Germany, backward as always, experienced her peasant disorders a century and more after they had passed through England and France. But by then the technology of violence had improved so that the German revolts were the bloodiest up until the Russian uprisings in the eighteenth century made even the Germans seem unskilled in cruelty.

All medieval social movements were likely to fall into the trappings and language of religion, just as those movements are likely to fall into the forms of nationalism today. The peasants had ample reason to go to religion for relief and rhetoric, for the poor receive benevolent attention in the Bible. Poverty was commanded by Christ in the Gospels to the rich young ruler who came to him, and when that young man turned away sorrowing and unwilling, Christ remarked sadly that it was far easier for a camel to go through the eye of a needle than for a rich man to enter the kingdom of heaven. Anyone with a taste for the literal interpretation of Scripture could believe that all rich men must be damned, and once anyone believes that a class of people is damned by God, biology, or geography, it is quite easy to advance to the conviction that one has a sovereign duty to aid in their extermination. Christ said, "Blessed are the meek, for they shall inherit the earth." He also said, "Blessed be ye poor, for yours is the kingdom of God." If one took the kingdom of God to be an earthly reign set up at the end of the age, one could imagine the poor ruling during a millennium when earth had been purged and the rich cast into hell.

Many of the peasants looked on Luther as their special prophet. His father had been born a peasant. Luther spoke continually of freedom. He meant freedom from a mechanical obedience to divine law in an effort to work out salvation. The peasants heard him speak of freedom from the sort of feudal obligation that oppressed them in body and in spirit.

Moreover, we must remember that Luther's language against the papacy and his other enemies rang with violence. He never really preached that Christians should be violent, but like most men who are fluent in language, he never truly understood the power of words. And when he preached that God would bring bloody vengeance against evil papists and princes, some of his listeners might be forgiven for believing that the agents of that vengeance would be blessed from on high.

By 1524 the south German lands were in a fever of peasant unrest, breaking out sporadically in a pox of violence. A few monasteries and convents were raided and sacked. The peasants usually made for the wine cellar, and nearly everyone who witnessed these outbreaks recalled a great deal of drunkenness and laughter. Some lords were killed along with their wives and children. Though these were mostly isolated incidents, rumor magnified what was a terrible situation. Still the great majority of peasants remained peaceful, though not serene.

In February 1525 a group of peasants in the region of Memmingen drew up a manifesto called the Twelve Articles, which sought redress of grievances from their lords. At the remove of nearly five hundred years what strikes us about these articles is their moderation.

The peasants denied that they were disobedient and rebellious. They asserted their love of peace. But they did want some wrongs corrected. For example, they asked for the right to choose their own pastors. Here we may recall the way white plantation owners imposed pastors of their own choosing on their black slaves before the American Civil War. We can perhaps better understand thereby the desire of the peasants to have one of their own kind to preach to them the consolations of religion rather than a hireling who would parrot the propaganda of their oppressors.

The peasants asked for control over their contributions to religion, tithes forced out of them as a tax to support the heavy ecclesiastical establishment. Now they were putting forth a medieval version of the belief that taxation without representation was wrong. If they paid the money, they should have some voice in how it was spent.

Most moving of all to our hearts is their pitiful request that they not be considered as mere property. The peasants wanted to be men —not free of all rule, not anarchists, but free under the law from the oppression of being treated like slaves by arrogant lords.

They asked also for the right to hunt and fish for food and for the right to kill game animals that destroyed their crops. Until then, hunting was a monopoly for the nobility. No one but the noble could kill a stag, a boar, a bear—even a fox. If any of these animals destroyed the crops of the peasant, the peasant could only try to chase it away—a tactic more likely to get the peasant mauled than it was to save his grain. To kill a game animal was to be a poacher, and the penalty for poaching was nearly always death.

The peasants wanted the right of poor men to cut wood in the forests in a day when the forests were kept as game preserves by the nobility. And they wanted an end to the corvée, that ancient system in Europe by which a lord required a certain number of working days from his peasants each year. What often happened was that the peasant might be summoned out on corvée during sowing time or harvest, there to do the lord's work when the peasant needed to be doing his own. The corvée gave the peasant's existence that psychological oppression most dreadful in the daily life—its unpredictability. For the peasant could never make a plan in the confident expectation that he could carry it out tomorrow. He was always likely to be thwarted by the lord's demand for corvée that, according to the law, took precedence over everything else.

Rents were attacked. The peasants pointed out that the rent on some of their lands was so great that they could not make a living on them, and they asked for reappraisal and adjustment. They did not ask that all rents be abolished! They wanted freedom of the public meadows to graze their cattle, and they wanted an end to the death duties.

Having presented their grievances in this mild and deferential fashion, the peasants asked the lords to negotiate with them on the basis of Christian toleration for the resolution of their differences.

Martin Luther felt compelled to reply to them, and from him they got no help at all. In fairness to Luther, we should recall that there had been enough peasant violence to make everyone edgy when the subject of listening to peasants came up. During the Vietnam War, the violence of some demonstrations against the war in the United States often blinded the eyes and stopped the ears of people in authority when other citizens peacefully petitioned their government for the redress of grievances. And Luther felt threatened to the marrow of his bones when he saw the peasants interpreting what he had said about Christian freedom to mean that they should be freed from their feudal obligations.

In some measure Luther sympathized with their grievances. It is also true that he reproached the nobles and the clergy alike for abusing both the gospel and the peasants. The clergy were included in his condemnation because the Church was the greatest single landholder in Europe. The accuracy of ecclesiastical records, kept by literate and methodical men for generations, meant that the peasants on church lands had a hard time evading any of their traditional obligations. Whenever there was a peasants' rebellion anywhere in Europe, the clergy and buildings belonging to the Church became targets of violent destruction. And so Luther told lords and clergy alike that peasant unrest was a sign of the wrath of God for their sins.

Yet his real burden is not the condition of the peasants but the persecution of the gospel by lords and clergy. He sees the roiling unrest of the peasants as having been stirred up by the devil and by false prophets unleashed by an angry God. He says that some of the demands of the peasants are just, but he is clearly not burdened by their justice—nor could he be. Luther saw everything in terms of cosmic significance and mystery. The earthly is always a sign of something else, a mask, a symbol. It becomes, then, a matter of finding the cosmic meaning rather than settling down in any pragmatic fashion to work out a compromise between the contending parties. Luther, caught up as he was in the sweeping conviction that the cosmos was veiled in tremendous mystery, could not really see that there was very little that was mysterious in the agitation of the peasants. They wanted relief from intolerable burdens.

To the peasants themselves he could give only one piece of advice: They should be humble and passive. Both the divine law and the natural law stand against rebellion. Though the lords are greedy, they still possess authority, and the peasants have no right to take that authority for themselves. Do the peasants complain about their suffering? They should rather accept it, for the Christian life is nothing but "suffering, suffering, cross, cross." Christ committed himself to God and was crucified by evil men. The peasants could not ask for more earthly benefits than Christ received, for Christ is the master of all Christians, and Luther always held that the servant could not be greater than his lord. The peasants should suffer and keep the peace and wait for God's pleasure. As to the Twelve Articles themselves, Luther could not find an unambiguous word of support to give to any of them. Some he condemned outright; others he said he would leave to lawyers to decide. And so he shut his eyes to the moderation of the peasants' requests, and he refused to try to mediate between peasants and lords to avoid the bloody war that soon came.

To a generation that has endured a long struggle for civil rights, for labor justice, and for a host of other causes, Luther's admonitions to the peasants to keep still seem dismaying and reactionary. Had Martin Luther, rather than Martin Luther King, been the champion of blacks in Montgomery, Alabama, in 1955, he would have advised them to sit in the back of the bus for the glory of God. It is no wonder that Lutheranism has never been a revolutionary faith and that Lutherans have usually stood for authority against change in Germany and elsewhere.

Yet we must remember that to Luther this life was so short and eternity so long that he would not have been himself had he seen the Gospels as a license for engineering social change. He believed that God was active in every moment and every event, working to bring harmony to creation, and that disorder was the sign of Satan's work.

He believed that if kings ruled, God must have a purpose in their authority or else God would change it. Certainly it was not up to the single person to seek any change for his own physical comfort or earthly good.

The position was otherworldly, but then Luther always saw the world as something to be endured until God brought in the fullness of time with the concluding trumpet. The basis of Luther's ethics was always some form of submission to the harmonies ordained by God, and somehow in that symmetry of creation the darkness had a place with the light, suffering with bliss, wrath with mercy. Jesus had said in Matthew 22:21, "Render therefore unto Caesar the things which are Caesar's; and unto God the things that are God's." The suggestion here is plain: The Christian should not be preoccupied with this world any more than he has to be and the business of God far transcends the grubbiness of politics.

One might ask here why Luther sought to change the Catholic Church, which had existed for such a long time. Is there a contradiction between his attitude toward secular rulers and his attitude toward the papacy? Yet Luther believed his own gospel was created not by himself but by God. The gospel attacked the Pope, and Luther must follow the gospel. He was possessed by the most terrible arrogance of all, the humility to believe that he was a mere beggar or a bag of worms and that all he did was not through his own power but by the ordination of God. In that terrible humility, he could give himself over to being the instrument of God to bring an old order down, while the peasants were trying to change the world into something more pleasing to themselves.

The nobles would not compromise. The failure of moderate leadership among the peasants brought the radicals to command. In the spring of 1525 the violence that had been random and occasional flared up into general rebellion. Everywhere in southwestern Germany, manor houses were burned, and noblemen, their women, and children were tortured and killed.

The savagery of the peasants must partly explain Luther's infamous reaction to their rebellion. He dipped his pen in fire and wrote a little tractate called *Against the Robbing and Murderous Gangs of Peasants.* Here he assaulted them for daring to use the gospel to justify rebellion, and in one notorious sentence he damned himself before the poor for all history. "So let anyone who can, strike, kill, or stab, secretly or openly, recalling that nothing can be more venomous, damaging, or demonic than a rebel." The peasants, he said, were no better than mad dogs.

The lords needed no encouragement from a preacher. When

Luther's nasty little tractate appeared, they were already butchering peasants by the thousand. Near Colmar in Alsace one can still see a great burial mound where slaughtered peasants were heaped up to rot, deprived of decent burial. Some peasants believed that they could not be harmed by bullets fired at them by their enemies; but like others, including some American Indians, who have gone into battle with similar illusions of magical invulnerability, they discovered conclusively enough that the entire world of the spirit does not suffice to stop one chunk of soft lead hurled through space by gunpowder. Trained and disciplined soldiers were already massacring the disorganized bands of roving peasants when Luther's tractate came spewing from the press. We cannot blame him entirely for the slaughter.

But still his vicious and unmerciful blast smokes in our eyes. Why did a man consumed with the suffering Christ write such a murderous tractate? Was this the best that Luther's gospel could do? Was this the true conscience of the sixteenth century speaking? It is of some comfort to know that some people in his own time were outraged by Luther's fury. He had to take note of this indignation by writing to justify himself before his numerous critics.

There is comfort in this knowledge because so many historians assume that we may excuse things in the past because men were not so advanced as they later became. Most of Luther's biographers have been uncomfortable about his reaction to the peasants. Few of them had felt the issue serious enough to raise questions about Luther's whole career. It was an unfortunate lapse in the glory of their hero, and having noted it with pain, they hurry on to other things. The times were brutal; Luther must be understood in the context of his times, and, in understanding him, it becomes easier to forgive him.

Yet times were not so brutal that everyone approved his bellowing for vigilante justice and lynch law. His little book shocked some decent people in his own days, and I like to think that the very existence of people who had the conscience to protest his brutality in the sixteenth century is a sign that some moral standards remain constant throughout history. No matter how bad the times are, there are always some to surmount the times in response to the call of human sympathy, and in their gallant breasts hearts drum civilization toward justice and mercy, without which society becomes only a robber band.

Luther's defense, published in the summer, did not retreat one inch from the position he had taken in his attack on the peasants. He only added footnotes, hauling out examples from Scripture to prove that rebellion was sin, that rebels should be destroyed, and that God was pleased thereby.

For his defense Luther relied chiefly on the Old Testament. Here there are many pages that reek of massacre. Rebellion against God's authority was one of the worst possible sins, and that authority was manifest in both kings and prophets. When David found Saul defecating in a cave, he glided up in the dark and sliced a piece from Saul's cloak, but he would not strike Saul because Saul was the king, the Lord's anointed. When Korah and his sons protested against the authority of Moses, the earth itself opened up and swallowed them down alive.

Mercy was out of the question against rebels, Luther said. He called up the example of Agag, King of the Amalekites, whom Saul had spared in battle. Samuel the prophet condemned Saul for being merciful when God had ordered Agag to be killed, and Samuel himself hewed Agag in pieces.

The New Testament was not likely to mitigate the wrath of anyone of Luther's disposition. In Acts 5 Ananias and Sapphira his wife were struck dead for lying to God, and the enemies of Christ were throughout the New Testament regularly consigned to a dark and burning hell forever. The notion of hell does not appear in the Old Testament at all, and it has always been an encouragement for Christians to do barbarous things. Luther thought rebels the hounds of hell itself, and soaked as he was in the uncompromising mentality of the Bible, he was doomed to scream for the peasants' blood.

It has been argued that Luther's aim was to save the Reformation. Certainly, had he taken the side of the peasants, his movement could have been stamped out by the bloody and unreasoning repression that followed the rebellion. Roland Bainton, the best of Luther's biographers, asks whether any peaceful social reform was possible in the sixteenth century. By keeping his distance from the peasants, Luther kept himself from the inevitable shipwreck of their hopes, and his gospel from drowning. At the time many people accused him of simple cowardice.

Both the explanation that depends on a desire to save the Reformation and that which accuses him of cowardice are too calculating to grasp Luther's mind at the time. He was not afraid for himself, and he was always sure that God would take care of the Reformation no matter what men did. His vehemence against the rebels came for the very reasons he gave, and the Bible is at the heart of it. To his mind they were rebelling against the clear Word of God. Whenever he saw such obvious malice, he was reduced to fury.

We would be equally furious if we should find a supermarket selling arsenic for sugar or heroin for flour. We are not relieved of the comparison merely by saying that we can be sure about arsenic or heroin but that we cannot be so sure of the Word of God. Luther was Luther just because he was as certain of the interpretation of Scripture as we are sure of some medical facts. Luther's God was the terrible God of the Bible, a deity of dreadful wrath and power, who required the appeasement of Christ's cruel death for the sins of man. That dogma about the nature of God was always more important to Luther than mere humanity or mercy.

There is a fierce integrity in Luther's position, but it is an integrity with a dimension of terror to it, reminding us of "Sea-green Robespierre, the Incorruptible," who, in his glimmering aqua-colored pantaloons, presided over the condemnation of thousands to the guillotine during the French Revolution, a man whose honesty was never questioned and whose memory was never loved.

The Bible had been converted into an elaborate tissue of allegory revolving around the suffering figure of Jesus by the time the Emperor Constantine was converted and Christianity became the favored religion within the dying Roman Empire. Had men remained stuck on a literal interpretation of Scripture, the Bible probably never would have appealed to the generality of educated men in the classical world. When Christianity did triumph, it was at least partly the consequence of a Bible that had had its fangs pulled, its coarse barbarisms translated into sign and symbol capable of filling philosophical minds with intriguing speculation. As I have pointed out earlier, in the Middle Ages the Bible was converted to a collection of divinely inspired proof texts, and hardly anyone paid any attention to the literal meaning of Scripture or to the study of the Bible as a literary document complete in itself. Erasmus and the Biblical humanists were on the verge of rebuilding the classical understanding of the Bible when Luther came storming onto the scene and demanded to look at the Old and New Testaments alike with a view to letting God be God. Letting God be God meant among other things that no mercy could be shown to anyone who affronted God's sovereign will. Here lies the fundamental answer to the questions raised by Luther's response to the peasants' revolt. And in many ways it is the most terrible answer of all.

23

As if to mock the screams of peasants still being chopped down by nobles who treated them like animals to be hunted, Luther chose this time—June 13, 1525—to get married.

We have encountered his wife, Catherine von Bora, in the Erasmus affair. The marriage shocked Luther's friends and delighted his enemies and may have lessened his influence in Europe at large. According to the canon law of the Church, he was now guilty of incest because he had married a nun. (Monks were brothers; nuns were sisters.) His enemies had always wanted to believe that he had begun the Reformation out of lust. Now they seemed to have their proof. This in spite of the fact that he did not marry until five years after the Pope had pronounced him a heretic and that there is not one particle of evidence that he had ever fallen into unchastity.

Part of the scorn that fell on Luther for his marriage must have originated in the stereotypes of humor that I have mentioned. One of the funniest scenes that his coarse age could imagine was a monk or a nun caught in sexual dalliance. Boccaccio, in his *Decameron*, tells of the monk who seduced an arrogant woman by convincing her that he was the incarnation of the archangel Raphael and that to lie with him was a celestial honor. Erasmus told one of the few Renaissance jokes still capable of raising a smile in the twentieth century. It was about a nun who turned up pregnant. The abbess of the convent was horrified. How in the name of heaven had this happened? The pregnant nun avowed that it had not been her fault;

a strange man had burst into her cell in the middle of the night and had raped her.

"But sister, why didn't you scream for help?"

"Oh, sister, you know there is a strict rule in the convent against making noise after curfew."

Stories like this are innumerable. Luther contributed to this attitude himself. In his attacks on monks, he made grim sport of the way they seduced women who came to them to confess. But when he married a nun, he seemed to incarnate all the obscene jokes that had been circulating about the lecheries of religious orders for centuries. It was just too good an opportunity for his enemies to pass by. Thomas More began writing voluminously in English against Luther and other dissenters from the Catholic faith soon after Luther's marriage. He pounded Luther so often for lechery, lust, and incest that More's works have become a pain to read. More evidently thought that he was being very funny.

Luther's marriage was a sign of his healthful decision to give the body its due, and that desire was a part of his faith that nature is good. If the body is tired, it should sleep. If the stomach is empty, it should be fed. If the body craves sexual expression, it should be satisfied. The key in Luther's thought was that bodily desire should never become an end in itself, making people forget the higher purpose for which they were created. Anyone may be a glutton, but that does not mean that everybody should cease eating and drinking. Anyone may be a lecher, but that does not mean that the cure for fornication is to allow no marriage at all. God has ordained marriage for the propagation of the race and the harmony of society, and within marriage the sexual drive may find an honorable release.

None of this was in theoretical contradiction with the teachings of the Catholic Church. At least since Augustine Christians had thought that all being was good by nature. Sin was a lack of something rather than anything positive in itself, just as darkness is an absence of light and sickness is an absence of health. Nature, possessing being, was good, and since reproduction was a way nature continued herself, sexual intercourse could not be evil in marriage. Yet in practice the Church treated virginity as a superior status, and no one who became a priest, a monk, or a nun could marry. "Chastity" became, in general, a synonym for not engaging in sexual intercourse at all, and if monks and nuns took vows of "poverty, chastity, and obedience," the implication seemed to be that even those who lived in marriage were vaguely unchaste.

Naturally enough, with his view of the priesthood of all believers, Luther could not permit a double standard in which a clerical caste had special burdens and special rights. Enforced virginity smacked of an attempt to earn salvation. The Catholic priest, monk, or nun could say, in effect, to God, "See how pure I am! See how I deserve to enter the Kingdom of Heaven!" To Luther the attempt to be purer than others by means of virginity reeked of that terrible human pride so lethal to the soul. By paying so much attention to the body, even in depriving it, one became much more materialistic than if he gave the body its due and passed on to more important things. If I am thinking all the time of how I may deprive my body, I really do not have much time left over to think of ways I may love my neighbor. Besides, if all Christians were priests, the same standards applied to all alike. If marriage was good for ordinary Christians, it was good for ministers, too.

All this sounds very much like common sense to us, and few people today are likely to be upset because Luther married a nun. We are more likely to become annoyed with such people as Thomas More, who seized upon Luther's marriage with shouts of grim pleasure as if this conjugal act finally showed the world just how evil Luther was. The very learned German Catholic historian Heinrich Denifle, in his *Luther und Luthertum,* written near the turn of this century, was bitterly hostile to Luther. And he summarized the traditional Catholic view that Luther was a lusty monk who could not keep his vows. But Catholic scholars are now embarrassed by Denifle in spite of his monumental learning, and in a day when the Catholic priesthood is experiencing a trauma of its own over the issue of celibacy, Luther's marriage does not seem to be such a stigma.

But our own change of attitude toward such matters should not blind us to the outcry raised at the time, for here was embodied one of the most profound changes in Western civilization in regard to the relationship between men and women.

For centuries the religious hero had been the one who fought off sexual intercourse. Jerome had seen dancing girls in Rome and could not get them out of his head. His fervid scholarship was a help in disciplining his body and his mind, for when he studied he was less troubled by the lusts of the flesh. Jerome studied so hard that he mastered Hebrew, Greek, and Latin and so translated the Old and New Testaments into a fine Latin version that is still the basis for study in the Catholic Church. Perhaps the great book is a relic of his sublimating sexuality in favor of learning. Augustine loved a woman faithfully in a relationship that we would call marriage by almost any definition. He had a son by her named Adeodatus, "Gift of God," but when he was converted, he put his wife away and lived to old age alone, and, like Jerome, he suffered the pangs of desire. There was no question in his mind; marriage and the highest dedication to God did not go together. Pope Gregory I, in writing to give common people examples of piety, told of the man who was converted, and who, though he did not cast his wife out of his house, still vowed not to touch her for the rest of his life. He kept this pious oath, and years later came at last to his deathbed, a wrinkled old man. In that extreme condition, his soft mouth trembled and his wife bent near to catch what he might be saying. As she did so, her ear brushed against his lips. The dying man jumped back in his bed as though he had been stung, summoning all his feeble strength to whisper, "Woman, get away from me! The fire is low, but it still burns!"

Bernard of Clairvaux fought the battle with sex and won. The story was told of him that he sat in cold water to quench the flames of desire, but then that yarn was told about many Christian saints. Of Thomas Aquinas it is told that he was locked in a room by his brothers, who disapproved of his wish to become a monk. They thrust a naked woman into the room with him to tempt him, but he drove the poor girl out by snatching up a blazing torch and running at her headlong.

Legends hung over the heads of great women, too. Saint Wilgefort vowed to remain a virgin, so the tale ran, but her father promised her in marriage to the King of Sicily. Yearning with all her heart to keep her vow, she prayed for a miracle, and God answered her plea by causing a beard to sprout on her fine face. So the King of Sicily would not have her to wife. Though her father was so annoyed with her that he had her crucified, she went to her death a pure virgin and died a saint. (She also became very popular among women in England and Germany who called her "Saint Uncumber." They prayed to her to uncumber them of husbands they already had but did not want.)

In spite of the female saints, the most popular view in the Middle Ages was that women were always seducing men, just as Eve had seduced Adam in the garden. There was something terrifying about the female sex as a consequence. This terror is reflected in the witch craze. Most witches were women, though in non-Christian cultures the witch is usually a man. The reason for fear of women was probably tied up with the general Western notion that woman had caused sin to enter the world.

At any rate, the eyes of Europe had been fixed on Luther after 1520, seeing in him a potential prophet, the harbinger of a new day. Though most Europeans did not formally adhere to his cause, there must have been thousands who were watching him in the cautious and hopeful expectation that he might prove to be just what he claimed to be, the spokesman for the true Word of God.

Luther became less and less viable as a general leader of Christendom as his vehemence and occasional viciousness spread on the wings of the printing press throughout Europe. (Of course Luther wrote a great deal in these years that was neither furious nor vicious, but irenic and devotional works are never quite so avidly read or so well remembered as are vehemence and satire. Jonathan Swift uttered an occasional benign prayer to God and preached funeral sermons of warmhearted consolation, but those are not the works for which most people remember Swift.) And when Luther married, he seemed to pass the nebulous line that distinguishes the hero from the clown in the public mind. When we consider that the devout Lutheran of today is likely to be shocked at the suggestion that Jesus might have had sexual intercourse, we may savor just a bit of the outrage and the ridicule that Luther's marriage provoked in his own day. Westerners prefer their religious heroes to remain above the normal passions of sex, and this sense of what is appropriate for a saint has extended to the point where few Protestants would like to believe that Jesus ever experienced a moment of sexual desire.

Yet Luther's marriage was a real beginning in convincing a great many people that the minister endowed with the divine gift of preaching could enjoy the passions of intercourse with his wife between the conjugal sheets without lessening his divine authority. In this way Luther represents a true exaltation of the goodness of nature and the place of the common life within a realm of sacred purpose. The idea was slow in catching on, and one might say that only in the nineteenth century did the notion of the sacred quality of the secular really come into its own in the West. The chief impulse then was nationalism rather than religion as people were encouraged to build strong families, to have many children, to raise them as good citizens, and to teach them loyalty to the state and willingness to die for the fatherland.

Few scenes out of that dreadful age are more touching than the image of Luther's young son, Hans, hardly more than a baby, sitting nearby and humming a tuneless song while Luther tried to work. Whenever we are tempted to see in Luther only that bitter and vengeful man assailing his adversaries with unrestrained vehemence and invective, we must pause just a moment before the recollection that he was a loyal husband and a generous, warmhearted father and that his children adored him.

24

After 1525 Luther became increasingly a sectarian leader, limited to the German scene. He remained for Catholics the worst heretic the world had ever known. For a long time the words "Lutheran" and "heretic" were synonyms. But in fact the divisions within the dissenters were becoming more and more acute. Soon the Reformation was to become fragmented beyond any repair, and no one could claim to be the leader of all the warring factions that sprang up to damn one another as well as the Catholic Church.

The division among dissenters brought scornful glee to Catholics. Thomas More chortled that by 1528 there were as many heretical sects as there were heretics, and all of them as frenzied as wild geese. It was not enough, he said, to know a man's town to know his heresy. Every street in a heretical city had a different confession.

Before the rancorous hatred of the dissenters for one another, a Catholic apologist could present the grand and imposing unity of the Catholic Church. The Church had stood for fifteen hundred years. Heretics had often arisen. They always quoted Scripture. They were always divided among themselves. And they always died away into oblivion. The Catholic Church alone endured and prevailed.

Luther and the swarm of malicious men who had risen up after him would go the way of other heretics. Or else Christ would return and bring the world to a crashing doom. Luther believed that the Pope was the Antichrist. Catholics repaid him the compliment. They thought that he was the man of sin who would arise on earth as the very incarnation of the devil. And then Christ would come storming back in clouds of glory.

The Catholic argument based on time is not overwhelming to us. Fifteen hundred years! What is that before the hundreds of thousands of years that mankind has inhabited this planet? Augustine, Thomas Aquinas, Thomas More, and indeed Luther himself believed that there had always been some people faithful to God on earth. God had not left Himself without a witness since Creation. But how does that notion square with the gospel according to Charles Darwin? And what of those millions who had never heard of Christ? They were by far the majority of the earth's population. One might ask a few sensible questions about the justice or mercy of a God who neglected to inform millions outside of Europe about Himself and then damned them for their ignorance.

But at the time hardly anyone in Europe understood how reality would be pulled out from under their questions. It has been only within the last century that most Christians have been willing to admit that the world was created somewhat before 4004 B.C. Luther said that it was impossible for the world to be more than six thousand years old. And it was only after Luther was born that those intrepid sailors of the age of reconnaissance ranged into the remote lands of the great globe and began to understand how few Christians there were on earth. Vasco da Gama came to Calicut thinking that the Hindus of the Deccan were Christians. His men puzzled over the fact that statues of saints in this region had six arms. But they dutifully prostrated themselves at a shrine where a female statue with very fine breasts seemed to be the Virgin Mary. Vasco da Gama began to have his doubts when one of the priests gave him a little package of sacred dust. It turned out to be cow manure.

All these events passed Luther by, and most Catholics could not understand their crushing significance. In his old age Luther heard enough of Nicolaus Copernicus to ridicule him. Here was a silly astronomer trying to turn the world upside down. Common sense told everyone that the earth stood still and that all the universe revolved around it. Most Catholics were equally scornful of Copernicus and the foolish idea that the language of nature was mathematics. There was no Newton to open space to infinity. There was no Darwin to open time to everlasting erosion and evolution. So Luther could argue that God was working out a cosmic and eternal purpose in the restored gospel being preached in Germany. And Catholics could stand on their unity in history and make most Europeans hold fast to the old faith.

Increasingly mutterings of bloodshed filled the air. More and more towns and princes were going over to the Reformation. Luther's stand against the peasants must have convinced some rulers that the new doctrines could be politically safe. Any government that went over to the new gospel also discovered a holy obligation to confiscate the lands that had been held by the papal Church. So the politically wise princes and city authorities looked for ways to protect their new faith and their booty.

The greatest dissenter with any political following besides Luther himself was Ulrich Zwingli of Zurich. Luther hated him and gloried in his violent death. Thomas More was willing to grant that many dissenters had been good men before they became heretics, but not Zwingli. Wrote More in his *Confutation of Tyndale's Answer*, "For as for Zwingli, I never heard of any good virtue in him. But all these other were the good children of God once, at such time as grace and devotion brought them into religion." Zwingli yearned for recognition from Erasmus, but Erasmus was embarrassed by him. And when Zwingli died in battle in 1531 and his body was burned on a dung heap, there was grim rejoicing in nearly every camp.

Yet it was Zwingli who posed in a most striking way one of the fundamental issues of Western thought. And there is a real sense in which it might be said that the dividing line between medieval and modern passes somewhere between Luther and Zwingli. Zwingli's question was this: What is the place of the sensual or the physical in religion? His answer was as little place as the Christian could possibly give.

Zwingli was only a few weeks younger than Luther. He began preaching reform in 1519, the same year Luther and Eck had their epochal debate at Leipzig. Zwingli was a thoroughgoing humanist. His humanism shows up in many obvious ways. Unlike Luther, he delighted in quoting from the great Greek philosophers. His sermons are studded with classical references and quotations. Luther's sermons are Scriptural and earthy, and one imagines that any shoemaker who wandered in off the street to sit under Luther's pulpit could have understood his sermons. Luther denounced classical paganism, and the wisdom of ancient philosophers scarcely made any impression on him. But Zwingli was sure that virtuous pagans had been transported to heaven.

Zwingli—like Karlstadt—believed that Christian worship should have as few sensual distractions as possible. He wanted no choirs, no organs, no stained glass, no statues, no pictures, no elaborate ceremonial. He believed in preaching the bare Word in churches that were whitewashed within and unadorned without. He could not find choirs, organs, images, and the rest in the New Testament, and he would not have them in Zurich.

He may have been doing battle against his own impulses, following an ancient logic that if one likes something very much, it must be bad. Zwingli was a sensual man. Unlike Luther, he had several sexual misadventures while he was a Catholic priest. When he applied for the job of preaching at Zurich, a rumor circulated that he had seduced the daughter of a powerful prince. The people of Zurich did not want the enmity of a lord who might cause them trouble if they hired the culprit who had seduced his daughter. Hearing of their doubts, Zwingli wrote the committee in charge a letter unlike most in the literature of Christian epistles. He admitted sorrowfully that he was unchaste. He had made a vow to abstain from women, but he could keep it only six months. But even in the weakness of the flesh, he resolved to be discriminating. He had never seduced a virgin, a nun, or a married woman. He had indeed had sexual relations with the daughter of a powerful man, a man who could touch the necks of princes with impunity. A barber! And the barber's daughter was a slut. *She* had seduced *him!* Since she had had so many affairs with so many different men, no one could prove that he was the father of her child. So, Zwingli believed, Zurich need have no fear of reprisals if he was employed to preach the Sunday sermons. The letter worked. Zwingli was hired. Perhaps what offends us is not his sexual exercise but his contempt for the barber whose daughter's pleasure he had enjoyed.

Zwingli loved music. He eventually married and had children, and he played the lute and the viol at home for his own delight and to quiet crying infants. Still he forbade music in the church service. Worship must be pure! The sensuality of music distracted people from the contemplation of God, who is above all sense. Some who followed him at first eventually rejected the sacraments and turned to a purely "spiritual" service that reminds us of the quiet congregating of the later Quakers. And, as we have seen, some even gave up the Bible as a physical thing.

But baptism and the Lord's Supper are in the New Testament, and Zwingli was committed to Scripture. The Anabaptists thought that Zwingli should cancel the baptism of children. There is no more evidence for infant baptism in the New Testament than there is for singing around the organ in church. Why not go all the way with primitive practice?

Zwingli, however, detested the Anabaptists. Perhaps he thought that they were trying to steal leadership in Zurich away from him.

Perhaps he viewed their frantic emotionalism with distaste. Perhaps there were too many lower-class, ignorant persons among them. Like Luther and traditional Christian thought, Zwingli held baptism to be for Christians what circumcision had been for Jews.

Zwingli also believed in theocracy. He thought that government had a divine purpose far beyond merely keeping order. Good government regulated the worship of its subjects, disciplined them in their moral conduct, and assured the teaching of the true faith. Godly government destroyed heresy and put heretics to death. Most important of all to Zwingli's mind, Jehovah called kings and governments to account if they allowed idolatry to flourish in their dominions.

Catholic powers all around were waiting to play the role of Babylon to Zurich's Israel. Under that continual, murderous threat, prudence dictated that the people of Zurich be united behind their godly magistrates and behind Zwingli, their very own prophet of the Lord. Infant baptism was desirable for a Christian city because the sacrament embraced the entire corporation. Anyone with half an eye for politics could see disaster ahead if adult baptism were made the mark of a true Christian. Perhaps half the adults in town would be baptized and half not. And then how would the Christian rulers rally their town to its defense? God's covenant was not just with individuals but with the nation. In Zwingli's view the nation was now Zurich. The mark of the divine covenant had to be on everybody, and the government of Zurich saw to it that the covenant was kept, for the covenant was the first wall of protection against both God and man.

So Zwingli stood by the baptism of children. He approved the ruthless persecution of anyone who dissented from his views. Zurich was the first city to punish Anabaptists by drowning. The practice was enthusiastically adopted by Christian authorities of various persuasions throughout Europe. Drowning seemed to be a fitting death for those who made so much of baptism. And the fact that Catholics and Protestants alike used drowning so zealously gives the practice the honor of being the first genuine ecumenical movement during the Reformation.

Important as it was to him, baptism remained for Zwingli only a symbol. For Luther it was a channel by which God's predestinating grace flowed into the life of the Christian. For Zwingli baptism was only an acknowledgment of community responsibility to the one baptized, and it was a sign that the new Christian had entered the household of God. William Tyndale, one of Zwingli's English disciples, thought that both the sacraments are like the sign in front of a tavern announcing that ale is sold inside.

The issue that provoked the most passion in Zwingli's doctrine was the Mass. Zwingli did not believe that the physical was worthy to bear the divine. He could not accept Luther's teaching that Christ was physically present in the Lord's Supper. To Zwingli the Supper was merely a symbol of the Passion of Christ. When Christians shared the Supper, they were supposed to remember how Christ had shed his blood for them on the cross. When Christ told his disciples, "This is my body," he meant to say, "This signifies my body." Such was Zwingli's argument. Its effect was to remove nearly all the sense of the holy that Christians had brought to the Mass for centuries.

Zwingli's change in the meaning of the Supper smacked of blasphemy to Luther. He had been nearly smitten to earth with awe before God when he performed his first Mass. That combination of terror and mystery never left him. To accept the words of Christ, "This is my body, etc.," became for him the very embodiment of that innocent and childlike faith with which he always thought all Christians should accept the clear commands of God. Luther said that he would eat shit if God commanded him to do so, though the command might be incomprehensible. And he would eat the body of Christ, though without understanding just how he did it, at the command of God. When Zwingli argued that the body of Christ was now in heaven and that a real presence in the Supper would be a duplication, Luther retorted that the argument was mathematical and refused to accept it. God could make the body of Christ be anywhere, everywhere, or nowhere. Zwingli's arguments were yet another attempt by proud men to subject God to the ridiculous bondage of contemptible human reason. And Luther could oppose Zwingli with all the arrogant authority of a man whose hold on the truth was sure. A part of Luther's truth was that people were subject to the mysterious whims of a hidden God, a God who was known only when He revealed Himself, a God who took inexplicable pleasure in commanding His followers among humankind to do what they could not understand.

Luther finally dismissed Zwingli with the comment: "We are not of the same spirit." Luther meant that he was possessed of the spirit of truth; his opponents were of the devilish spirit of pride and blasphemy and error. We might say that Luther's spirit was medieval while Zwingli's was modern. Luther believed still that the world was a domain of sacred mystery, the ground of a cosmic battle between Satan and God. On this stage, man was but a poor player, blessed or condemned to play the role assigned by God. Christians were to be patient, suffering, bearing always the example of Christ, who was silent before those who put him to death.

Zwingli believed that the resurrected body of Christ was in heaven and had no more connection with earth. He was alarmed when any Christian worshiped God according to the "flesh." "Flesh" was for Zwingli a word he rather mechanically made the equivalent of "body," though the Apostle Paul and Luther both saw "flesh" as the impulse that causes people to rebel against God. When Zwingli saw anyone adoring a physical Christ in the Mass, he said that the Mass became an idol. Sharing in the Mass became idolatry. The Christian was worshiping a physical thing instead of God. The later Puritans of England and America were to hold the same dark hostility to the idea that Christ could be in anything physical.

After 1525 Luther spoke less and less of predestination. He always believed in the doctrine, but he became more and more preoccupied with the means God uses to bring Christians to salvation. Baptism assumed a terrific quality in his mind. The Mass became increasingly a way God fed the physical body to prepare it for its everlasting destiny in the resurrection. Sometimes Luther sounds very much like the ancient Greek theologians who called the Mass the "medicine of immortality." To do any good, the Mass must be taken in faith. But faith combined with physical feeding to prepare the soul-body of man for the life everlasting.

Zwingli's view removed the divine mystery from the physical. The physical realm was no longer sacred; no longer did it even harbor demonic spirits. So Zwingli became one of many tributaries to a world scheme where scientists were allowed to manipulate the matter of the world, to convert alchemy to chemistry, to transform metaphysics to mere physics, inquiring not as to the divine purpose of the universe but seeking to know only in a practical way how it worked. Such questions are possible only when the physical universe itself is no longer a cloak for the mysterious presence of a personal God.

Luther himself helped contribute to this attitude—though, like Zwingli, he did so unwittingly. He discounted miracles. It is difficult to find in his works much evidence that he thought miracles still went on. Miracles had been performed by the apostles until the authority of Scripture was established, but his favorite Gospel was that written by John, and one of the reasons Luther liked it so much was that it told of few miracles but recorded many words of Jesus. The devil still did wonders to deceive, but these were like the magical tricks the magicians of Egypt performed before Pharaoh when they opposed Moses—only illusions. Zwingli concurred in this new and more skeptical attitude about miracles. William Tyndale, who translated the New Testament into English in 1525, promulgated this notion in England. The intention of all these men was to counter the Catholic claim that miracles happened every day within the Catholic Church. No one was quite willing to say that nothing at all happened at shrines or wherever else miracles were reported. The reformers were only willing to assert that Catholic wonders were of the devil and therefore not a manifestation of God. It was really not so far from that position to the belief that the order of nature was undisturbed by any supernatural power.

All of this means that the Reformation helped inject a sense of the regularity of nature into the European consciousness. People were taught by the reformers that nature was a self-regulating order, a system, and that when any irregularity appeared, the devil caused it. Nature was preserved by God; but God did not regularly make spectacular physical interventions in His creation the way medieval men had believed. Christ was the great miracle; Scripture was confirmed by miracle, and that was divine intervention enough. And if people do not expect miracles in their religious life, they may very well turn quickly to the idea that the order of nature itself is the true wonder. The spectacle of its meticulous working must then inspire with awe for its creator. So this respect for the orderly processes of nature could aid men in tracking nature's regularity through hypothesis and experience, for it gave them a confidence that made their patient research possible.

The foundations of modern science and technology were laid most firmly in Protestant countries. Sometimes principles of mathematics and astronomy developed elsewhere were put to work in such places as England, Scotland, the Netherlands, and the Protestant regions of Germany. Galileo had few disciples in Italy, but England produced a Newton to perfect his thought. David Hume could very easily pass from the puritan assumption that there had been no miracles since the New Testament to the thesis that there had never been any miracles at all. Luther and Zwingli alike would have been appalled by some of these developments. But no spring has the power to choose the bed its waters will find or the direction in which they will flow to the sea.

25

ZWINGLI WAS MORE AGGRESSIVE than Luther in making political plans. Luther was always one to wait and see what God would do in worldly affairs. Zwingli believed that being a tool of God meant the exercise of political wisdom for survival.

After 1525 the situation in the German lands was cloudy. Princes and towns were going over to the new faith, though the majority of Germans always stayed loyal to the old Church, and the Emperor remained steadfastly Catholic. But the Italian situation kept Pope and Emperor from cooperating to extirpate heresy in Germany. In 1525 imperial troops handed the French a crushing defeat at Pavia, twenty-one miles from Milan. Francis I, the King of France, was taken prisoner and hauled off to Spain, where the Emperor was living. By this time another Medici sat on the papal throne. He was Clement VII, and he was probably the most inept pope since Celestine V had incurred the wrath of Dante by resigning the papal office. The mercenary armies hired by imperial generals plundered Italy, and they posed an overpowering menace to the independence of the papacy. In 1527 the unpaid mercenaries, fed up with papal machinations and sweeping their officers with them, stormed the city of Rome. They scaled and breached its walls and ran amok through the streets, subjecting the city to the most savage looting it has ever known. Horrible stories of cruelty circulated through Europe about this dreadful sack. In England Thomas More heard that the mercenaries roasted children alive over fires to induce parents to disclose secret hoards of treasure. They attached cords to the genitals of men and pulled them into spear points to provoke them into telling of hidden wealth. Clement VII was shut up like a caged bird in Hadrian's Tomb, a round eminence of brick and stone converted by this time into a fortress with papal apartments on the Tiber. For weeks Rome was a scene of anarchy and desolation until plague finally killed off enough of the mercenaries so that the looting stopped. Order was slowly restored, and negotiations for peace were opened between the Catholic Emperor and the Catholic Pope. In these days neither Pope nor Emperor tended to think of Luther first thing in the morning.

The Turks were advancing up the Balkans in what seemed to be an irresistible wave portending either the fall of European civilization or the end of time. They were moving toward Vienna, and the domino theory of that day held that if Vienna fell, the Turks would overpower the rest of Europe. Many a German father must have looked at his chubby pink daughters and wondered darkly if they might end their days in a Sultan's harem.

In 1526 the German princes met without the Emperor at the First Diet of Speyer. There they tried to call a truce between Lutherans and Catholics for the sake of closing ranks against the horrors of the Turkish threat. They left every prince to decide for himself for the time being what he would do about religion for himself and his subjects. Everyone was to bear in mind his responsibilities to God. In effect, this decision meant that the Catholic princes imposed the old faith on their subjects, and Lutheran princes forced theirs to observe the new doctrines.

The outlook remained dark for some time. On August 29, 1526, the Turks won a great battle on the Hungarian plain near the village of Mohács. King Louis II of Hungary, brother-in-law to the Emperor Charles, was slain in combat. By September Buda and Pest had fallen, and Suleiman I, the conquering Sultan called "the Magnificent," took 100,000 Christians prisoner.

For the moment it was enough. The Sultan was forced to tend to disorders at home, and he could not pursue the conquest of Europe. Within another year Charles seemed to be the master of Italy. In 1528 he was preoccupied with affairs in Spain and the Duchy of Burgundy, which then included today's Belgium and the Netherlands. By 1529 the Catholic forces in the Empire seemed strong enough to turn again to religious affairs.

The Second Diet of Speyer, meeting again without the Emperor in April, revoked the religious agreement that had prevailed between Catholics and Lutherans for three years. Lutheran princes protested and so won for themselves the title "Protestant" that gradually came to mean anyone who left the Roman Church. In spite of the protest.

the lines were drawn. Rumors of conspiracy were afloat everywhere.

At this juncture, the Turks again came to the unwitting aid of the Protestants. In May Suleiman camped before Vienna with an enormous Turkish army and laid the city under siege.

At about the same time, the Landgrave Philip of Hesse, called "the Generous," appealed to Luther and Zwingli to meet at Marburg. Confessional agreement seemed to be a necessary prelude to military alliance. Zwingli and Luther had been waging a war of books. Philip, whose faith was as sincere as one could expect in a prince, possessed the reckless delusion that honest Christians ought to be able to agree on doctrine when the very life of the new faith was at stake. Zwingli quickly agreed to come. Luther grumbled and held back and finally appeared only out of respect for Philip. On October 1 the two great antagonists, accompanied by scholarly colleagues, sat down to talk across a table in Philip's picturesque and drafty castle.

The meeting was a failure, as were all those meetings with Luther intended to compromise on something. There was a little agreement. Both Zwingli and Luther hated the Pope. But on the most important issue between them, the Lord's Supper, there was no consensus. In the bitterness of debate, the two men came to detest each other even more than they had before. Zwingli seemed willing to grant Luther Christian friendship, but Luther persisted in treating him like an ignorant and malicious schoolboy who needed a good flogging to bring him to heel.

Zwingli had reason enough to be friendly. His situation in Zurich was becoming precarious. His Catholic enemies were above him in the high mountains, and his most dependable ally, Strasbourg, was too far away to offer him much aid in an emergency. The German princes still felt a certain cautious brotherhood that kept them from falling on each other for the time being, but there was no such feeling among the cantons of Switzerland. All that ever united the Swiss was that they hated outsiders and only disliked one another.

Luther was changing some of his opinions in these years. He had begun with such enthusiasm for his cause that he had seen the Turks as a scourge of God. Their rule would be better for Christians than the dominion of the Popes. Christians could be saved from the Turkish menace only by repenting and turning to God, not by fighting. But as the Turkish storm darkened across Europe, his attitude changed. He was angered by the steadfast pacifism of the Anabaptists and their withdrawal from government. In his tractate *On Whether Soldiers, too, Can Be Saved*, written in late 1526, he came out for the sanctity of the military profession. Government is a divine agency. Soldiers who obey orders uphold government. Their work in a just cause is blessed by God, and if they are obedient, soldiers can expect the crown of righteousness. Included in this hymn of praise to the good soldier was also the certification of war against the Turks. Such war was necessary and right, said Luther. In 1529 he published another work in the same cause, this one entitled *Concerning War Against the Turk.* Here he said that the Pope and the Turk were much alike and that anyone who defended his lands against either was acting righteously. In a mood of stern realism, he counseled the Christian princes of Europe not to take the Turk lightly but to prepare themselves for a terrible conflict. In October, when Suleiman suddenly lifted the siege of Vienna and withdrew, Luther called the retreat a miracle of God. He said that God had struck such terror into the hearts of the Turkish soldiers that they would not obey their officers' commands to advance and instead turned tail and fled. Luther also said that the Turks might have been frightened away by news that a Christian army was marching in relief. But, in any case, his earlier willingness to accept the Sultan's rule as a divine judgment was gone.

In spite of his willingness to fight the Turks, he still held back at consenting to oppose the Emperor by force. He still nourished the pathetic hope that Charles would finally see the light and be converted. Paul had persecuted Christians and had been changed into a great apostle for Christ by his vision on the Damascus road. God was still God; the Emperor, too, could become God's agent for the renovation of His Church. God decided the fate of princes, and to sanction violent resistance to the Emperor's authority seemed to be a kind of blasphemy. So Luther came to Marburg to meet Zwingli without any fatal sense that Christians had to get together in doctrine to make military alliance possible.

Philipp Melanchthon, an ardent student of Greek and of the early Fathers of the Church, still hoped for reconciliation with the Catholic Church. He came to Marburg with Luther, and at the time his hopes seemed plausible enough. If a general council overthrew the Pope . . . If Protestants and Catholics sat down in a spirit of Christian love . . . If the Bible was taken to be the norm of faith . . . If the Spirit of God was present . . . Well, who could tell what might happen?

But if Luther compromised with Zwingli on the Mass and on the nature of worship, any attempt to find common ground with Catholics was vain at the start. Melanchthon was especially enamored by the history of good in the Church. He was almost rapt before the vision of unity and consensus that he saw in the works of the early Church Fathers. The prospect of a recemented Christian unity in his own time was so enthralling that he nourished it until his death. He could only regard Zwingli as a dangerous radical to be converted, not as an equal in Christian debate.

So there was no real agreement at Marburg. Zwingli departed to die in battle two years later. Luther went back to Wittenberg, to his desk and his pulpit, and began to reformulate the order and practice of his churches. He trusted God to take care of politics. From time to time he ruminated about martyrdom, but that possibility seemed more and more remote as the years went on and there was work to do from day to day. Too much work, perhaps, for the Luther of these years was a haunted man, knowing spells of dark depression, believing even more, if possible, in the evil presence of the devil lurking in the background of all human affairs. I do not believe that Luther ever claimed to see the devil; but he heard the devil's noises, and he saw the devil's malign power darkly cloaked in the ordinary forms of this world.

One final difference between Zwingli and Luther is perhaps worth mentioning. This was the place of a grand design in Zwingli's thought. Zwingli believed in theocracy, and he held that Zurich had a place as a corporation in the divine plan for the universe. Luther always saw government under its more medieval and Augustinian guise, an authority set on earth to preserve order and to allow the common life to go on while the Church preached the gospel and administered the sacraments and testified to the presence of Christians in the midst of an evil world. He approved when Frederick and his successors exiled radical preachers from Saxony, for he thought that the radicals were disorderly. But he was never very comfortable about compelling people to live the Christian life. A theocracy requires a catalog of religious laws that all its citizens are obliged to obey lest God punish the government for allowing anyone under its jurisdiction to stray from righteousness. This sort of thing was in conflict with Luther's beloved fantasy that Christians could live with no laws at all. Luther was never quite willing to give up his true community of believers visible finally only to God. And he believed that true Christians were always a minority, even in those territories where the prince espoused the gospel.

Luther thought that all human institutions were saturated with sin, and no government could be seen as the incarnation of God's purpose in the world. Christ would wind history up like a scroll. Only then would all the world be regenerated and made perfect. No one could know when that doom and redemption would take place, and in the meantime the Christian must watch and wait, suffer and persevere, and trust in God.

26

IN 1530 the Emperor returned to the German lands for a Diet at Augsburg. It was his first visit to Germany since Luther had been condemned at Worms, and his return was nearly a triumph. He had settled his affairs in Italy at last. On January 24 the Pope had met him at Bologna and there, in the grand old church of San Petronio, had placed the imperial crown on his head. Clement VII was probably glad enough to keep Charles and the imperial bodyguard out of Rome itself for the splendid ceremony. Rome had seen enough of imperial soldiery, and Romans did not hanker to be burned or raped and robbed again so soon after 1527. Besides, Charles was in a hurry and did not want to descend to Rome. He had his eyes on Germany and wanted to hasten there.

Charles V was the last emperor to be crowned by a pope until Napoleon Bonaparte allowed Pius VII to hand him a circle of gold for his head in Paris in 1804. Charles thought himself to be standing in the amber dawn of a new Christian day. By noon the Emperor would have united all Christians under his benign authority. He believed himself to be a new Charlemagne, perhaps a new Augustus.

The times seemed promising and ominous at once. The Turks had fallen back from Vienna, but they still stood guard over the Balkans and ruled the Hungarian plain, and their ships patrolled the Mediterranean. The holy places in Jerusalem lay in the shadow of the Muslim standard. Charles yearned to go crusading, but first he must resolve the religious division in the German lands. Then, with the Empire secure, he could lead an army to Constantinople and even beyond. To that end he summoned Catholic and Protestant theologians to meet him in Augsburg in June. There he hoped to work out a compromise between the old faith and the new. In the meantime he belabored the Pope to call a new Council of the Church.

Luther could not come to Augsburg because he was an outlaw. He came to the Coburg Castle, a hard ride from the imperial city but close enough for him to remain in touch with events there. Philipp Melanchthon and some lesser lights appeared before the Emperor to represent the Lutheran cause. It was Melanchthon who was largely responsible for the confession presented by the Lutherans, a confession, now known as the Augsburg Confession, that remains the basic statement of Lutheran faith today. Melanchthon yearned for the restoration of Christian unity, and he tried to be conciliatory on many issues by leaving them out of the confession altogether! But John Eck, Luther's ancient nemesis, the avatar of orthodoxy, was at Augsburg, and he hooted at the Lutheran confession. He demanded submission, not compromise. Luther, waiting impatiently in his retreat as the hot summer dragged on, was hardly in a more mellow mood. He thought that the papacy must be abolished before Christendom could be united again, and he did not expect that to happen. Christ was going to come again soon, Luther believed. He was annoyed at the concessions Melanchthon was willing to grant. Before the looming end of the world and the day of doom, compromise about the gospel was pointless and perilous. He reproached Melanchthon for wavering and commanded him to stand firm. So the religious discussions broke up into recrimination and deadly menace.

The Emperor took the side of the Catholics. He may not have understood the central issues, but he retained the sense of the long history of his ancestors he had called up at Worms nearly a decade before. They had been Catholics. And chivalry still bound him up as tightly as a knight crammed into an obsolete suit of glittering armor; he could not escape his dreams. He ordered the Protestants to bend their necks to tradition. They would not. So the Diet ended in failure, and with it passed away the last real chance for reconciliation among Christians. Now the Catholic Church would drift toward the rigid formulations of the Council of Trent. And Protestants would harden their positions both against each other and against the Pope in Rome.

In February 1531 a group of Protestant princes met at the little town of Schmalkalden and formed a league for the common defense. Soon the Schmalkaldic League was joined by the Protestant cities, and in October Catholic Bavaria also threw in with the alliance! Bavaria joined not for religious reasons, obviously, but because she feared the dangerous power of the Emperor. If the Emperor grew too strong, all the princes must necessarily diminish.

Luther sadly and reluctantly came to the support of the League. In that same year he published a gloomy little tractate called *Dr. Martin Luther's Warning to His Dear German People*. In it he allowed a right of the princes to resist the Emperor by force.

He had always opposed defending the gospel by violence. Even now he said that he still believed God would defend the faith Himself and would not let it be overwhelmed by its enemies. And yet, he said, he was forced for a moment to speak as if there were no God, imagining as though in a dream that plots against the truth would go on and that Christians must then devise ways of protecting themselves.

He was at pains to say that if war came, it would not be because his followers had started it. They only wanted peace; they would not attack anyone first; Luther would not lead them in rebellion if the Catholics left them alone. Here he was speaking out of deep sincerity. A few years earlier a rather mysterious episode had threatened war in the Empire. One Otto von Pack claimed to have evidence proving that the Catholic princes were planning a surprise attack on the Protestants. Young Philip of Hesse wanted to strike the Catholic princes first in a preventive war. But Luther would have none of it. He withstood Philip with all his might. Such an attack, he said, would be infamy, and he demanded that Philip talk the thing out with the Catholics. This had taken place in 1528. So Luther could claim the peaceful intentions of the Lutheran princes with a pure conscience in 1531. If war came, it would have to be started by someone else.

As far as he was concerned as a single person, Luther said that he was willing to die if God wanted his death. He thought that any ordinary citizen who found himself caught in Catholic oppression should share that sentiment. Every Christian should be willing to die for the faith. Death could hold no terror but only bliss for anyone who died in the Lord.

But then Luther raised a sharp note and sang it into an angry war cry against all the Catholic powers. God could raise up another Judas Maccabeus to fight for His people. Judas Maccabeus had been the Jewish champion who led a successful rebellion against Antiochus Epiphanes in 166 B.C. Antiochus had profaned the Jewish Temple with pork blood. He had also introduced a vigorous Hellenizing policy. He loved gymnastics. Under his rule Jewish boys competed naked in the public games so popular wherever Greek culture spread. Pious Jews were horrified. So there had been rebellion, and the Maccabean leaders had driven the Hellenists out of Palestine.

Here was a sentiment that Luther had developed before. It appeared in 1523 in his tractate on secular authority. The times of all princes, he said, are in the hands of God. An evil prince may well be a divinely sent scourge for a sinful people, but in time God will bring the evil ruler down. Assyria had been the rod of God's anger when Israel sinned; but the Assyrians were themselves evil, and eventually God brought their fine cities to desolation. Evil rulers did the will of a good God, and other evil rulers were raised up by that same almighty rule to destroy them. And although Luther in his younger days did not allow rebellion to Christians, still he could argue that the rebel did the will of God. It was a subtle point, and an ordinary man might be forgiven for missing it. One doing the will of God by insurrection was still deemed wicked for the insurrection itself.

But now in 1531 came an important change. Luther mentioned Judas Maccabeus with evident satisfaction. In the very same sentence he uttered a more terrible warning. "God . . . taught us to make war and peace through the Bohemians." Here he recalled for the Germans the bloody conflict that scalded Bohemia and the Empire when John Huss had been burned at the stake after he had been tricked into coming to the Council of Constance. Luther meant that God Himself would now fight against the Catholics; blood would flow, and the men who fought to accomplish God's will were not evil, as the Assyrians had been, but were themselves pious Christians. The scourge of God had become the blessed of God, not a mere crude instrument in God's hand to be cast away when the job was done. Luther was threatening a sort of crusade in self-defense, a just war against the Catholics who had themselves crusaded for so many centuries.

Luther said that he would not now condemn those who defended themselves. Curiously enough, he still claimed that he would not urge people to war, even in self-defense. Always for him there was that gnawing desire to make Christians passive, to let God do their striving for them, while they watched and waited. He could tell the papists in this work that they could make themselves necklaces of shit to hang under their chins. But he could not become a crier for violence. He would do no more than to tell people who did defend themselves that they committed no sin. He was sure that Catholics were violating the ancient customs of the Empire, natural law, and their own consciences. "They themselves know that our teaching is true!" It was his old fallacy about the conscience of his enemies. And what he imagined to be their hypocrisy made him furious.

Yet he retained his futile hope that the Emperor would not attack, and indeed the war did not come until after Luther was dead. Throughout this little work he flattered Charles whenever he could. As always he blamed the ills of the Empire on the people who gave Charles advice, especially on the Pope. Should the Emperor raise a call to arms against the gospel, true Christians should not obey. Was this not rebellion? No, said Luther. Such an edict from the Emperor would come down only because the Pope had duped Charles into issuing it. Luther seemed to be arguing that because such an edict did not represent the Emperor's own true sentiments, Christians would not be in rebellion by ignoring it.

It may be that he was flattering Charles out of a calculation about how people would read this tractate. On the surface his strategy for winning the Emperor over was similar to that which he used in trying to gain the support of Pope Leo X in 1520. Tell both Emperor and Pope that they are good men surrounded by evil counselors. Tell them that wicked men have seduced them so that neither can see the truth, that each is being led about like a pig with a ring in his nose. This was really to say to Leo in 1520 and to Charles in 1531 that they were not knaves but merely fools, and very inept fools at that. It is not a flattering estimate of either man, and neither was converted. Only in recent American history has a ruler been willing to profess to the public that he was too inept to see how his closest advisers were running the government exactly contrary to his wishes. Charles V would have considered such a confession of incompetence as an affront to his imperial dignity and even to his manhood. And we may be justified in thinking that Luther was foolish to employ such a tactic. But it may have been that the flattery was a rhetorical device. By saying to the people that the Emperor was not in control of himself, Luther could hold that resistance to his decrees was not rebellion, and Christians could take up arms with a clear conscience. Luther, by praising the Emperor, could impress the average reader with his own goodwill toward an ancient and sacred office. Again we cannot be sure. Luther always has the mark of deep sincerity stamped on his works, and it is difficult to suspect him of scheming.

Though he allowed resistance, Luther was circumspect at how it should be led. No private citizen had any right to rebellion. But that citizen could respond to the call of his prince. The Catholics, in fighting against the gospel, were assaulting all three persons of the Trinity, the blood of Jesus, and Creation itself. They were more loathsome than Turks. The Pope presided over an institution that spawned whoredom in convents and fornication in cathedrals. The Pope and his cardinals were perverts, fouled with sodomy. The Fifth Lateran Council, Luther said, had restricted the cardinals by limiting the number of boys they could keep for perversion. Pope Leo, Luther said, had suppressed the decree lest the Roman Church get a bad name. All this was only the wildest gossip. But Luther's hatred of the papacy and the papal court was so fierce that he believed any evil he heard about them. The papacy, he said, had invented the doctrine of purgatory for its own profit. It had shed blood. It had instituted a tyranny of the clergy over the laity. And the Pope had tried to subvert good government in all the world. The German princes could resist such atrocities, and their people could follow them.

Luther believed that besides the Emperor, only the princes in Germany possessed an authority like that sanctioned by Paul in Romans 13:1–10. He thought that they were among the powers ordained by God to punish the wicked, and they were worthy of support and honor from the people they protected. The princes had a divine right to defend their people from evil. If evil should be found in the edicts of the Emperor himself, the princes had the right to resist him. This came to be called the doctrine of resistance by the inferior magistrate. It meant that the Emperor (or the King in other countries) did not possess a monopoly on divine magistracy. All who exercised governmental authority in any realm possessed a power granted by God to be used for the good order of their subjects. When the greater authority commanded blasphemous worship, the lesser authority had the right to resist his will by force.

Calvinists would later extend the doctrine of the inferior magistrate to parliaments. But in the German situation Luther's teaching was to enlarge the place of the princes in German life. They alone were to direct the prodigious leap from loyal subjects to heroic defenders of liberty in response to the demands of God and their office. Only they, in Luther's view, could grant the authority for such resounding remarks as "Give me liberty or give me death," or something equally memorable. Common people must wait for their lead. And in Luther's mind the only tyranny that could be resisted by anybody was religious. He would not have been sympathetic to the American Declaration of Independence of 1776. Taxation without representation? The quartering of troops in the homes of citizens? Luther would have seen such afflictions as these only as a part of the cross to be borne by good Christians. They would not have justified revolution. George III would have had to impose the Mass and the

Pope on Thomas Jefferson before Luther would have been at all sympathetic to the American War of Independence. Even then he might have held back, for Jefferson was no prince.

So the princes became the real winners in the Reformation. By granting them the sole responsibility for the military defense of true religion in their domains, Luther effactually sanctified the ancient divisions of the German lands. German particularism had kept Germans divided during the Middle Ages; Germany was to remain divided until Bismarck united her in 1871. Religion did not create the disunity, but it conferred a holiness on it and helped to preserve division. And even in the ramshackle Empire that Bismarck made, the religious strife from the Reformation era continued like a fever in the German blood. It might even be said that the virulent form of German nationalism so dreadfully familiar to recent history was a calculated antidote to the old religious hatreds between Catholics and Protestants. Since Christians of various persuasions could not meet each other with trust in a united country, Christianity itself would be burned away by a new and virulent paganism. And eventually even old symbols like the cross were twisted into the signs of a new faith and a new order.

Luther must be judged partly responsible for the sense of divine mission that let the German princes justify their autonomy in the world. That autonomy contributed to the rest. Perhaps no other course was open to him. The princes were his only reliable political allies. By supporting them, he could also limit their ferocity. As we have seen, one of the great burdens of this tractate is that Luther would not support anything but self-defense. He would not grant his authority to the Schmalkaldic League to attack first. We have seen how he mistrusted the mob. He craved order in the world, and he wanted freedom for his gospel. So the princes became his only hope on earth.

Luther's feeling that the Christian should be passive went beyond the question of political duty. It extended to every aspect of life where the Christian might be tempted to live for himself. In his sermons and his pastoral writing and in his lectures of the next decade, he developed a doctrine of vocation that has often inspired his disciples with admiration. The Catholic Church had taught that only the priest had a calling from God. But now Luther extended the doctrine of divine calling to everyone who did a useful service in the world. The scullery maid or the prince in his palace alike had their jobs to perform. The world depended on them, and each should do his duty to the glory of God.

Some have said that this doctrine of vocation gave a dignity to labor that had been lacking in the Middle Ages. There is something to this claim. It is dismaying to see just how people in previous centuries had held peasants and other common laborers in contempt. We have noted with what scorn Ulrich Zwingli regarded a certain barber. But it could be that Luther's view of calling is not so modern as some have thought. To say to the scullery maid that God has called her to the kitchen may confer dignity on her sweeping, but it is also to imply that she should not seek to improve her lot. For if she is called by God to sweep, how can she dare decide that she would rather dance? And if God has called the cobbler to his bench, how can that man dare dress himself in long boots and ride out as a knight in the wide world?

Luther's doctrine of vocation is little more than the medieval view that held things to be the way God wanted them to be. If He had desired something else, He would have made the world different. Coupled with this was the New Testament understanding of the indifference the Christian was taught to assume toward his earthly condition. Paul said in I Corinthians 7:20–24, "Every man should remain in the condition in which he was called. Were you a slave when you were called? Do not let that trouble you; but if a chance of liberty should come, take it. For the man who as a slave received the call to be a Christian is the Lord's freedman, and, equally, the free man who received the call is a slave in the service of Christ. . . . Thus each one, my friends, is to remain before God in the condition in which he received his call."

Alexander Pope, in the eighteenth century, said, "Whatever is, is right." But that conviction was much more typical of the medieval mentality than it was of Pope's own day. This is the best of all possible worlds—at least given the inescapable circumstance of a mortal life dictated by Adam's sin and God's plan for redemption. Luther believed in social classes, with some people made for high position and others for menial tasks. This was how God had designed the world. This was how the world should remain until Christ returned to make a new heaven and a new earth. Everyone should do his duty in his place and be content until God brought change to pass. The destiny of all men was to do God's will. Hope lay not in this world but in the glorious life to come.

Perhaps these facts help us to understand Luther's consistent hostility to the merchant and banking classes. He often condemned them because they devoted too much time to success in this world. He disliked the new capitalist spirit for much the same reason medieval theologians hated trade. Capitalism made men seek to climb out of the place where God had put them. Luther believed that people should stay put and be content. Everyone should work to earn his daily bread and to supply the needs of the people who depended on him. Luther castigated the monks for idleness and by implication exalted useful labor. But he also thought the best work was agriculture. Capitalism carried within itself manipulation and a dangerous instinct for change. Capitalism reeked of ambition for worldly things. It was directly contrary to that spirit of patient, passive, and watchful obedience in Christ that Luther took to be the suffering of the Christian life: "Suffering, suffering, cross, cross!"

Conservative attitudes are increasingly dominant in the aging Luther. His evaluation of the law is a part of the trend. At an earlier time he suggested that Christians could live without the law altogether. He meant that Christ in their hearts would make them live spontaneously the life that conformed to the nature of Christ, at least insofar as their own corrupted natures would permit. The Christian was always a sinner, but he was also always warring against the sin that he found in himself. And the young and exuberantly hopeful Luther believed that spirit in the Christian's heart was sufficient to let him live by the gospel alone.

But as time passed, Luther became more and more gloomy about the power of Christians in the world. The peasants' rebellion permanently unnerved him about the masses. The princes who came over to his gospel led the way in plundering the old Church for their own gain. They did not even support the impoverished pastors who preached the new faith that had sanctified the confiscation of church property. Luther was also shaken by the way some of his would-be disciples seemed to interpret Christian freedom as license for the flesh. More and more often he confessed that the superiority of his followers to Catholics lay not in living but in doctrine. It was a confession that took reality into account. Still we must note the change in spirit. Gone is the sublime hope that shines in Luther's great *Freedom of a Christian* of 1520.

And so he became a vigorous preacher of the law. He never did say that anyone could be saved by keeping the law, but he did think that the law gave a standard necessary for society. The true Christian was perpetually humbled by his inability to keep the law with his whole heart; the law made him seek the mercy of God. Those who were not Christians were made by the law to keep its outer demands. They did not murder. They did not steal. They did not swear falsely and so on. Or, if they broke the law, they were punished by government, by parents, and by the penalty of public disaster. Any government that allowed killing or stealing to flourish was headed for destruction. No government could endure that did not force its citizens to observe the natural law. The Christian might live in humility before the law. But there were not enough Christians in the world to assure stability unless the compulsions that enforced the law were retained for the masses of men.

The magnitude of Luther's conception should not be overlooked. He deftly plied his way between two extremes. He had long since surrendered any hope that the world was going to be renovated by Christians. He did not believe that the purpose of God could be incarnate in any visible human corporation, whether it might be the institution of a church or the constitution of a government. He was no Savonarola, no Zwingli, no Calvin. Their frantic moral activism in the observance of Christian forms was not his way. He thought that Christians were always a minority, and that they were always sinners and justified at the same time. They could not regenerate the world before Christ came. They could not even regenerate a city from tavern to tabernacle so that it might be a light unto the world; for even if everyone was forced to attend church three times on Sunday, sin was still present.

Neither did Luther assume that Christians should let the world go to hell while they withdrew to conventicles. He would not follow the Anabaptists into making the isolated community of true believers the object and guide for Christian practice. Anabaptism was monkery with wives and children and a code of eccentric beliefs destined to separate its practitioners from the world as sharply as the old Benedictine rule had severed monks from society. Luther would have none of it.

God had made the world. The world was corrupt. It would remain corrupt until Christ came back to restore it to the purity of the original creation. But Luther's stress on the divine authority of the law for this earthly life is only another face to his steadfast conviction that Christians must stay in the world. They must be willing to get their hands dirty, doing their share to keep the world under the rule of law even if most people in it were bad. Why? Such was the mysterious will of God.

In his earlier days Luther had preached that a Christian should be willing to be damned if that should be God's will. His preaching about the Christian's obligations in the world under the law is akin to his resignation to inferno. One cannot decide on one's own to give up what God has ordained. So the law must be preached. The world must be governed. Christians must bear their afflictions, and they must stay at the task God had given them even when they, like Luther himself, could not clearly perceive the good of their efforts or the reward for their suffering and their toil.

231

27

OWARD THE END OF HIS LIFE Luther is an enigma in some ways. There is much in his lectures and in his sermons on the tenderness and the mercy of God. But there is also a dark and brooding stress on God's awful mystery, and most of Luther's late works are vicious and hateful and a pain to read. His power to convince seemed to be gone, and he responded in the way vehement men usually do to such a situation. He raised his voice to a ranting squeal.

By 1540 God's ways must have seemed mysterious indeed. The papacy had not died. The Catholic powers remained strong. The world was disorderly. Robert Barnes, Luther's most influential disciple in England, was burned at the stake by Henry VIII's government. (Barnes had earlier been instrumental in seeing to it that a Zwinglian named Lambert was burned.) How could anyone perceive God at work in such chaos? Luther's steadfast answer was what it had always been: God worked in the world in ways that seemed to be just the opposite of what He was really doing. When man drew back in perplexity before the mystery of things, God's purpose was already partly accomplished. Man's reason was humbled. The true Christian was thereby made to throw himself on God's mercy. The true fear of God, Luther wrote in 1539, was not to become grim at His incomprehensible judgments, but to love, praise, thank, and adore Him for everything that happens, whether good or bad. The mystery extended to history. Why was it that the Fathers were so often in error? Luther could not tell. He could call men like Augustine blessed and beloved. But he could not explain why the "dear fathers" so often disagreed with the gospel as Luther saw it. Once he suggested that they might have been strangely misled by God Himself for some secret purpose. But whatever the cause, he knew that their words were the words of men. They should always be judged by Scripture, for Scripture alone of all written works came from the hand of God.

In 1540 Philip of Hesse decided he wanted to put his old wife away and take a younger woman to bed and hearth. As we noted earlier, he asked Luther's counsel. Luther fell back on a thought he had espoused in 1520: Bigamy was better than divorce. Let Philip take the young damsel he loved, make her his wife, and keep his old wife, too!

Luther's solution was humane and Biblical. In the sixteenth century a woman divorced and cast out into the world was helpless unless she owned great lands or had a strong family to look out for her. Even then she was most likely to live out her days in shame. A woman divorced was considered little better than a harlot; her social isolation was terrible. Without the care of her family, she might even starve.

Bigamy preserved Philip's obligation to his first spouse. It was in no way contrary to Scripture. Even Pope Clement VII suggested bigamy as a way to cool the raging heat of the marital problems of Henry VIII in the Anne Boleyn affair. Bigamy did happen to be contrary to the law of the Empire and to the morals of the age. Luther said that the affair should be kept secret. But such news has a way of leaking to the world. The resulting scandal damaged Luther's influence tremendously and left him raw and bitter.

A much more important issue is Luther's hatred of the Jews. Here we touch on an aspect of his thought that is embarrassing to his warmest admirers. Roland Bainton, whose fine biography *Here I Stand* nearly always praises Luther, says that one might wish that Luther had died before writing a little book called *Against the Jews and Their Lies*. William L. Shirer, whose *Rise and Fall of the Third Reich* was one of the first efforts to assess the history of Naziism, quoted from this book and implied that Luther was a spiritual ancestor to Hitler. W. H. Auden, in "September 1, 1939," his poem commemorating the outbreak of World War II, could write,

> Accurate scholarship can
> Unearth the whole offence
> From Luther until now
> That has driven a culture mad.

Luther's partisans have defended him. Bainton is typical and far better than most. Luther was old when he wrote so hatefully. (Actually he was only fifty-nine.*) He was beset on all sides by enemies. Some Christians were taking up such Jewish practices as worship on Saturday. Bainton implies that Luther's outbursts are to be seen as an eccentricity, a terrible offense, but one that is to be understood by reference to the times. And Bainton seems to believe that Luther is not to be judged for something that was only incidental to his life's work. He says, with apparently careful discrimination, that Luther's attacks on the Jews were religious and not racial in origin, and this view has been taken by others who have written not to bury Luther but to praise him.

But this is really to say that Luther's hatred of the Jews was not based on the pseudoscientific theories of "race" that came from the social Darwinism of the nineteenth century. In fact, Luther shared abundantly the fierce and terrible hatred of the Jews that had made their lives hellish in Christian Europe from at least the time of the Crusades, when Christian warriors were sent down into Palestine to slaughter infidels. Many of these exuberant and sanctified killers thought they might as well practice murder on the "infidels" in their midst—the Jews. And so a series of pogroms began that has continued until modern times in spasmodic outbreaks against those helpless people whose only distinguishing mark is not racial at all. (There is no such thing as "race" except in the minds of some who want to simplify human existence so that their prejudices may seem to be more rational.)

But the main problem is this: Is Luther's hatred of Jews merely an eccentricity? Or is it rather a natural consequence of the way he looked at the world? I believe that the latter is the case and that it is an error of critical historical misunderstanding to make his loathing for the Jews only a consequence of a supposed crabby old age. Luther's loathing for Jews is a predictable extension of his view of the Bible and of the way the Bible must be understood.

It is true enough that his view of the clarity of Scripture was combined with a growing pessimism about the future of his movement. He could not for the life of him understand how people could deny anything as evident as Scripture. He felt himself threatened within the ranks of Protestants who disagreed with him. And throughout Europe the power of the Catholic forces was swelling in the way a thunderhead will build in the hot sky of still summer afternoon, sucking the light out of earth below. When people are threatened,

* Roland Bainton is now eighty, as kind and generous as he has always been and showing no sign of the hatefulness he excuses in Luther because Luther was so old!

they are likely to become vicious. And so Luther exploded in 1543 with two vitriolic screeds that assaulted the Jews. One was *Against the Jews and Their Lies*. The other, much shorter, was entitled *Concerning Schem Hamphoras and Concerning the Lineage of Christ*, a work in two parts. Both were written in German so that their popular dissemination would be large, but in fact neither had a wide circulation. Here Luther said almost every hateful thing that had been said about the Jews for centuries.

Many have pointed out that at the beginning of his public career Luther had said some surprisingly kind things about the Jews. In 1523 in his tractate *That Jesus Christ Was Born a Jew*, he wrote, "What good can we do the Jews when we constrain them, malign them, and hate them as dogs? When we deny them work and force them into usury, how can that help? We should use toward the Jews not the pope's law but Christ's law of love. If some are stiff-necked, what does that matter? We are not all good Christians!"

The reason for this early kindness was that Luther expected the Jews to be converted. The Pope had blinded the eyes of Christians, and he had also been so cruel to the Jews that they had been driven to reject Christianity. Now that Luther had come preaching the unfettered gospel, he thought that the Jews would surely turn to Christ. He said again and again that the word of Scripture was clear enough for any honest man to see. Now that he had freed Scripture from the bondage of the Pope, he thought that the Jews should see its clarity, too. And everyone in the Middle Ages knew that when the Jews were converted, the time for the coming of Christ again was at hand. In the Gospels Jesus had made the fig tree a symbol of the Jews. And, he said, when the fig tree put forth new leaves, his disciples could know that summer was nigh and the end of the world near. All of this went naturally with the great hope Luther possessed in the beginning. He was a tool in a cosmic drama that would soon come to an end in the great Judgment Day. Satan and his minions would be bound and cast into hell. The era of redemption would dawn for all the regenerated world. So the Jews were a sign to be regarded with hopeful joy; Luther expected them to do their part.

But they did not. The Jews remained persistently Jews. Some even tried to convert Christians. Luther himself was approached by rabbis who thought that he might be ready for conversion or at least ready to live in peace with them.

Luther thus turned on them with the same charge he flung against all his other opponents. The Jews were obstinate. They knew the truth about Jesus and would not confess it. They willed to believe a lie because they were too proud to confess that they had been in error. All his work against them was intended to show how obvious it was that Jesus was the true Messiah. Naturally, if such a thing was obvious those who did not see it must want to shut their eyes to the truth. In medieval theology, such malicious blindness was viewed as the unpardonable sin.

Even in his youth Luther rarely had anything good to say about the Jews. At best his attitude was like a benevolent warden who hopes that the felons in his charge may be reformed. Usually he mentioned them with contempt. He hated their trust in the law. He was annoyed at their attention to ritual. "Jewishness" in his mind was always associated with ritual efforts to earn salvation. One of the worst things he could say about the Pope was that the papacy Judaized the Christian Church. "Jew" to him was a bad word, and he regularly flung it against his enemies like oozing mud.

Luther was a Biblicist, and hatred of the Jews can easily come to anyone who takes the Bible as a standard for faith and morals. Jesus had a hard time with the Jews, and some of the more dramatic episodes of the Gospels portray his conflicts with the letter of the law. He broke the Sabbath by healing the sick; and when he opened the eyes of the blind, the leaders of the Jews could only think of how they might kill him. Such fantastic yarns are absurd on the face, but they are cracking good drama, and only a few people have perceived the element of propaganda in them. The message of the Gospels agrees with the sentiment of Luther. Why did the Jews not accept Jesus? Because they were malicious. Why were all the miracle stories tossed in to embellish the stature of this strange man Jesus who had been put to death by the Romans? They made the Jews who rejected Jesus seem all the more evil. Jesus himself was said by Matthew, Mark, and Luke to have predicted the destruction of the Jewish Temple. The only implication one can draw from the story they tell is that the Jews deserved it.

Paul, in the epistle to the Romans, changed the definition of "Israel" so that it no longer meant the Jews at all. In the epistle to the Galatians, he made a stringent demand for the abolition of the Jewish law. By the time the Fourth Gospel, called "John," was written late in the first century, the phrase "the Jews" was used almost as a choral effect to stress the murmuring, greedy, obstinate, and murderous quality of those who opposed Jesus. Most people nowadays recall the Bible in much the same way they remember childhood. They think only of the good parts. But Luther, absorbed as he was in all the words of Scripture, rather naturally imbibed the deep hostility of the New Testament against those who had rejected the Messiah. And so it is difficult indeed to argue convincingly that he ever really changed his estimate of the Jews at all. The most that can be said is that he went from thinking of the Jews as reformable felons to perceiving them as criminals who must be damned and that right quickly and forever. It takes a real wrenching of the evidence to say that his hatred of the Jews is an eccentricity, an aberration, a fault of the hardening of his arteries in old age. And surely in this present age people who want to cling to the Bible as some special revelation of divine truth should perceive Martin Luther as an example of how the Bible may be taken seriously.

In his *Against the Jews and Their Lies,* Luther turned to the Bible to "prove" that the Jews lied in the way they interpreted it. They lied in their understanding of the Old Testament, which they regarded as divine, and in their slanders against the New Testament, which they rather naturally saw as a fraud. He thought they were wicked because, he said, they called the Virgin Mary a whore and Jesus the son of a whore. They said that Christians worshiped three gods. And they questioned the divinity of the miracles performed by Jesus. (Just as Luther believed that Satan did wonders at Catholic shrines, many Jews seemed to think that Jesus had done wonders but by means of a magical use of the divine name—the so-called "Schem Hamphoras"!) And Jews for some mysterious reason did not believe that Christians were always kind and good and peaceful.

Luther refuted all these positions at great length and with irrepressible fury. The substance of his argument was unchanged from his lectures on the Psalms at the beginning of his career. The Old Testament cannot be understood without reference to Jesus; Jesus is the only possible Messiah. If one is determined to find Christ speaking in the Old Testament, one has the example of the New Testament writers to follow. These men wrenched every Old Testament text they could lay eyes on to prove that Jesus was the fulfillment of Jewish history, and Luther only followed their example. Others have found the secrets of the universe hidden in the dimensions of the Great Pyramid, and some have found spacemen from other planets cavorting through the mythology of ancient societies. All proof enough that the industrious believer in anything can prove his faith anywhere he wants. Always Luther's conviction is that the New Testament is right because it says that it is right, a variety of the common Christian assumption that the Bible is inspired because it says that it is inspired.

Terrible indeed were the inferences Luther drew from the fact that the Jews disagreed both with the New Testament and with himself. Perhaps most puzzling to us is his gloating at their sufferings. The Romans destroyed their Temple. Their miseries ever since have been proof of God's wrath against them. And God will continue to afflict them until they turn at last to Christ. It is passing strange that Luther could say that suffering was proof of God's anger. He had said to the peasants in 1525 that the mark of the true Christian was "suffering, suffering, cross, cross." He had always seen the true Christians as a small and persecuted minority in a world of wolves. God worked in paradox. What appeared to be one thing was really another. Affliction was a sign of God's blessing. One's faith was tried here below so that one might enjoy the bliss of heaven forever and ever. With this sort of theology one might very well have expected Luther to sympathize with the sorrows of the Jews. But no. He only gloats at their anguish and chortles because God has shown the Jews His wrath so mercilessly.

The Jews, Luther says, are proud. And how is that? Well, they demonstrate their arrogance by their prayers, their hymns, their synagogues, and their whole life. They boast of their lineage. They believe that they can accomplish the law of God. In short, Luther thinks the pride of the Jews is in their very effort to be religious. In this he is consistent with his earlier denunciations of any claim to righteousness arising from religious observance. But by his definition there is no way for Jews to be humble at all unless they turn to Christ.

Then Luther passes to mere vituperation. The Jews, he says, are the most bloodthirsty and vengeful people who have ever seen the light of day. They love the Book of Esther, says he, because that book recounts a great slaughter of Gentiles by the Jews. (We have seen that Luther had never liked the Book of Esther, but here he seems to loathe it.) The Jews have always delighted in murder. They killed the prophets. They murdered the Son of God. And how does Luther know that they are still murderers? Well, says he, if only they had the chance they would put the bloody fantasies of their hearts into operation, and then we would see for ourselves. It is an argument tediously similar to that made by Southerners in the United States about blacks. White people who looked at the afflictions of the slave knew what vengeful feelings *they* would have if they were enslaved; so they read their own fantasies into the minds of the helpless blacks they ruled. Luther had never learned the patient resignation and quiet strength that real suffering brings to those who are exposed to it for generations. Revenge then becomes pointless. Luther, enthralled with his vicious ruminations about Jewish vengeance, said that there were no pious Jews. They were whores masking as virgins. All they could teach was how to misunderstand the divine commandments. The devil possessed them. They were beyond help. No prophets had come to them for centuries. His catalog of abuse goes on and on.

Like nearly everyone else who has hated the Jews, Luther casti-
gates them for their greed. He thought them parasites on society,
making their living universally by the interest (he always called it
"usury") they charged on money they lent to Christians. By 1543 he
had forgotten his earlier declaration that Christians had forced the
Jews into usury by exiling them from most other occupations. No one
could trust them, he says. Only an occasional truthful word dribbled
from their lips. The Jews are idlers, sitting around their stoves fart-
ing and eating pears while Christians work like slaves for them. The
Jews make foreigners out of Christians in Christian lands by possessing Christian money and Christian property. (Hitler was to make
a similar argument, holding that Jews controlled the wealth of Germany.)

Luther says that the Jews were sorcerers. He often attacked them
as practitioners in the black arts. A pious Jew would not pronounce
the name of God, called the "tetragrammaton" because it was written
with four characters. The accusation by Christians that Jews used
it as a magic sign was very old. The charge of familiarity with the
black arts had been leveled against the Jews during the Reuchlin
controversy that had flamed up in Luther's young days, a dispute that
has been seen as a forerunner to the Reformation. Johann Reuchlin
believed that Christians should study the Jewish language and Jewish
books. His antagonists, who included many conservative churchmen,
said that all Jewish books ought to be burned. Many saw the conflict as
a battle between civilization and barbarism, and later on many of the
same people who had opposed Reuchlin also opposed Luther. Luther
himself became one of the greatest Gentile Hebrew scholars of the
sixteenth century. But still he shrilled the old cry, that Jews used
their language for magic.

There is an inharmonious rhapsody of violence clanging through
these terrible denunciations of the Jews. The Jews, he says, eat no
food, wear no clothes, and support no wife and child except by the
theft of usury that they practice daily against Christians. We hang
and behead thieves, trumpets Luther. The usurer is the worst thief of
all; he should be hanged on a gallows seven times higher than that
for other thieves. The equation seems monstrously clear. All Jews are
usurers; usurers ought to be hanged. If some humble Christian wanted
to conclude, "Well then, all Jews should be hanged," there is precious little in Luther to condemn the thought. Indeed, he says in this
book that God has cursed the Jews and that Christians are guilty for
not killing them!

Why do the Jews insist on being enemies to Christians? Luther
poses the question in ridiculous self-pity. We do not, he says, call their

women whores as they do the Virgin Mary. We do not call them the
sons of whores as they call Jesus. (In this same tractate Luther does
call them devils, thieves, robbers, and various other names that somehow seem to fall short of perfect Christian benevolence!) "We do not
curse them but wish good things for them both physical and spiritual!" And how do the evil Jews repay this pious Christian generosity?
They kidnap Christian children and crucify them! Here was one of
the most ghoulish Christian slanders against Jews, and Luther accepts it at face value and shrieks it to the multitudes! The Jews
poison the wells of Christians, he says—another hoary libel. The Jews
thirst for blood. . . . On and on he goes until we are worn out by his
fury. The sum of these horrors seems clear enough to anyone who
takes the trouble to make the addition: Anyone who kills a Jew serves
society, though in one place Luther piously declares that Christians
should not avenge themselves! This small afterthought commending
restraint is hardly convincing amid this avalanche of murderous
accusation.

What are Christians to do with the Jews? First, says Luther, the
synagogues and the Jewish schools are to be burned to the ground.
Christians may join in throwing in sulfur and pitch to make the flames
hotter. If they can find any hellfire lying about, they can toss that in,
too. Anything left over should be covered with dirt so that not a
trace remains to pollute a good Christian land. Anyone who sees a
Jew knows that he sees someone who curses Christ every Saturday.
For Christians to allow that blasphemy to go on is to consent to it and
to share in its dire punishment by God. So the fires must burn, and the
schools and the synagogues must fall, all to the glory of Luther's
merciful and tender Jesus.

Destroy their houses, too! Luther says that the same blasphemies go on under Jewish roofs that rage in the synagogues. Jews
should be forced to live in barns or else in the open like Gypsies. The
Talmud and their prayer books are to be destroyed. Not even a page
of the Bible is to be left to the Jews, since they use the Scripture only
to curse the Son of God. That means, Luther says, that they curse
God Himself. Rabbis were to be forbidden "by body and life" to
teach. I can read no meaning into this phrase other than a threat to
mutilate and to kill any rabbi who violated the law against Jewish instruction. Such was the common practice in the executions of that
barbarous age.

One of Luther's more dismal proposals was that Jews should be
granted no safe-conduct on the highways. This would have meant
that anyone could have attacked any Jew who might be found on the
open road, robbing him, killing him, or doing anything else that a

cruel fancy might dictate—all without fear of penalty under the law. Let the Jews stay home! That was Luther's advice. They had no business running around, said he. He seems to have forgotten that only a few sentences before he had recommended that their homes be destroyed and that they be made to live like Gypsies in the earth. Apparently he expected them to be sitting Gypsies—or sitting ducks.

He wanted the Jews banned from usury. This meant that he wanted them forced out of banking. He suggested that whenever a Jew was sincerely converted, he be given enough money to set himself up in an honest occupation. For the Jews who remained Jews no such retraining program was proposed. They should have tools thrust into their hands, and they should be driven into the fields and set to laboring like peasants. The women should be taught to spin and weave at home—as if no Jewish matron had ever mastered those skills before Luther came along!

But having proposed to make the Jews into peasants, Luther turns with dizzy speed to his final solution to the Jewish question: The Jews should be driven out of the country. Let them all go back to Jerusalem, he says. There they can prey on one another and leave Christians alone. He cites with approval the Christian lands that have already expelled the Jews. These territories are better for it, and he urges all Christian rulers to do the same.

Rulers have usually tended to be less bloodthirsty than prophets. Saul was willing to let Agag live; it was Samuel who demanded death for all the Amalekites and killed Agag himself before Jehovah. Many governments in Luther's time tolerated the Jews. The Jews paid taxes. Some of them were in banking and commerce, though not nearly the number Luther (or later Hitler) supposed. Banking was a help to governments. It made society itself more rational in an age when rulers were slowly imposing order on turbulent lands.

But Luther demanded implacable punishment for the Jews to prove to God how serious good Christians are in their devotion to Christ. Woe to any rulers who allowed the Jews to remain in their territories in exchange for services rendered! Rulers must rather act like physicians who, when they perceive gangrene in a member, ruthlessly cut, saw, and burn it off! Again Luther's rhetoric implies massacre.

Some things strike us as truly cancerous in this sick work. Luther comments repeatedly about all the kind things Christians have done for Jews! He boasts that Christians have never used force but have only preached the Word—as if there had never been a pogrom in Europe before his time! This is clearly a headlong book, foolish, wicked, filled with inner contradictions and thoughtless violence.

Even the later Russian czars seem almost mild by comparison to Luther's recommendations for the Jews, and it is really no wonder that Luther has been claimed by many as a spiritual ancestor to Adolf Hitler. But of course Hitler and Luther differed profoundly in most things. Hitler was much more akin to the Spiritualists in the Reformation, the so-called "Heavenly Prophets" whom Luther detested for their claims of direct, special revelation from God. The dismal fact remains, however, that we cannot find much in Luther to mitigate Hitler's decision to exterminate the Jews. There is much in Luther's rhetoric that could have urged Hitler on, though in fact Hitler was not interested in Luther and did not need a voice from the Reformation to inspire his madness. It is not so much that Luther was an ancestor of Hitler's that may strike us with foreboding when we read this tractate; it is that Luther is yet another example of that nearly ritual bloodiness that in our history is so frequently associated with men whose lives are tied to desks and theories, isolated from the red ground where the blood is shed. Hitler is gone, but the almost ritual propensity for abstract violence among the theory class is still frighteningly with us. Maybe Luther was one of the first of that horrible ilk.

His other important anti-Jewish work, *Concerning Schem Hamphoras and Concerning the Lineage of Christ,* is made of the same shoddy stuff. When it appeared in 1543, Zwingli's dismayed heirs in Zurich wrote, "If it had been written by a swineherd, rather than by a renowned pastor of souls, it might have some justification—but not much."

Here Luther attacks a curious belief reported among some Jews that Jesus did miracles by means of a magical incantation, the "Schem Hamphoras," related to the sacred name of God. He also defends the reputation of the Virgin Mary against those who accused her of whoredom. In his unrestrained praise of the Virgin, he even goes so far as to profess her Immaculate Conception, the doctrine that she had been created without original sin, conceived without spot in the womb of her mother. Such a doctrine has no foundation in the New Testament Luther professed to revere, and it was not universally accepted in the Middle Ages. Thomas Aquinas, whose name Luther despised, disputed the Immaculate Conception on the simple ground that if Christ died for all, he must have died for his mother, too; but her redemption would not have been necessary had she been born without original sin. Indeed, it was only in 1854 when the reactionary pope, Pius IX, got around to proclaiming the Immaculate Conception as Catholic dogma! Luther's hatred of the Jews was such that even his doctrine of the universal power of sin over humankind and his reliance on the Bible as the standard of doctrine were both repressed when he had a chance to make a point against these people he despised.

We might at least have hoped for Luther to have relegated the Jews to the mystery of God. Many Christians have done as much. Even Paul with all his vehemence did not condemn Jews to hell. But in the *Schem Hamphoras* Luther held that the Jews must accept the New Testament, baptism, and the Christian faith or be forever damned. He went even further by saying to Christian rulers that to allow Jews to flourish among them was to share in their blasphemies and abominations. Here was the impulse to theocracy that so exercised Zwingli and Calvin, men who tried to build the city of God in Zurich and Geneva. Any Christian who tolerates iniquity in his fellow citizens shares in that iniquity himself. If he does not stamp out evil wherever he can, God will judge him and his government. A new Babylon will come down, and the would-be Christian regime swept away. Such was the rationale for making even those predestined to be damned for eternity nevertheless conform to the outward pieties puritans demand. Luther seldom indulged himself in such follies, perhaps because he never dominated any government in the way Zwingli or Calvin did. But here in his tirade against the Jews, Luther turns to the theocratic motif. We must show God that we are in earnest about our faith, says he, in advocating harsh measures against Jewry. It is as if for a moment he had forgotten all about the God who knows all the secrets of men. Here is Luther fallen into the trap of works-righteousness as surely as any Pharisee or any Catholic who ever did a work of satisfaction in penance to persuade God to be merciful to him. Here is Luther seeking to prove his sincerity to God, and by a work of merit—persecuting the Jews—seeking to gain the favor of a loving God.

Luther's other polemics toward the end of his life are equally harsh. His blistering assaults on Catholics are full of hate and raucous obscenity. But at least the Catholics wished him the same evil that he predicted for them. The Jews were helpless. Luther castigated them for their supposed desire to massacre Christians. But he could not prove any of his slanders and was willing to devour them for their imagined silent intent. It was a tactic used by the Spanish Inquisition, and one should consider it before making of Martin Luther one of the great heroes of our civilization.

28

*L*UTHER DIED on February 18, 1546. Sick and weary, he had made a hard journey in the midst of a frozen winter to help settle a petty dispute between two quarreling brothers who were Counts of Mansfeld. On January 28 he was smitten with a fever, and in that condition he was escorted into Eisleben, the little town where he had been born nearly sixty-three years before. He had departed from the town as a baby, the son of poor and struggling parents, unnoticed in the great world. He returned as an old and dying man, guarded by a troop of more than a hundred armed horsemen, welcomed like a conqueror, and toasted like a lord.

For a while he seemed to regain his strength, and he labored to reconcile the contentious counts, but then the fever returned. He wrote to his wife fearless and loving letters, told her that she must not worry, and commended himself to God. Weakness overwhelmed him, and he took to his bed and passed into a deep sleep. Two friends, eager to have some last affirmation from his lips, shook him awake and shouted a question: "Reverend father, are you prepared to die trusting in your Lord Jesus Christ and confessing the doctrine that you have taught in his name?" It was an act reminiscent of extreme unction, the Catholic sacrament for the dying that Luther had long since rejected, but he did what centuries of Christians had done before him in the hour of death. He assented to the confession yelled in his ear by muttering a single word, "Yes." Turning over on his side, he slept for a few minutes longer, sighed deeply, and stopped breathing. It was three o'clock in the morning, and beyond the dimly lit room both the Pope in distant Rome and the German people scattered through village, forest, and town lay sleeping in the same wintry night.

Almost at once the evaluations of Luther's life began, and they have continued to this day. His followers saw him as a saint and a hero, and in only a short time most Lutherans came to regard his every utterance as only slightly less authoritative than Scripture itself.

Johannes Cochlaeus, one of Luther's most bitter and persistent Catholic opponents, set a Catholic standard for the estimate of Luther's life by publishing the first book-length biography of him in 1549. A preface, written by one of Cochlaeus's friends, tells us that we study history because a knowledge of the past gives us wisdom for the future. From history we learn what is wise and honest and what is evil and pernicious. History gives us prudence. As Livy says, orators are not to be trusted as much as historians are. The orator seeks to be eloquent, but the historian seeks only the truth. With that Cochlaeus set out to tell the truth about Luther—that he was possessed by devils in his youth (Cochlaeus uses language that might suggest Luther had committed sodomy with demons); that once he was flung out of a choir by a deaf-and-dumb demon who left Luther shouting, "It is not I! It is not I!"; that he bought his doctorate by fraud; that he was angry with the indulgence traffic because he did not get a commission to sell indulgences himself; and so on *ad nauseam!*

We may well scorn Cochlaeus and his headlong polemic that pretends to be honest history. Yet nearly all writing about Luther has been couched in words saturated with value judgments. Most studies about him have been done by clergymen. Even those removed from the clergy have sought to use his giant figure out of the past to teach us something about the present.

Luther's works began to be edited at Weimar at a moment in the nineteenth century when German nationalists were seeking to prove to the world that Germany, too, had her intellectual heroes. Kaiser William II became one of the sponsors of the Weimar Edition in much the same national enthusiasm with which he sponsored a great German navy.

As a consequence of the great Weimar Edition, the twentieth century has been flooded with Luther studies. Heinrich Denifle produced the first modern consideration of Luther's works done with meticulous concern for Luther's own writing. But Denifle was only Cochlaeus with footnotes. He sought to prove that Luther was dominated by lust, that the Reformation came solely from his hankering for sexual intercourse, that the theological reasons Luther gave were mere lies to cover his guilt, that the lies were easily refuted, and that Catholics had been perfectly right in condemning him as a heretic.

245

Denifle wrote at a time when the Catholic Church was under furious attack throughout Europe and the world. Socialism, nationalism, secularism, and the philosophical spirit that had become jaded with nostalgia and romanticism wanted to sweep the Church under the rug of history. Within the Church itself some American Catholics were coming dangerously close to teaching that activity was the way to salvation. And some French scholars were undermining the very foundations of the Church by a radical historical study directed at the origins of Christianity. In that troubled context, Denifle's attack on Luther became a defense of the Church that stood in the world as a champion of decency and right reason against perversion and madness. By studying the righteous judgment of the Church against Luther in the greatest peril the Church had faced in its history, a troubled Catholic might infer the righteous judgment of the Church amid the dangers of the new twentieth century and so be moved with courage and hope to do his religious duty.

Protestants naturally enough responded with books that vigorously defended their hero. Denifle forced them not so much into biography as into minute textual analyses to prove that Luther's statements about himself reflected a genuine personal struggle with sin, but not sin conceived as sexual lust. No, the concupiscence Luther talked about meant a selfish desire of the heart to make the self the center of the universe. Denifle did have an incalculable general effect. He made students of Luther pay close attention to the details of Luther's life in their relation to his theology, and he also turned scholarship to a consideration of the flood of works from Luther's pen that had been neglected. Everyone had looked at the ninety-five theses, *The Babylonian Captivity of the Church,* the *Freedom of a Christian,* the *Address to the Christian Nobility of the German Nation,* and some of the devotional works. But now scholars were forced to look at other works that were less inspiring.

The old Catholic-Protestant division in Luther studies began to break down in the 1930s as both Catholics and Protestants found themselves fighting a losing battle against the culture of the twentieth century. One of the more startling contributions to Luther literature appeared in 1939. This was not a biography but rather a great, two-volume monument called *The Reformation in Germany,* by Joseph Lortz. Lortz became the first Catholic scholar of any great reputation to praise Luther as a monumental religious personality. Lortz naturally enough condemned Luther for "subjectivity"; that is, Lortz said that Luther was wrong for placing individual judgment in religious matters over the consensus of the Church. Still he praised Luther for the earnestness of his religious conviction, and he defended him against the old Catholic charges of sexual immorality. He blamed Catholic theology in the sixteenth century for the Reformation, saying that theology was so unclear on so many vital points that heresy was difficult to identify. He also condemned the secularization of the papacy and the lack of religious spirit in most of the German bishops. Lortz especially condemned Catholic champions such as John Eck for their harsh and thoughtless interest in winning debates. Lortz, like Luther himself, believed that Eck was more concerned with his own reputation than with the health of the Church.

Lortz disliked humanism in general because it tended to exalt culture over theology. Some of his harshest judgments he reserved for Erasmus. Erasmus was superficial and more eager to make jokes than he was to right the wrongs of the Church. He was not a sincere Catholic. Lortz's book has been hailed by many scholars ever since as a great document in the hopeful ecumenical dialogue between Catholics and Protestants, especially since the pontificate of Pope John XXIII.

Yet there is a darker side to this book that must give us pause. Lortz was one of those Catholic intellectuals who saw in the Nazi party of Adolf Hitler the hope of Germany. Lortz joined the party soon after Hitler came to power, and he wrote an enthusiastic book in favor of Hitler. He sought to convince German Catholics that to support Hitler was perfectly compatible with their faith and that the fate of the German nation was inextricably bound up with the survival of Catholicism. Lortz claimed, after the war, that he had dropped out of the party in 1936, but there is no evidence that he did. His dossier in the files of the party, captured intact by the American Army at war's end, makes no mention of any resignation. And certain it is that he never spoke out against Hitler until all the Germans like himself who had supported the Nazis discovered in the ruins of defeat that Hitler had been a madman who had led the great and good German nation astray.

Whether it is conscious or unconscious, a powerful sense of German nationalism permeates Lortz's *Reformation in Germany*. We can easily read these ponderous two volumes as an exaltation of one of the great German national figures who fit well into the Nazi view of the heroic German past. Lortz's aim could have been to show the Nazis that religion should contribute to the spirit extolled by the German regime of 1939. Perhaps, then, his book should be read not as a source for the ecumenical movement but rather as a part of the Nazi policy of *Ausgleich,* the word Nazi theoreticians used to express the harmonizing of all the inner forces of the German nation.

Certainly Lortz holds that intellectual strength comes from the soil of the homeland and from a sense of nationalism. Erasmus was weak and trifling because he was a citizen of the world and thereby a foreigner to all countries. He was a partisan of secular cosmopolitanism, says Lortz. *"Kosmopolitismus,"* the word Lortz uses to damn Erasmus, was in Nazi terminology the very crime for which Jews were being stuffed into concentration camps as Lortz wrote. Is the word itself thereby so tainted that whenever we find it in this period our minds and our hearts must go on the alert like hunters in the forest dark hearing a crackling twig? Is it possible for a language such as German to become so corrupt by the moral barbarism of its speakers that it becomes impossible for even simple nouns to be used indifferently? The question is serious and should not be dismissed lightly by those superficial souls of today who yearn to rush in with forgiveness for all the past simply because forgiveness is easier than justice. There are some crimes that should never be forgiven, and in some sense the very notion of a moral climate in the present depends on our willingness to make moral judgments about the past. To forgive the past simply because it is gone is likely to lead us to moral impotence in our own time.

Lortz filled his work with value judgments about Luther, and it is just this collection of value judgments that has been so enthusiastically greeted by Christian scholars in the present ecumenical movement—those embattled and desperate people who now grasp at any straw. That being the case, it is a serious matter to investigate the sources of those judgments to see if they correspond at all to the spirit in which they are received today.

Even the best treatments of Luther are likely to be tracts for the times. Roland H. Bainton's *Here I Stand* was published in 1950, in the midst of an American crisis. It was the beginning of the McCarthy era in the United States, a moment when the country was hysterical over Communism, a time when a national orthodoxy was being loudly formed. Heretics from that orthodoxy were losing their livelihoods if not their lives. Once, during a pleasant walk in the country, Bainton told me that a motive for *Here I Stand* had been to provide an example from history of one who had stood steadfastly for his convictions during a moment when such convictions meant the chance of horrible death. Again Luther was brought into an arena of public debate to speak to the times. And although Roland Bainton is a man and a scholar of utter integrity, throughout this work he tends to excuse Luther time and again for excesses. Bainton strives for objectivity in the tradition of that liberal school of historians who seek to understand rather than to condemn. And so this becomes an "objectivity" that shows Luther at his very best. For example, Bainton quotes Luther in three passages where Luther spoke kindly of the Jews in 1523. But the vulgar polemics of 1543 are passed over briefly, with no quotations, all as if they had been so terrible that no detailed account of them should be made. There is nothing in them to inspire the present, and so they are quickly dropped. The bias in Bainton's work is almost unconscious, but it is nonetheless distorting.

In 1958 Erik Erikson brought out his *Young Man Luther*. Here was an attempt to bring a century of psychological science to bear on the understanding of a historical character. It came during the same year in which William L. Langer, then president of the American Historical Association, urged historians to use psychological tools in their study of the past. It seems somehow fitting that Luther should have been one of the first and most interesting objects of such study. Historians have never been happy with Erikson's slapdash use of the evidence. And most people who have talked to me about Erikson's book have found it intriguing not for what it revealed about Luther but for what it seemed to say about their own psychological development. Thus, if only indirectly, Luther has become once again a voice for this time rather than for his own.

Protestant and Catholic scholars alike have met in several conferences in recent years to discuss ways of interpreting Luther. At these affairs Catholics usually present papers showing how devout Luther was, and Protestants usually speak long and learnedly about the many Catholic elements in Luther's thought—as though the man might have been suspected of being a Hindu or a Buddhist. The point of these inane affairs is said to be serious. The way back to Christian unity is taken to lie through a careful reconsideration of Luther's works. And again he becomes contemporary.

But what of his relation to the present for those of us who are not churchmen, not psychologists, not rulers, not leaders of any causes that he would have approved? Can Luther be in any way an example for us to imitate? Does he have any lessons to teach us? Should he be a hero and a champion to our times? These questions must inevitably arise in connection with any survey of Luther's thought just because the overwhelming tendency in contemporary Luther studies is to make him speak words of wisdom to our own embattled age.

The use of the past to inspire the present is a hallowed tradition in the writing of history. History has often been used as a repository of examples, usually to be imitated in the time of the historian. Every American schoolchild learns of George Washington, of Thomas Jefferson, of Abraham Lincoln and other great men of American history. The aim of that instruction is to present the young with a glorious tradition and so to make them aspire to contribute something good of their own to the American commonwealth. All other nations have done the same with their histories. Or if the examples of history are not to be imitated, they are by a sort of negative inference to be taken as lessons about what is to be avoided. If only Hitler had died in 1937, he would have been seen as a great German statesman. If Napoleon had stopped short of the invasion of Russia . . . If Lyndon Johnson had not sent fighting men to Vietnam . . . The implication is that the person we write about was engaged in something good and necessary but did it badly, even did it to the point of catastrophe, making mistakes that led to doom when he might have won glory.

Martin Luther claimed to be the most perfect expositor of the Bible in Christian history. Of course, the words in which he asserted this claim were not so bald as these, but the pretension is implicit in everything he ever said about the manifold errors of every commentator before him. Augustine, Jerome, Origen, Gregory, Cyprian, and all the rest made many great and grievous mistakes. Sometimes they did happen to stumble onto the truth. Augustine was right on grace and predestination at least up to a point. Luther quotes him favorably more often than he does any other commentator. But Augustine erred, too, and on several important points where Martin Luther after many centuries proved him wrong.

Luther was willing to admit that he had made a few errors himself. But always his were the faults of a young man too much in love with the papacy. He was never willing to admit that he might still be ignorant of Scripture in any way truly important to the Christian faith. It is true that among his last words were these: "We are still beggars, and that is the truth." That sentence and others claim a certain humility in principle. But it is rare indeed to discover that humility in Luther's practice. He said that he merely expounded the obvious meaning of Scripture, the divine words. In his commentaries, in his sermons, and in his harsh and bitter polemical works, he seemed to think that to admit his own interpretations to be even slightly doubtful was also to admit that Scripture itself was unclear in things that counted. And this admission he was utterly unable to make.

We should consider this estimate Luther made of himself—the expositor of the clear Word of God as gleaned from the sacred text of Scripture. Does the twentieth century with its world civilization need such an almighty interpreter of the Bible? Can we transpose Luther on his own terms and set him in our world? That question really becomes a question about the place of the Bible in our time, and here the differences among people are profound. Some still find Scripture to be divine. But there are others for whom the burden of modern critical scholarship has crushed forever the claim that any consistent, divine message can be found in the disorderly array of books that make the Bible. It is one of the stranger aspects of religious studies that scientific Biblical criticism has gone on beside the theological discipline in seminaries and yet seldom the twain have met. Theologians go on blissfully interpreting the Bible as though it were the same book medieval expositors thought it to be. For such people Luther may have a place for a long time. A few have seen the enormous implications to theology of critical Biblical scholarship, and they have tried to deal with them. Some determined Lutheran scholars such as Gerhard Ebeling have laboriously tried to come to terms with modern Biblical studies. But their painful distinctions, qualifications, and arbitrary definitions are utterly unconvincing except to the frantic and rather pitiful crowd that yearns for proof of what it is already determined to believe. There is no reason in the world on the face of it now to accept the Bible with any more reverence than we might accord the Vedas of India, the Buddhist scriptures, the Koran, or any account ever spun out by anybody in any time about any gods.

Some might claim Luther to be a spokesman for Christ, Christ who makes the Scripture shine, Christ who somehow stands above all written words. Christ is still revered in the world. Novelists write stories about him. Some sensitive poets and a great many adolescent girls still write verse about him. He has turned up as the typically loving and typically abused young freak in several musicals that have become rollicking movies. He figures in the art of the West all the way down to the present. And there has been an almost universal appeal in the paradoxical notion that Almighty God, the Creator of the universe, suffered alienation and horrible death as a man among men.

But once we have begun to approach Scripture critically, what really remains of Jesus? How do we get to him through the accounts written about him? Did he heal the sick, restore the blind to sight, make the lame walk, and raise the dead? Was he born of a virgin in a stable in Bethlehem, and did angels sing to shepherds abiding nearby in the fields of Judea? And did a special star shine in the east to bring wise men from afar? Did Christ himself rise from the dead and ascend into heaven? Did Zeus get Leda with child when he disguised himself as a swan? Did Orpheus descend into the underworld to ransom his beloved Eurydice from the kingdom of the dead? Did Gilgamesh journey to the far land where Ut-Napishtim lived and there hear the tale of the great flood and learn the lesson of the fish-wife, that his quest for immortality was in vain because he was a man?

We may answer yes to all these questions when we nod by the fire on a snowy evening and the wind sings its song in the chimney and the world beyond our windows lies shut away in the magic isolation of a cold and dark that do not quite touch us. But in the heat of open day, we know as surely as we know anything about the past that whoever Jesus was, his bones lie rotting or else are already dust in a grave long since forgotten. We do not really know who he was or what he was, and our ignorance about him will never be enlightened by knowledge. Westerners in every generation have indeed made him the ideal man according to whatever their values might be at the time. But to use him in art or in literature or even in theology does not make his story true, and it does not make him our redeemer.

Where is Luther then if Christ is not risen? Well, he might be looked upon as a prophet of that loving and personal God so many millions would like to find filling the emptiness of space. There are many who want to believe that all religions finally point to the same reality, that there is a God who rules the cosmos, who keeps His eye on the sparrow, and reveals Himself partly here and partly there. Then we may take Luther as one more spokesman for the religious life, and religion will always be with us.

This is not to say that the Church will survive. The Church does still lie coiled in the dust of this present age, dying in the parching and invincible sunlight, though still able to strike the unwary pilgrim should he tread too near its venomous head. Luther will go on being used for a while in a vain effort to restore the Church to health through heroic doses of ecumenical saccharin. But the Church will go on dying, and Luther will live for some when the last priest lies in the grave and the last preacher stands mute and bemused in an empty auditorium.

To say that religion will live though the Church will die does not relieve us from all consideration of whether this vaguely religious use of Luther is to be commended. I think it is not. The great majority of humankind will always seek to hide its fears in the embrace of fantasy, and though the fantasies of religion are not so bad as others that might be invoked, they are bad enough. For the rest of us, our obligation as thinking reeds requires us to make the painful discrimination of reality from dreams. And for many of us the magnitude of the earth's savagery exposed in this century has ended forever the capacity we might once have had to believe in any god whose essence is goodness and mercy. There is not room in the universe for both Auschwitz and Jehovah, and the fact that Auschwitz has been is proof enough that Jehovah never was.

Luther would have answered that the mystery of Jehovah is

infinitely more than our feeble sight can see in horrible events. But suffering for Luther was always either a deeply subjective feeling of his own heart or a prosaic anxiety for his kith and kin or else only the bare news of torments that he in his small and narrow world never saw. One of his children died, and he grieved for her. Occasionally he witnessed a visitation of the plague. But he never saw a heretic burned. He never saw a battle. He never saw a mob on the rampage. He never witnessed the massacre of hundreds, much less of millions. And so in his limited and provincial way he could make suffering a mystery that had some reason, hidden in a God who seemed very near.

In our world suffering has become an absurdity, and Luther's God to this century has been as silent as stone. In Ingmar Bergman's great film *The Seventh Seal*, the knight playing at chess with death says, "I want to know your secrets." And death responds, "I have no secrets." And so to the assurance of faith—the faith of Dante, of Aquinas, of Luther—that we shall finally understand God's mystery, we can only respond with the wisdom of Paul Henri Thiry, baron d'Holbach, who wrote more than two centuries after Luther died. If God cannot halt the suffering of the innocent, then He is not truly God. If He can but will not relieve them of their afflictions, then He is not worthy to be adored. For what possible reason could there be to judge God on a moral standard any different from that which we might use to judge a man who rained death down on children from the skies or demolished whole cities in the name of an abstract glory forever unknown to those who died in its name? Here is where Luther would answer with a tirade against reason the whore. And he would advise us to cling to the faith that is above reason, for only such a faith is pleasing to God. Yet though our will to believe may be the best in the world, our reason in such matters is as difficult to forsake as our skins and our bones.

Then, someone else may say, even in a world without God we may yet praise Luther for the courage of his convictions. He possessed that quality so rare in our days—integrity. He wanted neither fame nor luxury. He stood when the wind was a hurricane. He risked death for his cause, and we should admire him for being such a man.

To this theory I can only respond with a piece of wisdom I heard once from the philosopher Paul Weiss in a lecture he gave at Yale. Courage is really a neutral quality that may be used for many different ends. Soldiers have courage, and so do firemen and policemen and men who resolve to tell the truth when their superiors command them to lie. But bank robbers and burglars also have courage, and so do murderers and assassins and those who plan revolutions against democracy.

So do we, then, admire Luther for the courage to stake his life and the life of Europe itself on his personal assurance that he alone understood the divine meaning of an absurd collection of folktales and fantasy? In our time we might better choose examples from the past who had that rare and remarkable courage to compromise, to be tolerant, to admit ignorance, and to survive by keeping the heat of crusading passion damped down by reason.

We could find some such examples from Luther's century if we require heroes to affirm the virtues we need. Erasmus might be a good one. And Rabelais, I think. And after Luther's death we might revere Montaigne and Shakespeare. Even among the more conventionally Christian men of the time we might find a few. Sebastian Castellio, run out of Geneva for denying the divinity of the Song of Solomon, said that the Bible was not clear enough to let any man burn another over its interpretation. John Foxe, who wrote of the acts and monuments of the Protestant martyrs under Catholics, resolutely resisted all efforts of the Protestant government of Queen Elizabeth I to make martyrs of its religious adversaries. But not Luther. The very qualities that made him notorious would destroy our civilization if everybody practiced them today; indeed, under their modern and more secular forms they may still do so. We may yet perish for the interpretation of a book or the exegesis of a document. The qualities we might genuinely admire—Luther's gentleness to his children, his heartiness, his brilliant gift for language, his blistering wit, his hilarious obscenity—we may find in many another without the evils that Luther hammered onto them. Hitler liked children, and he was kind to dogs. But we must measure the effect of a man on his times in something larger than the perspective of isolated personal virtues that are a part of the daily life.

Then why study Luther at all? The answer sounds like a tautology, though it is really only common sense. We study him because he is studied. He is one of the giants in our history, a great bulk of a name heaving itself out of our past with the insistent demand that we pay attention to him. The past always exercises a dominion over the present by its quality of being so easily translated into mythology. Myths explain our being and our destiny with such authority that they may well prevent us from creating that being for ourselves or making a destiny that is truly our own. Priestcraft of one sort or another has often fixed on these myths about our past to flail us into being whatever the priest wants us to be. That is why history as well as death have so often been bound up together in the arsenal of religion. But ordinary people—and some not so ordinary—are often vastly relieved by having the puzzling questions of life answered already for them by the giants of the past. And so history can become a cherished excuse not to think, a great warm mother of sorts who tells us that we need only cling to her and shut our eyes to the world just beyond her comforting arms.

The good historian is always seeking to look the myths in the face, to surmount the enchantment lent by distance and, as best he can, to try to see the past as it really was. It is often an unpopular occupation, and historians have frequently been in trouble with the political powers who dictate what is useful and thus what should be discovered in the past. For the historian is likely to tell us that the great stone face looming on the mountain is only a pile of rock or that our heroes walked the earth in muddy boots. Yet in the process of his study, the historian is always at work to free us from a slavish adoration of the past that may make us less than men in the present.

Our age, our minds, our thoughts, and the possibilities for good and evil are different from anything that has ever faced mankind before. That may seem like a senseless statement to some, for every age possesses its own spirit, and men in every century are different from those who lived before them. But in our time we face differences of a colossal magnitude such as no one has ever experienced in the previous history of the world. We are rushing headlong into what one sensitive observer has called "future shock." No generation has ever been quite so removed from its history as has our own. Our children will find the past even more alien than it is to us. And in this world of ours the true social task of the historian must be to make the transition as easy as such a wrenching and terrible process can be.

When we look back at Luther from our autumn of the twentieth century, we discover that both the man and his time are stranger than almost every reality we can imagine. We may be awed at his prodigious influence. We may dissect his thought in appreciation of the vigor of his mind and the power of his imagination. But still he perches there in the past like a great pterodactyl, brooding with folded wings into a world that has vanished almost utterly away, a past four centuries gone that might as well have been in some remote geological epoch before the glaciers came. Perceiving him so, we are freed from his special burden of myth, and we can turn away from him to discover our own being in this new day.

A part of that being is to understand that we have no god to help us and that there will never be any divine shaft of illumination to make our night shine like the dawn. We turn from the study of Luther, the theologian of arcane lore about an arcane deity, knowing that there is no help for us but that residing in our own heads and hearts, and confessing wryly, too, that that help is feeble enough. If there is anything else that his life can teach us, it may well be that all our striving, like his, must finally be hidden in the long cold that comes for great and small alike, and that life at its best and all history, too, are but parts of a process whereby we make our own terms with the dark.

Done in camp
The Wind River Mountains
By Lander, Wyoming
August 1973

BIBLIOGRAPHY

A Note on Sources

BIBLIOGRAPHIES, like books themselves, are reflections of the personal experience in study of the persons who write them. In this book I have sought to reconsider Luther's life by an analysis of those works of his that I find most important. The works I have discussed are nearly all readily accessible in English translations. Luther has been frequently Englished ever since the time of Henry VIII, but the most ambitious translation of his works into English is only now nearing completion from Fortress Press, the Lutheran publishing house in Philadelphia. Eventually fifty-five volumes, edited by Jaroslav Pelikan and Helmut T. Lehmann, will appear. Most of the works that I have discussed will be found in this series, called, appropriately enough, *Luther's Works, American Edition*. The volumes are well done, and the format is such that each corresponds in one particular at least to one of the requirements Ernest Hemingway insisted upon for a good book: it can be easily read in the bathtub.

For some works that I have treated—such as the *Against Henry King of the English* or the *Concerning Schem Hamphoras*—one must still go to the basic printed source for all Luther studies, the great Weimar Edition of his works. None of these ponderous volumes can possibly be read in the bathtub without the risk of an involuntary baptism of the work itself and a consequent damage to the reader's ribs that may make him turn quickly from Luther to liniment. The Weimar Edition is something of a monument. It has been issuing steadily from the presses in Germany through war, revolution, inflation, depression, invasion, and prosperity since the year 1883. When completed, as it soon will be, the Weimar Edition will number some 110 volumes. Here is Luther in his fluid Latin and hammering German sweeping on and on like some vast and irrepressible river for thousands and thousands of pages. One can only wish that when the present editors are done with their textual labors, they will turn to a critical historical dictionary of the German language that will do for German what the *Oxford English Dictionary* has done for English.

Books and articles about Luther are more numerous than what anyone can read in a lifetime. Most of them are dreadfully dull. In Luther studies a curious scholasticism has sprung up. Some writers believe that they must rehearse everything every other writer has said about Luther before they can say anything themselves. In the midst of these tiresome tomes, the weary reader is likely to have the nightmarish fantasy that he has been transported to a maze manufactured by Cretans (if not cretins), with the writer become a Minotaur and Luther himself a distant promise of sunny air impossible to find across the bending of authorities.

The best way to get to Luther is to read his own works, read them again and again. Take the table talk with a grain of salt, be wary of those lectures that we possess only in the form of classroom notes taken down by students, read the letters for pleasure, study his translation of the Bible, concentrate on the theological tractates that were intended to explain special problems, and do not neglect the polemical works.

Obviously enough, there are some books about Luther that the serious student should consider in addition to Luther's own works. The following are a few that have been helpful to me. It is not an exhaustive list, but the student who spent a year with these books would emerge with a profound knowledge of Luther and the Reformation of the sixteenth century.

BEFORE THE REFORMATION

Huizinga, Johan. *The Waning of the Middle Ages.* London, 1924. One of the great books of medieval history. Huizinga's thesis is that, at the end of the Middle Ages, the forms of cultural expression were extraordinarily rich and complex. But the very multiplicity of the forms with their mechanical conventions was such that spontaneity was no longer possible within the old assumptions of medieval civilization, a thesis that helps explain the larger context of Luther's yearning for spontaneous simplicity.

Oberman, Heiko A. *The Harvest of Medieval Theology.* Cambridge (Mass.), 1962. Written in the appalling style of some maritime insurance policies, this book is nonetheless one of the most important contributions in years to our understanding of the late medieval theological world whence Luther came and against which he so strongly reacted. A revised edition was published by Eerdman's in 1967.

GENERAL SURVEYS OF THE REFORMATION

Bainton, Roland H. *The Reformation of the Sixteenth Century*. Boston, 1952. Short, interesting studies of various religious movements and their leaders within the Reformation. Delightfully readable and illustrated with contemporary woodcuts.

Dickens, A. G. *Reformation and Society in Sixteenth-Century Europe*. New York, 1966. A short, gracefully written, beautifully illustrated book, on the side of the Protestants.

Elton, G. R. *Reformation Europe 1517–1559*. New York, 1966. An excellent survey of medium length by Great Britain's most brilliant living historian.

Grimm, Harold J. *The Reformation Era*. Second Edition. New York, 1973. A plodding, encyclopedic study of the Reformation, very dry and dusty. All the names, dates, and events are assembled here as though they had been neatly laid out in a morgue. But they are here.

Hillerbrand, Hans J. *The Reformation: A Narrative History Related by Contemporary Observers and Participants*. New York, 1964. An entertaining and enlightening collection of sources from a throng of people who observed the Reformation and shared in it.

————. *The World of the Reformation*. New York, 1973. A fine short summary of the Reformation, somewhat weak on the Catholic reaction but excellent on Luther, Zwingli, and the radicals.

Holborn, Hajo. *The Reformation, Vol. I, A History of Modern Germany*. New York, 1959. Not very strong on religious thought, this book is enlightening on the political and economic situation of the German lands during the Reformation. The section on the peasants' rebellion is especially good. Excellent maps.

Lortz, Joseph. *Die Reformation in Deutschland*. First edition. Freiburg, 1939. 2 vols. Comprehensive and controversial.

Marc'hadour, Germain. *L'Univers de Thomas More*. Paris, 1963. Much more than the title suggests, this book is a detailed chronology of European history from 1477 to 1536. A compressed, comprehensive, invaluable reference tool, marred by several important errors.

Spitz, Lewis W. *The Renaissance and the Reformation Movements.* Chicago, 1971. A comprehensive textbook of medium length, well illustrated, mechanical in style, accurate but unimaginative; here Luther is the paladin of God. The mediocre best from the present school of clerical historians.

LUTHER: LIFE AND TIMES

Bainton, Roland H. *Here I Stand.* New York, 1950. The standard biography, generally in praise of Luther and certainly admiring in its final estimate of the man, but much more critical than many other works. Immensely readable.

Boehmer, Heinrich. *Martin Luther: Road to Reformation.* New York, 1957. A readable, interesting account of Luther from his birth to the Reichstag at Worms, 1521. Somewhat old-fashioned, but detailed and witty.

Cochlaeus, Johannes. *Commentaria Ioannis Cochlaei de actis et scriptis Martini Lutheri saxonis, chronographici, ex ordini ab anno Domini MDXVII usque ad annum MDXLVI inclusive fideliter conscripta.* 1549. The first full-length biography of Luther, this one done by an inveterate foe whose slanders ruled Catholic thought about the German reformer until the twentieth century.

Dickens, A. G. *Martin Luther and the Reformation.* London, 1967. A short, readable account, full of praise.

Erikson, Erik H. *Young Man Luther.* New York, 1958. The celebrated attempt by a noted psychologist to find a great identity crisis in Luther that led to the Reformation. Erikson's work is subjected to a detailed and blistering attack by Roland H. Bainton, "Psychiatry and History: An Examination of Erikson's 'Young Man Luther,'" *Religion in Life,* 1971, pp. 450–77.

Friedenthal, Richard. *Luther: His Life and Times.* New York, 1970. A vigorously written, detailed account, not profound with regard to Luther's thought but fascinating for the drama of the Luther affair in Germany, concluding that Luther was a failure. Grumpily reviewed by clerical historians.

Reuter, Fritz, editor. *Der Reichstag zu Worms von 1521.* Worms, 1971. A splendid collection of essays on the various aspects of the Reichstag at which Luther made his celebrated refusal to recant before the Emperor. Especially good is the contribution of Rainer Wohlfeil, an analysis and narrative of the politics of Luther's appearance at the Reichstag.

Schwiebert, E. G. *Luther and His Times*. St. Louis, 1950. A prolix and adoring biography, uncritical and tedious, but nevertheless valuable for its simply enormous quantity of detail.

LUTHER'S THOUGHT

Aland, Kurt, editor. *Martin Luther's Ninety-Five Theses*. St. Louis, 1967. A faintly amusing book, demonstrating the almost frantic tendency of some Lutherans to defend every layer of paint on the idol they have made of Luther's career. Aland labors mightily to prove from contemporary documents that Erwin Iserloh was wrong in saying that the theses were not posted. Aland fails.

Aulén, Gustaf. *Christus Victor*. New York, 1957. A short, exciting survey of Christian understandings of just what Christ did to redeem humanity. Excellent on Luther, showing how he reflected the primitive idea of the New Testament against the more sophisticated philosophical notions that came in the Middle Ages.

Bizer, Ernst. *Fides ex Auditu Eine Untersuchung über die Entdeckung der Gerechtigkeit Gottes durch Martin Luther*. Third edition. Neukirchen, 1966. Bizer says that Luther arrived at a full understanding of "justification by faith" only after the beginning of the controversy over indulgences. Bizer proves his point and in the process presents an extraordinarily clear definition of Luther's meaning about justification.

Hägglund, Bengt. *Theologie und Philosophie bei Luther und in der Occamistischen Tradition*. Lund, 1955. Heiko Oberman has criticized this little book for some of its generalizations about nominalism. Still, it is stimulating and helpful for Luther's notions of "faith," "knowledge," and "reason."

Harnack, Theodosius. *Luthers Theologie*. 2 vols. Munich, 1927. An old but useful study, especially for its treatment of Luther's practical concern with predestination. Harnack thinks that Luther seldom used the doctrine after 1530.

Headley, John M. *Luther's View of Church History*. New Haven, 1963. History, dark to reason, is understood by faith, though only to the extent that the Christian knows that Christ is in charge. A meticulous study, showing how Luther classified history into periods, used history in arguments, and thought history would end.

Holl, Karl. *Gesammelte Aufsätze zur Kirchengeschichte*, Vol. I. Tübingen, 1927. A worshipful collection of essays on Luther by a brilliant scholar utterly devoted to the memory of the man. Detailed footnotes on every page make an interesting index to Luther's thought.

Iserloh, Erwin. *The Theses Were Not Posted.* Boston, 1968. Lutheran antagonism to this little book is demonstrated by the amusing fact that Aland's attempted refutation of it (noted above) appeared in English a year before Iserloh's work was translated. Thus the counterattack was launched before the attack was available to most people.

Kaufmann, Walter. *The Faith of a Heretic.* New York, 1961. Kaufmann and I disagree mildly on Luther's use of the Old Testament, but this excellent book contains a splendid short critique of Luther's view of Christ. Beautifully written in the manner of all Kaufmann's books.

Kawerau, Peter. *Luther: Leben, Schriften, Denken.* Marburg, 1969. A superb account of Luther's early development combined with an excellent history of historiography concerning Luther.

Ozment, Steven E., editor. *The Reformation in Medieval Perspective.* Chicago, 1971. A rich collection of essays on the relation of several strands of late medieval thought to Martin Luther (*not* to the entire Reformation as the title erroneously suggests). The contributions of Bernd Moeller on piety in Germany on the eve of the Reformation, of Heiko Oberman on Luther and mysticism, and of Ozment himself on Luther and late medieval theology are especially valuable.

Prenter, Regin. *Spiritus Creator.* Philadelphia, 1953. In intent a study of the use Luther made of the Christian idea of the Holy Spirit. In fact, a summary of the best in Luther's piety and his view of human psychology.

Rupp, Gordon. *Luther's Progress to the Diet of Worms.* London, 1951. A short, readable, loving account of Luther's development to 1521. Excellent.

———. *The Righteousness of God.* London, 1953. The best single volume on Luther's thought done by a warm admirer of the man.

Sensible, well-written, and witty, though Rupp always sees Luther in the best possible light.

Spitz, Lewis. *The Religious Renaissance of the German Humanists.* Cambridge (Mass.), 1963. The best book Spitz has written, a collection of short analytical essays on various German humanists, including Erasmus, who was not really a German, and Luther, who was not really a humanist. The group that does conform to the title is a barren lot, revealing how dismal was the cultural life of the German lands at the time of the Reformation. Spitz shows how humanism both contributed to Luther's movement and hindered it.

Törnvall, Gustaf. *Geistliches und Weltliches Regiment bei Luther.* Munich, 1947. A brilliant account of Luther's view of government. Shows that the apparent dualism in Luther's thought between the private morality of the Christian and the Christian in public service is really a means Luther used to preserve a view of God ruling the entire universe.

Wicks, Jared. *Man Yearning for Grace.* Wiesbaden, 1969. A careful study of Luther's thought from its beginnings to 1517 by a sympathetic but critical Catholic scholar influenced by the work of Ernst Bizer.

OTHER FIGURES OF THE REFORMATION

Bainton, Roland H. *Erasmus of Christendom.* New York, 1969. A careful, magisterial account that refutes the ancient charge that Erasmus was more rationalist than Christian.

Brandi, Karl. *The Emperor Charles V.* New York, 1939. The standard political biography, showing Charles in the midst of his worldwide concerns.

Fraenkel, Peter. *Testimonium Patrum.* Geneva, 1961. An immensely learned, copiously annotated, miserably written study of the use by Philipp Melanchthon of the traditions of the early Church Fathers. Difficult but rewarding for the way some of the great issues of the Reformation—such as the relation of Church, Scripture, and history—are thrown into relief.

Garside, Charles, Jr. *Zwingli and the Arts.* New Haven, 1966. An elegant, beautifully written study of sterling scholarship, comprising much more than the title might imply.

Huizinga, Johan. *Erasmus.* New York, 1924. A classic work stressing the deep ambivalence in the personality of Erasmus, gentle and very perceptive.

Pollet, J.-V.-M. "Zwinglianisme," *Dictionnaire de Théologie Catholique,* vol. 15/2, cols. 2745–928. Paris, 1950. A detailed, suggestive, imaginative study interesting for its consideration of what Zwingli's view of the relation between body and spirit meant for Western thought.

Tyler, Royall. *The Emperor Charles the Fifth.* London, 1956. A learned, critical, witty, beautifully illustrated, and strangely neglected study, written with verve.

Walton, Robert C. *Zwingli's Theocracy.* Toronto, 1967. A fine study that illuminates not only Zwingli's ideas about theocracy but also the theocratic motif in the sixteenth century. Careful and readable.

INDEX